POETICS OF CRITIQUE

for

J.D.

Poetics of Critique

The Interdisciplinarity of Textuality

ANDREW W. HASS

Routledge
Taylor & Francis Group
LONDON AND NEW YORK

First published 2003 by Ashgate Publishing

Reissued 2018 by Routledge
2 Park Square, Milton Park, Abingdon, Oxon OX14 4RN
711 Third Avenue, New York, NY 10017, USA

Routledge is an imprint of the Taylor & Francis Group, an informa business

Typeset by MHL Production Services Ltd, Coventry

A Library of Congress record exists under LC control number: 2002043953

ISBN 13: 978-1-138-70995-9 (hbk)
ISBN 13: 978-1-138-70994-2 (pbk)
ISBN 13: 978-1-315-19822-4 (ebk)

Contents

Foreword

Interdisciplinarity is a difficult term, opening up a language of the in-between, a borderland of no space or time. Living on the borders is dangerous and perplexing, beyond the comforts of settled truth and being. In the academy we define ourselves by our 'discipline', in the religious life we seek God by the discipline of spirit, mind and body. To abandon such comforts seems foolish and a risk we rarely dare to take. Yet we still acknowledge and even celebrate the need and call to be interdisciplinary. For a long time in universities and colleges such intellectual activity has been publicly applauded and privately deplored by subject-specific experts and administrators who prefer clear categories. Andrew Hass pursued his doctoral studies in the field of literature and theology – perhaps one should say 'fields' – which became for him a kind of utopia, 'in the strict sense of the word: a "no place" which brings together the best of all worlds and allows a vision to flourish'.

In this book the vision grows to a new maturity, and interdisciplinarity is explored not at arm's length but from within the very fabric of the writing and criticism. Be warned, therefore, this is not an easy book to read. As literature in its own right it has its distinguished forebears in such works as Sir Thomas Browne's *Religio Medici* (1642) and Samuel Taylor Coleridge's *Biographia Literaria* (1817). For, like them, it is not so much *about* the books, writers and thinkers to which it gives attention, as written in dialogue with them – a conversation that transcends the limits of history, genre, and place. We might say that both its theme and its nature is 'textuality', texts exploring each other while we the reader listen to them, sometimes as partners in the discussion, and sometimes as those who overhear conversations between others, like passive participants in the Socratic dialogues.

What are we concerned with if not truth? But what is truth? Pilate's question to Jesus in the Fourth Gospel resonates in the Western tradition alongside Augustine's question on time in the *Confessions*, or the revolutions in our perception of space in Galileo, Newton and Einstein. These great mysteries, to which there can never be final answers beyond critique, lie at the heart of the labors of philosophers, theologians, novelists, playwrights and poets; above all poets, for they are the true makers. Thus Hass's book is, as it must be, a book of voices in conversation. Like the poet, he readily sheds his own voice to inhabit the voices of those whom he addresses, so that thinkers find new partnerships, and companionship, in each other's worlds. Most startlingly, Nietzsche enters the world of Goethe's Faust, playing his role in it to perfection. Nor is this just Goethe's Faust, but behind and in front of that figure are all other Fausts, from Marlowe's Faustus to the world of Mann's genius Adrian Leverkühn. For to be interdisciplinary is precisely to be ready to speak in many voices, and not to withdraw as a solitary speaker against and in the face of others. We all live in a world, or worlds, constructed and defined by Sophocles, by Kant, Kierkegaard and Nietzsche, by Heidegger and Gadamer –

even if we do not know it. In order to hear them, therefore, we have to look also within ourselves and not be afraid of that which we do not readily understand.

Thus this book is also necessarily postmodern, in the sense that it deconstructs our safety zones of understanding and releases texts from the security of the study or the academic department to be the worlds that they create – truly there is nothing outside this text. It is a book which speaks in endless discussions and arguments with others, not caring where it will be placed on the library shelf, for it must be in all places – and perhaps none. It offers no answers, except the answer that the truth is always that which comes and is coming in a living poetics and in a hermeneutics of suspension. The truth lies within the struggle with the text and is not 'out there'; it is in the struggle of each of us. *Poetics of Critique* has in common with the *Biographia Literaria* a concern not principally to instruct us in a particular philosophy or writer, but more to make us think about how we are thinking and how we address difficulty. (This is, of course, why Heidegger is also a crucial dialogue partner.) There is always the option of giving up, but that too is a judgment upon ourselves as much as upon the text. What is it that we profess not to understand?

Finally, this is a deeply religious book, even a deeply Christian one, though that term is not and cannot be in any sense an exclusive one here. It opens up spaces for the sacred for all which too often sacred traditions have closed down or barricaded against outsiders. But to those who will listen and persevere, Hass's writings are endlessly hospitable, welcoming all, listening to all, critiquing all. Here is interdisciplinarity from within, with a rhetoric which deconstructs the languages of professional critics, yet is itself learned and urbane. I believe this book is that rare thing in the literature of the academy, a genuinely original contribution to thought, by the nature of what it is and does as much as by what it says. It takes the study of literature and theology on to a new level, beyond its present borders to new heights of Pisgah. But far more than that. It thrives within the great traditions of the history of ideas and literature of all ages, and it welcomes each one of us afresh into the precarious processes of thinking so that we may ask with renewed confidence and resources the ancient question, what indeed is truth?

David Jasper
University of Glasgow

Acknowledgements

This text engages with many voices, both from the past and from the present. Some of these voices are given a name, explicitly and repeatedly; other voices move through the pages unannounced, though a discerning enough ear will hear them, sometimes clearly. In this manifold of conversation, two voices deserve particular mention. The first is that of David Jasper. His encouragement, support, advice and abiding friendship over the years have allowed me to embark upon this ambitious project with a measure of assurance, if never quite an equal measure of confidence. As the project took shape, his ongoing commentary proved, as always, insightful and suggestive, extending the limits of the field in view. I owe him much gratitude; the text owes to him much of its inspiration. The second voice resonates on almost every page of this text – and I do not exaggerate. It belongs to Robert William Sherwood, whose exacting eye, refined ear, and precision of mind has, through exceptional commitment, improved this text on virtually every level. His emendations were a privileged gift, and I cannot express enough thanks for his generosity, and for the many hours of input that came at the expense of personal work. This was a sacrifice only a deep friendship could sustain. But then, it is perhaps the personal nature of this friendship that deserves the better of the praise, for it is this very nature, expressed through countless conversations into all hours of the morning, over many years and through varied experiences, that has done more to bring this book into the light of day than all the detailed textual comments combined and multiplied.

Thus the seventh day – which in our age is supposed finally to have arrived in so many ways – is used not to rest from historical work but to criticize.

Søren Kierkegaard, *The Concept of Irony*

A Beginning

It has been claimed we live in a 'post-critical' age. What this means exactly, amid all the other claims of supersession for which the prefix 'post-' has been marshaled into service over the last decades, is anyone's guess. For the term 'critical' has had an array of affiliations. Even the expression 'critical theory' finds many distinctions, with differing subscribers, so that whatever the 'theory' being referred to actually is, it is hardly uniform. But then, those who supposedly originated this phrase as a label or a formal designation, the Frankfurt School, were themselves hardly uniform, and even individual proponents within the school changed significantly over the course of their thought and the movement's varied existence. Marcuse, for one, spent half of his 'critical' years, like most of his colleagues, living on another continent, well away from the institutional, if not the theoretical, wellspring. Even so, if the term 'post-critical' looks back to anything specifically, it looks back, one should think, to the Critical Theory of the Frankfurt School. For the theoretical thrust of its thinkers, variegated as they were, and often at odds with each other, has now lost its general force as a Marxist critique, and not because Marxism has been overtaken by the economic ideology of capitalism, which practically, in the West (and arguably now most of the world), it has, but because the Marxist dialecticism that propels this theory forward has been unable to shed completely its totalizing and utopian tendencies. And even those contemporaries who try to dispel these tendencies, such as Thomas McCarthy and David Couzens Hoy, admit that in order to do so, we must now employ critical theory within postmetaphysical and reconstructionist understandings (McCarthy) or alongside poststructuralist and deconstructive lines (Hoy).[1] Perhaps then we *are* in a post-critical age, if we take the Frankfurt School to have been properly, and respectfully, superseded.

But critical theory has always gone beyond the confines of one school, and critique has always taken more forms than simply Marxist dialectic. It has other roots even besides Hegel – not all critical theorists are 'Left Hegelians'. Though the formal idea of critique is a modern invention – the word arose at the beginning of the eighteenth century, as both reliant upon and in response to Enlightenment rationalization – its practice is at least as old as Socrates, whose critique against the Sophists, using a dialectic of his own, continues to be a model of critical enlightenment. Have we gone beyond this kind of critique, in which the dictates of reason are brought to bear upon themselves in a necessarily limiting and questioning fashion? Have we really superseded the critical spirit, by which we call into question not just our rational procedures, but the logic which stands behind them and ratifies their very *raison d'être*? Is not to go beyond critique fundamentally dependant upon a critical move, a critical intention, a critical disposition? Can we talk about being 'post-critical' in any general way without, at the very heart, contradicting ourselves?

Some see contradiction in the very notion of critical theory. The oxymoronic nature of a theory that posits a critique of theoretical structures has always been a tension at work within formalized critical theory from its very inception. This tension finds its source in dialectical thinking, which in its Hegelian form (but even

[1] See David Couzens Hoy and Thomas McCarthy, *Critical Theory* (Oxford: Blackwell, 1994).

in the earlier Socratic form) has contradiction built directly into the system. *Aufhebung*, we know, cancels as much as it preserves. And this sublationary effect is carried over into our use of the prefix 'post-', which indicates both a succession from the phenomenon to which it has been attached, and a furtherance of that phenomenon. However 'postmodern' our culture may have become, we are still carrying forward our modern legacy. The day we cease being modern, we cease being postmodern. And the same we can say for critical and 'post-critical'.

Let us therefore remain within the purview of critique. At least for now. For we have not yet finished with the critical spirit, if our logical structures, and even the para-logical structures that have come to mark postmodern thought, have not yet fully yielded to their own critique. And for evidence that they have not we need only look to the academy, where, in the institutional nature of its structure and its discourse, it continues to conform to the rational ideals laid down by the Enlightenment: that all knowledge is open to our grasp and our power, and that such grasp and such power are contingent upon the logical arrangement (or the logical economy) of our pursuits into categories that define disciplinary fields: theoretical and applied, natural and human, scientific and artistic. Even the para-logical discourse of contemporary thought, which has arisen predominantly within the university system, and not, as one might think, in spite of it, owes its existence to the academy's disciplinarity, as it maintains its critical distinction by setting one discipline against the other. Literary criticism is a good example here. It does not, for all intents and purposes, exist outside the academy. And though it has recently adopted many of the 'post-' terms from other fields, while offering one or two of its own, it nevertheless has tried to hold its own disciplinary boundaries by claiming, in its most imperious moments, that all other fields of enquiry, whether philosophical, psychological, political, economic, or others, are in fact all dependent elements of a literary dimension. The 'criticism' here has remained territorial, but this territorialization is a result of the institution that it serves. What it criticizes, and indeed how it criticizes, is wholly dependent upon the logic of the disciplinary economy around which it gains its own identity and currency. And it has not, as yet, made any significant inroads into questioning that logic. It cannot afford to, despite much of its own rhetoric. It may adopt para-logical approaches on the margins of its own discipline, but we have yet to see the adoption, whether by literary criticism or by another other disciplinary criticism, of the term 'post-logical'.

The term that has been seized upon instead, the term that is meant to suggest both a canceling out of disciplinary autonomy (or disciplinary hegemony) and a preservation of disciplinary borders, is the much heralded term 'interdisciplinarity'. Under this banner we are taught to expect the latest evolution of academic pursuit. Here the freedom to move from one discipline to another, from one body of thought to another, while maintaining a respect for all the traditions and histories involved, is given its full license, we are told. And literary criticism may well have led the way, when from a less imperial position it has crossed over to neighboring fields simply to show the great cultural repository that we call a text, even a fictional text.

But such an academic 'interdisciplinarity' has remained problematic. The wider institution, however much it espouses a nominal notion of interdisciplinary studies, is not set up for the ground-breaking disruption and dispersal of a pure interdisciplinarity. The academy functions by virtue of its disciplines, not in opposition to them. Precise and defining boundaries are set rigidly in place through the creation of institutional compartments – faculties, departments, schools, and colleges – that become dividing lines of bureaucratic organization by which each discipline is held in check and each field of study demarcated one against the other. These divisions are not simply pragmatic, they are also prescriptive. For they have come to define our Enlightenment and 'post-Enlightenment' world, our inherited understanding of reality built upon that Cartesian model of clear and distinct ordering, of methodological exactitude, of reduction to the smallest and simplest components, of the manifold taxonomies by which the objects of our propositional analysis are arranged and enumerated, and of our ability to grasp and appropriate knowledge to our own end. To question the basic tenet we call a discipline, to question its separation out from the conglomeration we call the University, is to question the very core of the modern Western liberal tradition. The University resists and will continue to resist any interdisciplinarity that disrupts the structural logic upon which it has prided itself for so many centuries. This resistance emerges at the very center of its operations: in managerial control, in curriculum design, and in hiring practice. The academy loves to applaud interdisciplinary rhetoric, and does so by employing the language of interdisciplinarity itself. But we know that this kind of rhetoric goes only so far. It must of necessity go only so far, if the academy is to remain what it is.

But if the critical question remains in view, we must ask: is the language of interdisciplinarity only rhetorical? What is its underlying logic? Can a critique resurface here, under the force of that ancient Socratic query which challenged the rhetoric of the Sophists? It seems that here is the place at which a critical spirit must again rise. For interdisciplinarity, if it is to be a solution to the question of our rational projects and their limits, to the question of knowledge and its appropriation, to the question of power and its authority, must come under the scrutiny of its own claims, and yield to critique even in its most advanced 'post-' phases.

If the spirit of critique should rise again from the grave, let us for the moment look elsewhere than Socrates' resting place. Let us go rather to a modern site. For the kind of interdisciplinarity we hear being expressed is a thoroughly modern creation (we could even say postmodern, though it makes little difference here), and so to put interdisciplinarity properly to the test, we ought to invoke a thoroughly modern spirit. Of course we mean Kant, the first great source of modern critique.

By the German term *Kritik*, Kant assumed two things: that criticism will function over dogmatism, and that criticism will be critical of its own powers. In his Preface to the First Edition of *Kritik der reinen Vernunft* (*Critique of Pure Reason*), Kant labors under what he calls an 'age of criticism', fueled by a prevailing mood of indifference towards 'illusory knowledge' and 'groundless pretensions'.[2] This knowledge and these pretensions had subjugated themselves before the regal claims

---

[2] Immanuel Kant, *Critique of Pure Reason*, trans. Norman Kemp Smith (London: Macmillan, 1929, rpt. 1990), p. 9.

of metaphysics, the 'Queen' of all sciences, as Kant calls it. But the more 'matured judgment' of Kant's time would no longer subjugate itself. From indifference it developed a critical stance, a refusal to let metaphysics reign with unimpeachable authority, a demand that metaphysics be called to account by a greater authority. If Kant can distinguish his world with such indifference, how much more then can we in our world, where indifference has developed a post-critical stance, and maybe even a cynical posture, as the reigning claims to authority are put into unremitting question. Let us then also convert our indifference to a criticism, but now one aimed at the newest claims of an interdisciplinarity.

Of course our critique cannot follow the exhaustive nature Kant claims for his critique. Indeed, such presumption of comprehensiveness, of totality, of *a priori* absolutism, is the very thing we can no longer hold in our post-Kantian world, whether as regards the faculty of reason, or as regards any other human faculty. Nor do we preclude experience and illustration, which Kant so easily dismisses in the name of logical or discursive clarity. *Intuitive* or *aesthetic* clarity is what he must forego, he says, as they are necessary only from a 'popular point of view', and interfere with the rigors of speculative knowledge or 'the coherence that follows from unity of principle: ... The reader is not allowed to arrive sufficiently quickly at a conspectus of the whole; the bright coloring of the illustrative material intervenes to cover over and conceal the articulation and organization of the system, which, if we are to be able to judge of its unity and solidity, are what chiefly concern us.'[3] But what is this 'conspectus' we are to arrive at? On the one hand, it is the very thing the rhetoric of interdisciplinarity holds out as its promise. And yet on the other hand interdisciplinarity has not been averse to cross over into the realm of the *intuitive* or of the *aesthetic* as part of its licensed border crossing, and again literary criticism affords us one of our clearest examples of such an incursion. Can interdisciplinarity justify this double claim, a conspectus of the whole and yet at the same time an aesthetic incursion? Kant will struggle with this very dilemma, as he treats the question of the *aesthetic* first in its ancient Greek sense (that which is intuited through the senses) in the First Critique, and then later in its more modern sense of artistic beauty in the Third Critique. To address the problem of interdisciplinarity, we first need to do as Kant did: reduce the question to its 'pure' form. From there we may then proceed more critically towards the aesthetic in all its 'impure' senses.

What might be a 'pure interdisciplinarity'? For Kant the term 'pure' took on an important new sense: that which comes before all experience and which denotes the very structure of a given faculty or principle. Under this rubric, a pure interdisciplinarity becomes not only that which precedes a practical interdisciplinarity, in the same way that Kant's pure reason precedes his practical reason, but also that which grounds the practical version, in the same way that Kant's practical version is predicated upon the pure version.

Let us push this further. In its purity, interdisciplinarity would provide the structural possibility by which any one particular discipline might emerge. To study any one science, for example, one must have an understanding, however previously

[3] *Ibid.*, p. 13.

determined or made conscious to the mind, of that which allows science to arise in the first place. To study the humanities, one must have an understanding of what constitutes the 'human' or the 'humanity' from which the humanities take their various disciplinary departures. To practice interdisciplinary studies, we must have something that allows or accounts for the existence of the 'inter-', that prefixing feature which binds all our disciplines together. This notion of binding purity is what the term 'university' first tried to capture in its Scholastic origins – a purity claimed foremost by theology, the study of the divine that binds all our reality together. We have lost this sense of the cosmological and theological 'universe' in our academy, and now understand its 'universe' in a more summative sense: the university is an entity which, in the theory of our great liberalism, may be greater than the sum of its individual parts, but which, in the pragmatic reality of academic life and procedure, does little more than gather all our disciplines under one roof and validate their occupation. Practically, the term 'university' is now a cipher into which we pour our own particular disciplinary identity. If we were to return to a pure interdisciplinarity, this identity would become greatly disrupted.

If we were to dare such a disruption, we would find ourselves once again seeking out the aid of a critical theory to ground our newly constituted selves. But amid the rhetorical polyphony that would ensue, if only because competing forces would never let one disciplinary discourse be sovereign over another, we would find that any criticism, under the Kantian drive, would require a self-criticism as well, a subjection of its own powers as part of the critique. To this end, a new discourse or a new language might emerge, not as a totalizing structure that allows for the Kantian 'conspectus' to be founded as a unified system, but as a modal structure that keeps its own mode under the force of the criticism. For pure interdisciplinarity would be just that, a *mode*. And we know from Kant that the questions concerning mode, those regarding its mechanisms, its procedures, and its limits, are the very questions for which *Kritik* was first introduced. Thus we would stand in a more strategic position to help orient us to the rhetorical nature that such a purity of interdisciplinary mode would unavoidably carry with it.

We may have already seen the foreshadowing of such a critical strategy within the broad wake of Kant's critical legacy, at least as it pertains to the history or historicity of a possible interdisciplinary development. The critical strategy laid out for us by Michel Foucault owes a direct debt to Kant, as Foucault himself admits.[4] If Foucault is right, the language of any one discipline is a product of many other languages, or discourses, which together have created the necessary constituents of and conditions for an environment in which it is first possible for another language to become a discipline. These 'discursive formations', as Foucault calls them, are by no means homogeneous entities, but arise themselves out of varying bodies of preconceived knowledge, some of which are situated within the mainstream of social understanding and acceptance, many of which are marginal to that mainstream. The knowledge itself is not grounded upon a universal or absolute base, upon the authority of an original and transcendental act of giving, as Foucault

[4] See David Couzens Hoy 'Foucault vs. Habermas' in Hoy and McCarthy, *Critical Theory*, especially p. 146.

describes it,[5] but emerges organically through the various sedimentations of discursive practice built up over time. He gives us an example of such an emergence in the rise of a nineteenth-century psychiatric discipline, in which we might see the possible prototype of an interdisciplinarity at work:

> This discipline had neither the same content, nor the same internal organization, nor the same place in medicine, nor the same practical function, nor the same methods as the traditional chapter on 'diseases of the head' or 'nervous diseases' to be found in eighteenth-century medical treatises. But on examining this new discipline, we discovered two things: what made it possible at the time it appeared, what brought about this great change in the economy of concepts, analyses, and demonstrations, was a whole set of relations between hospitalization, internment, the conditions and procedures of social exclusion, the rules of jurisprudence, the norms of industrial labour and bourgeois morality, in short a whole group of relations that characterized for this discursive practice the formation of its statements; but this practice is not only manifested in a discipline possessing a scientific status and scientific pretensions; it is also found in legal texts, in literature, in philosophy, in political decisions, and in the statements made and opinions expressed in daily life. The discursive formation whose existence was mapped by the psychiatric discipline was not coextensive with it, far from it: it went well beyond the boundaries of psychiatry.[6]

Foucault's critical apparatus here, 'archaeology', even in this extremely abridged view of it, exposes the multiple factors by which a practice becomes a recognized practice, factors which go well beyond the practice's own immediate concern, and take us to wider cultural and intellectual forces.

The work Foucault has done in the human sciences is unsurpassed in showing discursive buildup, its many stratifications, and its unsettling lack of a primary or original substratum. What if we were to think in similar terms as we try to describe interdisciplinarity in its purity? We would find that what allows *all* our disciplines (not just the natural and social sciences) to take their specific shape, and mark themselves off from the totality of the body politic, the academy as an administrative institution, relies on a certain structural priority which furnishes individual disciplines their ability to function as a distinct discourse. That this priority was once the divine Word – in a Scholastic sense, the eternal reason that issued forth from the Godhead; in a Protestant sense, the specific revelation of the Word of God, the Holy Scriptures – is something we cannot ignore, nor will we. But we must emphasize that this discursive priority, for Foucault, is not in any way originary. What provides the structural basis of our discourses does not come from some transcendent place, but from heterogeneous languages and formations which, although preceding our discourses, precede without any fixed location as a starting point, except insofar as they are fixed within the fluctuating and often competing natures of our human history. This way of conceiving the 'origins' of discourse (which Foucault terms 'genealogical', following Nietzsche, as opposed to 'evolutionary') might help us to understand a pure interdisciplinarity not as a

---

[5] Michel Foucault, *The Archaeology of Knowledge*, trans. A.M. Sheridan Smith (London: Routledge, 1972, rpt. 1989), p. 192.

[6] *Ibid.*, p. 179.

stable theological or epistemological site which grounds any discipline that emerges from it, only to turn silent as that discipline articulates itself, but as the place which grants any discipline its discursive grammar, and which is always in some sense vocal in that grammar. This place, with its 'vocality', we could justifiably call a place of rhetoric, bound as it is to discourse, and self-conscious as it would become if we called attention to it from whatever disciplinary vantage of criticism we may have first begun. But of course by 'rhetoric' we would now mean something different than the rhetoric we presently find paraded up and down the halls of academia in the loose name of interdisciplinary studies. We would mean something that approximates a 'truth' of what first allows us to speak.

Truth? Amid rhetoric? How can we talk about a truth here? Do we not now invoke the spirit of Socrates whether we intend to or not, as it rises seethingly, to denounce the bastardization of truth in the guise of any rhetoric? And yet the question of truth properly belongs here. For truth is what has been so often invoked in our present interdisciplinary approaches, as an attempt is made to unify our discourses in the name of something higher and more absolute. Indeed, truth is what all liberal education has always claimed as the principal object of its pursuit, through disciplines both traditional and new. Yet we also know that truth, in the tradition of Platonic critique, is that which opposes rhetoric. Rhetoric's mandate is merely to persuade its audience towards what seems most convincing, without any consideration for the high ideals of truth. Thus Socrates relentlessly dismissed the Sophists and their rhetorical ploys. If then a pure interdisciplinarity is rhetorical by virtue of its nature as a mode of discourse, how could we advocate, in the name of truth, its priority? Here is precisely where a new grammar, a new language, a new discourse, a new consciousness must begin to take shape, as it leaves behind one understanding of truth, one that has guided the Enlightenment project since the seventeenth century, and takes on a reformulated understanding of truth within the horizon of a non-originary purity.

Foucault's archaeology, with all the disruptions it has brought to our traditional notions of truth, set its sights chiefly on the human sciences. But the question of *truth and rhetoric* takes its starting point well before the rise of modern science in all its forms. If we are to treat this question critically – because it is, fundamentally, a question of critique – then we must now, under the guiding force of philosophical intention and rigor, not only include that space which Kant had purposefully eschewed in his First Critique, only to return to it later in qualified form, the space of aesthetics, but also set our sights on that realm which has long held sway over the question of truth – religion. Here, in the crossover where truth and rhetoric most powerfully meet, that aboriginal ground which has been prepared long before science's schism from the humanities, we find ourselves facing anew the critical question which has driven humankind in all its cultural variations and densities for as long as humankind has expressed itself in developed language. But now we face it with the need for a critical language to develop with yet another modulation. *This* side of the modern scientific project, *this* side of the Enlightenment reign of reason, in the interdisciplinarity of a world where borders continue to be erased between old competing sectors, and new allegiances are being daily formed and tested, truth once again must turn and face its old rival rhetoric, though in modernity's new arena of 'post-' determinations. We stand then before a strange mutation in the question of our destiny, for it seems now our destiny must of necessity come to us from within the question of language.

But any language we adopt will have to be a language of *self-reflection*. Our critical powers must turn inward upon themselves. In this move, though akin to the Kantian move, we do not embrace any transcendentalism. The reflexivity is not towards a position of pure anteriority or exteriority, not towards a speculative ascendancy with magisterial rights, superseding all other claims to knowledge. It is towards a perpetual critique of the critique, the critical force turning upon itself in a manner that abrogates all rights, even for itself. This self-assessing, self-rivaling force functions under the critical structure of a *hermeneutic*, which exposes not only the interpretive strategies that make up the critique, but the provisional and always tenuous hermeneutical frame that allows for the existence and operation of those strategies. A transcendental positioning is thus frustrated and rendered impossible by such a hermeneutic, as it admits no closing off of its logical structures into something foundational or originary, but only an opening of continual self-evaluation and self-perpetuation. If we seek any 'grounds' in this self-reflexivity, they are to be found here – not in the abstracted stability of the metaphysical, the transcendental, the ideal or the universal, but in the fertility of a hermeneutical field which is forever undergoing re-creation, issuing forth possibilities from within that *existential* drawn for us so painstakingly, if problematically, by Heidegger, and which invites the cross-pollination of the conceptual with the intuitive, the philosophical with the aesthetic, the discursive with the illustrative, the ratiocinative with the instinctual, the noetic with the imaginative, the abstracted with the concretized. It is at such a critically hermeneutical and purely interdisciplinary site that we can begin to harvest our new formations.

Dare we embrace a pure interdisciplinarity? Dare we take truth to a new level and dimension, where rhetoric is found necessarily, and found as necessary? Dare we forge a new language? Are we ready for the risks that might accrue? Or do we remain indifferent to it all? But it seems we cannot remain indifferent, since we have already made a move, even in our current interdisciplinary rhetoric, towards *difference*. This is what makes our situation unique and unprecedented: our age has become the first to produce from indifference a new valuation of difference. As borders fall, difference becomes the new paradigm *contra* homogeneity and universality. That is to say, our indifference is hardly neutral, hardly an overriding mood or feeling that nothing matters. Quite the opposite – things matter now to us more than ever. The problem is that what matters is difference itself, and out of this difference we have developed a pathos too singular for its own good, too obsessed with maintaining its own difference that it is continually threatened by a thoroughgoing relativization. And we have found that such relativization, the main charge against, and a rising attitude within, our 'post-universal' world, tends in turn to lead to an apathy, a weariness and exhaustion under the realization that all our private actions are nothing more than evidence of a comprehensive and overwhelming inertia. Hence *indifferentism*, Kant's word for his own age of tired dissenters. We are worn down not only *by* the center which cannot hold, but *because* the center cannot hold, and in this knowledge we lapse into an indifferentism, and there valorize difference as a means of dealing with the dispersal. Indifferentism and difference – we have curiously merged these two words. And this is what passes for interdisciplinarity now. Can we, alongside Kant's hope, lift ourselves out of the defeated spirit of this age, on the back of our indifference and its indifferentists, to revitalize ourselves towards the thing that matters to us most, truth? Can we find new ground (and new grounds) for our pressing concerns, a critical language that gives new voice to our pathos, that transposes our indifference *and* our difference into an open, creative, intuitively rigorous mode of critical, and perhaps rhetorical, reflection? Do we have the courage for such a venture?

If we are to move forward in this postmodern world, we can no longer accept a lack of courage, like that of the young Nietzsche, to permit ourselves a new way of speaking. Nietzsche, in overcoming himself, has already opened up the way for us, has even called out the way to us, as the first modern thinker to bring truth out of the jurisdiction of the sciences and, more significantly, back into the district of rhetoric and play. Truth, he said, is a sum of human relations 'poetically and rhetorically heightened, transferred and adorned', and this claim is not an indictment against humankind so much as it is a celebration of its possibilities.[7] Nietzsche gives new meaning to the term 'humanities'. It is not simply that the realm of human conduct and thought reasserts itself over the natural world of scientific logic and law, but that natural science was only ever human, as the Greeks in their mythology so perspicuously and artfully saw. Thus in his later 'attempt at self-criticism' of *The Birth of Tragedy*, an attempt which embodied the critical spirit at its apogee, Nietzsche writes,

> And science itself, our science – indeed, what is the significance of all science, viewed as a symptom of life? For what – worse yet, *whence* – all science? How now? Is the resolve to be so scientific about everything perhaps a kind of fear of, an escape from, pessimism? A subtle last resort against – *truth*? And, morally speaking, a sort of cowardice and falseness? Amorally speaking, a ruse? O Socrates, Socrates, was that perhaps *your* secret?[8]

Even in the unmerciful critique of his own first effort in *The Birth of Tragedy*, with its borrowed voice and formulas, Nietzsche still praised the audacity of the book, praised it for what it 'dared to tackle for the first time: *to look at science in the perspective of the artist, but at art in that of life*.'[9] And we see now that his borrowed voice and lack of courage to strike out with an 'individual language' prompted a new manner of speaking, a new consciousness, a new path forward for the relation of art and life, of which the self-criticism fourteen years later was a ripe manifestation. 'How differently Dionysus spoke to me!'[10] How differently indeed, that God who possesses humans with the raw primal force of creativity.

---

[7] Friedrich Nietzsche, 'On Truth and Lying in an Extra-Moral Sense', in *Friedrich Nietzsche on Rhetoric and Language*, eds. and trans. Sander L. Gilman *et al.* (Oxford: Oxford University Press, 1989), p. 250.

[8] Friedrich Nietzsche, 'The Birth of Tragedy', in *Basic Writings of Nietzsche*, ed. and trans. Walter Kaufmann (New York: Modern Library, 1968), p. 18.

[9] *Ibid.*, p. 19.

[10] *Ibid.*, p. 24.

Nietzsche's Zarathustra would later state the matter clearly in his assertion that life itself can only be seen as an activity of art – '*First, peoples were creators*'.[11] Such is the very essence (if we can speak here of 'essence') of Nietzsche's critique, which sends its echo, sometimes openly, but often muffled, through the interdisciplinary chambers of our cultural spheres in science, politics, art, language and life. But now the Nietzschean reverberation must retune itself into something other than the necessary pessimism that Nietzsche claimed not only for himself, but even for Kant, and for his other great German predecessor, Luther. All creators are annihilators, and must destroy in order to rebuild, but we who have now experienced a century of destruction, at every conceivable level, stand to gather the various strands of our heritage and to wind them around new 'posts' and new pegs. The cutting and the hewing is over; it is time to arrange these strands into new harmonies under the tension of a deep and abiding critical force, whose exertion produces neither tonal nor atonal sounds, neither consonance nor dissonance, neither perfect nor imperfect intervals, but an entirely new 'harmolodic'[12] structure, upon which scales never before heard will emerge with strangely familiar pitches to sound out new songs and hitherto unheard orchestration. The prelude to this movement, the overture, is neither Wagnerian nor Nietzschean, nor is it even Kantian. It is the atmosphere of the last several decades which, though ringing with the overtones of these great innovators and their successors, has been calling out of its indifference for something radically different.

And so, how do we proceed?

Right at the outset, let us establish at least one mode of approach. Let us be what Nietzsche in his Preface to *Die Morgenröte* (*Daybreak*) calls 'friends of *lento*'.[13] This musical term asks for care and circumspection in the face of an impatient, indifferent, and hurried temperament, often so characteristic of our day (and far more so than in Nietzsche's). This term Nietzsche transcribes from the discipline of music to the wider realm of reading and texts, dictating against a blinding haste that wants to get everything done at once. We cannot get everything done at once, obviously. But let us say of any new consciousness we may conceive: 'this art does not so easily get anything done, it teaches to read *well*, that is to say, to read slowly, deeply, looking cautiously before and aft, with reservations, with doors left open, with delicate eyes and fingers ...'.[14] This art of *lento*, may it be inscribed above the first page of our overture, upon the proscenium arch of our stage. For as we shall see, the art of reading well is necessitated within any new critique we adopt, and may well become the determining characteristic of our new age.

---

[11] Nietzsche, 'Thus Spoke Zarathustra', in *The Portable Nietzsche*, ed. and trans. Walter Kaufmann (New York: Viking Penguin, 1982), p. 171 (italics added).

[12] A term coined by musician Ornette Coleman to denote a convergence of harmony and melody.

[13] Friedrich Nietzsche, *Daybreak*, trans. R.J. Hollingdale (Cambridge: Cambridge University Press, 1982), p. 5.

[14] *Ibid.*

1 John

What is truth? In what does its essence consist?

That question is always already included in the guiding question and the grounding question of philosophy. It runs ahead of them and yet is most intrinsic to these very questions. It is the primal question of philosophy.

Martin Heidegger[1]

Τί ἐστιν ἀλήθεια; 'What is truth?' This question has come to us in every language, and, we might say, in every discipline. It is the driving force behind not just philosophy proper, but every serious inquiry into the reality of our existence and our experience. By it we seek out more than what meets our eye, for truth has always suggested something beyond our eye. Hence its longstanding association with the divine. When we pose the question, we always bring with it an invocation of divinity, and the deep history which our understanding of divinity has produced, regardless from what stance and set of presuppositions we direct the question, and regardless of how conscious we are of this theological import. By virtue of asking the question we face the possibility of the divine, even if we retreat from that possibility. And the answer we expect, if not the answer we actually find or receive, always anticipates something numinous, since to ask the question is already to acknowledge a possibility beyond what reality here and now affords, beyond what we can here and now grasp.

Yet as spoken by Pilate to a tired and beset Jesus, the question remains ambiguous. With what tone did the Pilate of John's Gospel pose that question in his praetorium? Was it a tone of curiosity, derision, dismissal, interrogation, disputation, perplexity, fascination, or exasperation? More importantly, why did Jesus furnish no answer? Because he himself could not divine the tone with which the question was put? Or because divining the tone all too well, he knew it fruitless to answer? Or was the question *rhetorical*, as most translators imply, and thus required no answer? But rhetorical or not, here was an opportunity for Jesus to answer. Here, before the arbiter of his fate, a question is put that could not possibly have had any bearing on his fate, but could have set the record straight once and for all. Jesus, the one who bears witness to the truth, the one who earlier claimed he *was* the truth, could now speak to the one authority who, for all intents and purposes, had no vested interest in his person, a third and neutral party, so to speak. Yet this most powerful ally, a sympathizer not to Jesus' cause but to his very being, who even vouchsafed the chance for self-defense and vindication, now asks the most fundamental question of all to this strange prisoner, this self-proclaimed witness to the truth. And Pilate receives no answer. Why was Jesus reticent on the very matter that plagues us all so incessantly and profoundly? Was Pilate not the perfect kind to whom Jesus could divulge the truth, a second-tier Roman official whose very political need to mitigate strife amid dangerous local factions qualified him as perhaps the safest ear for a truth which surpassed all local programs, ideologies, theologies, and fidelities? Surely the answer, were it sought in faith,

[1] Martin Heidegger, *Nietzsche, Volumes One and Two*, ed. and trans. David Farrell Krell (New York: HarperCollins, 1991), p. 141.

would not have jeopardized the divine destiny of the one they called 'The King of the Jews'. Surely, on the eve of a most dramatic end to an extraordinary mission (foreknown and foretold), Jesus might have laid the truth bare, if not for his adversaries and disciples – those who could not see past the religio-political aspect of his teaching – then for one who, in an honest privacy and with a crucial indifference, gave him the benefit of an all-too important doubt.

But perhaps Pilate was not the perfect sub-witness to the truth. Perhaps his question was not sought in faith, at least the faith of an open and sincere inquiry. Perhaps the question *was* purely rhetorical. Perhaps Pilate was too disinterested – or perhaps not disinterested enough. Perhaps in the end his tenuous alliance and fleeting sympathy could lead only to mocking tones, inevitable with one in a position of power for whom such religious eccentricity as Jesus, a man who seemed pathetically naive before the law, must ever appear as simple and petty. Perhaps. But let us recast our own line of questioning.

Let us ask rather why the Gospel writer did not record any answer. Why do we have this glaring gap in John's account, set up by a question which does not appear in any of the Synoptic Gospels, and in which, upon the falling pitch of its interrogative, we find ourselves nowhere, in silence, until the next action in the narrative when Pilate leaves the praetorium and returns to the accusers who wait outside? Why this odd lacuna in the dialogue, bridged by the ambiguous services of a following participle (εἰπὼν) in John 18:38, which could be rendered many ways, but is probably the surest in its least defined form, 'having said' – 'Having said this, he again went out to the Jews, and said to them, "I find no crime in him" '? What transpired immediately after this 'having said'? Is the fact that the question was 'said' (εἰπὼν) and not 'asked' (ἠρώτησας) close the matter as rhetorical without question? Or, in the lingering ambiguity, did the dialogue continue, unrecorded? Was there a great conference on the nature of truth? An earnest and intense debate? A brief parley? A quiet reflection? A sagacious monologue? A succinct and revelatory pronouncement? Why, whatever the case, are we not party to the event? Why do we peer over into the darkened abyss of this textual gap and hear no echoes, no murmurings? Why are we not told whether Pilate's question was in good faith or bad, genuine or rhetorical, a pivotal question for any exegesis? Why are we left with nothing, when the author seems in the best place to give us something?

Pilate's question is in return to Jesus' statement πᾶς ὁ ὢν ἐκ τῆς ἀληθείας ἀκούει μου τῆς φωνῆς – 'Everyone who is of the truth hears my voice.' But we hear no voices following Pilate's response to this. We do not even hear the Gospel writer's voice. Given the nature of this affair, what are we to make of this taciturnity? Is the writer telling us that we, the readers, could not possibly be ὢν ἐκ τῆς ἀληθείας, counted among those being of or from the truth, and therefore that we cannot be privy to any ensuing conversation? More poignantly, is the writer telling us that he (or she?) is not ὢν ἐκ τῆς ἀληθείας, and thus has not heard for himself (or herself) the voice with which the truth is unveiled? What does it mean to be ὁ ὢν ἐκ τῆς ἀληθείας? The text never reveals whether Pilate was someone from the truth or not. We are kept from the secret, in the dark. The interrogative decays into a nothingness, only to be re-invoked again and again from within the various structures and disciplines of human inquiry we have built for this very purpose. Τί ἐστιν ἀλήθεια;

What we encounter here in the text is more than a narrative strategy. Granted, John has presented us with a case, Jesus before Pilate, on which the immediate fate of the accused Jesus hinges. In this narrative a political and legal tribunal turns private and philosophical. But this meeting takes place within a larger narrative of passion, of ministry, and of proclamation. We can read this one episode as part of a sequence of events, and, as so many have worthily done within traditional theological and literary criticism, render the story according to a larger narrative momentum, as the various currents of meaning are traced along historical, linguistic, redactive, figurative, symbolic, formal and/or structural(ist) lines. All these analyses, whether from confessional or purely philological positions, yield similar readings in regard to Pilate's interrogation of Jesus: the encounter marks an apex in the confrontation between two differing authorities, and a point of departure from which two incommensurable realms (βασιλεῖαι) move their separate ways, one back to the world, and one to another place altogether, foreign and unknown. But the question of truth that emerges here, and acts as a fulcrum in the confrontation, this pivotal moment when decision hangs in the balance, is itself a point of departure. If we take the very presence of the question as anticipation, an anticipation inherent in the question itself, then the question, far from ending matters, becomes another kind of beginning point. This point of beginning becomes the realization of the lacuna that exists as the quintessence of the question, and that is brought into greater relief by the rhetorical suggestiveness with which the question is left hanging. This lacuna is the very gap that separates the human from the divine. Here in John it is textually arranged and set forth to bring out all the more the profound nature of that separation we as humans have never ceased trying to overcome. This point of beginning is not an invitation to start this attempt all over again. The point of the beginning is rather to acknowledge the gap's existence in all its silent but swallowing depth. The point is to gaze into its dark chasm, as Pilate did into Jesus' eyes, in an attempt to plumb the mysterious region for something that does not meet the eye, something unknown.

If Pilate's question remains rhetorical, it is not because the answer is known. A rhetorical question is one in which some response is already implied in the asking of the question. It is asked merely for 'effect', we say. By asking, we have already 'effected' to some degree the answer which the interrogative sets up. Pilate had already given us a prime example of such rhetorical questioning only a few verses earlier. If we return to the beginning of this pericope, we can see a development in the succession of questioning. Pilate's first question to Jesus upon their initial encounter in the praetorium was one very opposite to the rhetorical, one demanding as direct an answer as possible, given that the fate of all parties involved – Pilate, Jesus and the Jews – was at stake: 'Are you the King of the Jews?' Yet Jesus supplies anything but a direct answer: 'Do you say this of your own accord, or did others say it to you about me?' (John 18:34–35, RSV). Jesus is the first to cross into rhetorical territory here, as his question implies an answer – 'you are asking this only because my reputation precedes me, not because you have come to this possibility of your own accord.' But Jesus' psychology is far more penetrating than simply a clever retort. What Jesus' question in fact effects is a complete shift in the line of questioning – from the political intentions and ramifications of ferreting out a possible rival, who may be gathering a band of zealots for insurrection against the established sovereignty of Rome, to the personal intentions and existential ramifications involved in questions of belief. If Jesus' reply is rhetorical, it is of the kind where the implied answer is less a mutually accepted and pre-established factor than it is a change in the nature and scope of the inquiry. The effect is upon context, not upon predication. And in this change, Jesus is drawing Pilate into a private space to which Pilate is unprepared to go. Thus he resists with a perfectly rhetorical response to Jesus' question: Μήτι ἐγὼ Ἰουδαῖός εἰμι; 'Am I a Jew?' (John 18:35). Three questions in a row, leading from a pure interrogative to the purely rhetorical. The answer to the third question is obvious because, of course, Pilate is not a Jew, and both parties know it. Hence the emphatic Μήτι that begins the question, a Greek participle which in questions expects a negative answer. With this emphatic response, as proclamatory in language as the interrogative can be, Pilate puts up a wall to Jesus' probing. The rhetorical is used here as a shield.

As the encounter proceeds, Pilate continues to stand his ground by deflecting the line of the question back to his domain, the political and legal: 'Your own nation and the chief priests have handed you over to me; what have you done?' (John 18:36). The emphatic 'no' implied in the preceding Μήτι now carries through to this following statement, which 'in effect' says, 'Obviously I am not a Jew; it is not I but your own people who have charged you with illegitimacy. Don't blame me for your troubles. Account for yourself.' Thus the questioning returns to the pure interrogative with imperative force, demanding an unambivalent answer: 'what have you done?' But Jesus yet again pulls back the line of questioning from Pilate's context, stating that his kingdom or kingship (βασιλεία) is not of this world. Pilate's realm carries no jurisdiction over Jesus' realm, nor does the realm of the revolutionist Jews or the realm of the dogmatic chief priests. Jesus, in redirecting the heart of the matter from this politically-charged world to another, is magnifying the incommensurability of the two authorities at stake. His βασιλεία is neither of Rome nor of a separate Jewish state. It resides elsewhere.

Having no context for this βασιλεία, Pilate makes one last attempt to reestablish his ground. Οὐκοῦν βασιλεὺς εἶ σύ; 'So you are a king?', he asks (John 18:37). Here the adverb Οὐκοῦν is inferential, giving the question an affirmative directive. The questioning thus moves again within the perimeter of the rhetorical, as the answer is forced along an assenting response implicit in the question. But Jesus now dismantles Pilate's rhetorical construction and contextual armor once and for all. He finally responds with an unqualified statement: Σὺ λέγεις ὅτι βασιλεύς εἰμι. '*You* say that I am a king.' Individual decision and belief is now marking the context and controlling the direction of conversation, as Pilate is made fully responsible for the logical grammar of his Οὐκοῦν. Now Jesus can draw Pilate into the fold of his βασιλεία: 'For this I was born, and for this I have come into the world, to bear witness to the truth. Every one who is of the truth hears my voice' (John 18:37, RSV). εἰς τοῦτο, 'for this', for the question of belief, for Pilate's ability to come now into the jurisdiction of belief, Jesus has left one domain and one authority and entered another, this world. And now, standing before one who epitomizes this world's power, and who can enforce his departure, Jesus confronts this worldly authority with the question of truth – the truth of himself and the truth of Pilate. μαρτυρήσω τῇ ἀληθείᾳ – Jesus bears witness to the truth (John 18:37). John has already told us that he came into this world full of truth (John 1:14), but if in fact there is more to this, if in fact he *is* the truth, as Jesus had self-proclaimed (John 14:6), then here he bears witness to himself, and witnesses for himself, as the authority of his own, far different, kingdom. Thus, πᾶς ὁ ὢν ἐκ τῆς ἀληθείας ἀκούει μου τῆς φωνῆς: whoever is of the truth hears Jesus' voice. But we have already asked: what does it mean to be ἐκ τῆς ἀληθείας, 'of [or from] the truth'? Is Pilate now 'of the truth' by virtue of hearing Jesus' voice in the privacy of his praetorium, and of coming into Jesus' sphere of authority, however reluctantly or unaware? Or is Jesus trying to draw Pilate yet further into this sphere, to get Pilate to embrace more fully this authority and thereby embrace a different truth than what Pilate's world can afford? How does one become ἐκ τῆς ἀληθείας? But Pilate does not ask this question. Pilate asks a more fundamental question. Pilate asks, what *is* truth? If this question is rhetorical, it is out of the anticipatory nature of the question at its most basic level. But it is not rhetorical in the conventional sense of anticipating something *known*. It is not like his previous question Μήτι ἐγὼ Ἰουδαῖός εἰμι; ('Am I a Jew?'), or even Οὐκοῦν βασιλεὺς εἶ σύ; ('So you are a king?'), where the known was not just anticipated but already in some degree obtained. It is rhetorical in the sense of anticipating only something unknown. For there is nothing directly at hand for Pilate to know, except Jesus, the man he stands before and surveys. And this fact he does not yet know, which is why he asks the question he does. For if he knew that there was nothing to know but Jesus, he would ask a question with a rhetoric more effecting of that which can be affirmed or denied.

John does not supply us with any answer to Pilate's question because the truth here is caught up in the in-between. Just as the verdict on Jesus is suspended in the halls of this Gentile praetorium, where even the Jews will not go because it is ceremonially unclean, and just as commensurability is suspended in the collision of radically dissimilar worlds and authorities, so the question of truth sits over a gaping chasm that cannot be closed. That Pilate has not been able to understand what it means to be 'of the truth' we can see from the other side of his question, when he returns to the Jews outside for direction, when he flogs and parades Jesus with mocking display, when he twice exonerates Jesus according to the legalities of the Roman system ('I find no crime in him', John 18:38, 19:6), and, most significantly, when he returns to Jesus for one final encounter in his inner and private court. Here the gap we have been suggesting is outlined in bold strokes. As Pilate not only exonerates Jesus but tries to absolve himself, as he pronounces Jesus innocent of any crime for a second time and gives the matter back into the hands of the Jews, he is told: 'We have a law, and by that law he ought to die, because he has made himself the Son of God' (John 19:7). At this, the narrative tells us Pilate became even more afraid, and immediately returned to Jesus in the praetorium for one last set of questions. 'Where are you from?', he asks. But we read that 'Jesus gave no answer' (John 19:9). This silence is an echo of the silence that follows Pilate's previous question about truth. We see the nature of the first silence, the textual lacuna, now reinforced: it is a question of divinity. 'Where are you from?' becomes a reprise of 'What is truth?'. And the gap that separates the human from the divine becomes the gap entextualized here by John's narrative, while in the narrative itself it is embodied in Jesus. Pilate's rhetoric then can only give way to the exasperation of a demanded answer unforthcoming: 'Will you not speak to me? Do you not know that I have power to release you, and power to crucify you?'

(John 19:10). But these words, these questions, resort to the known reach of Pilate's jurisdiction, his realm of authority, which is now frustrated by the insistent silence. When Jesus does speak, his final words to Pilate are not about his question of truth. They are about authority, and about culpability: 'You would have no power over me unless it had been given you from above; therefore he who delivered me to you has the greater sin' (John 19:11). Now it is Jesus who offers exoneration to Pilate, and it is Jesus' authority that closes and seals the interrogation. But the gap, the unanswered center of the conversation, remains, in the same way that Jesus remains standing before Pilate.

What we are isolating here is certainly a phenomenon of the text. The narrative deliberately falls silent at the place where we most want an answer, in order to let the rhetoricality of the posed question carry us, in anticipation, backward (or forward) to the individual who claimed he was truth. And this is John's theological and textual 'strategy', if we can designate him one. But even John, like his Pilate, gets more than he bargained for, as the created gap leaves open the question in all its permutations to a silence that will not close down the interrogation with propositional assertions and unambiguous explanations. The silence has rattled Pilate, but it rattles through the entire pericope as that disturbing in-between site that marks out the ineffable separation of the human from the divine. This is the space Blanchot has so painfully and so exquisitely demarcated in all his work, the one modern writer who is most willing to occupy this gap as a matter of course. (But how? He is strangely silent, except insofar as he calls the inhabitation of this space an 'essential solitude'[2].) Pilate then becomes the great human symbol of one who peers over the edge into the abyss with both irrepressible fear and irrepressible need. His question of truth distills this fear and this need with an almost other-worldly condensation. Goethe once wrote of Pilate: 'All power, skills, feeling, abstraction, all science, acumen, all examination, all deep feeling of humanity, in all its circumstances and its merits ... he leaves behind, he throws away, in order to hound breathlessly after the unattainable.'[3] What is truth? Is it only and always unattainable? The gap in the question leaves us breathless, and even John has no voice with which he can describe or utter. All he can do is point to the blank space between Pilate and Jesus.

It was Heidegger who suggested we cannot ask a question without first having a sense of what its answer could be. If this has merit, our question of truth becomes an even greater disturbance. Perhaps this is why Heidegger sees it as 'the primal question of philosophy', running before all other questions. Yet if it is indeed primal, if it is intrinsic to the most 'grounding' questions of the philosophical endeavor, then we must shift our understanding of truth completely.

As Heidegger points out in *Sein und Zeit*, truth has been traditionally bound with *assertion*: 'assertion has been accepted from ancient times as the primary and

---

[2] See Maurice Blanchot, *The Space of Literature*, trans. Ann Smock (Lincoln: University of Nebraska Press, 1982).

[3] Johann Wolfgang Goethe, 'Ein Wort Über Den Verfasser Des Pilatus', *Sämliche Werke*, gen. ed. Karl Richter, *Vol. 2.2, Erstes Weimarer Jahrzehnt, 1775-1786*, eds Hannelore Schlaffer, *et al.* (Munich: Carl Hanser Verlag, 1987), p. 471: *All Kräfte Fähigkeiten, Empfindung, Abstraktion, alle Wissenschafte, Scharfsinn, alles Anschauen, alles tiefe Gefühl der Menscheit und ihrer Verhältnisse und mehr Vorzüge ... läßt er zurück, wirft er weg, um dem unerreichbaren atemlos nachzuhetzen.*

authentic "locus" of *truth.*'[4] Truth is something we can point to, and yet assertion, he goes on to extrapolate, is only a *derivative* mode of understanding and interpretation: assertion as 'a pointing-out which gives something a definite character and which communicates' already assumes, on the basis of being-in-the-world, a prior knowledge or a prior grasp of that something. This assumption involves Heidegger's famous 'fore-structures' ('fore-having', 'fore-sight' and 'fore-conception') with which we come to understand anything through our interpretation.[5] They pre-structure our ability to assert: 'in any approach when one gives something a definite character, one is already taking a look directionally at what is to be put forward in the assertion.'[6] We could apply the same to questioning: the fore-structures pre-structure our ability to question, as we are already taking a look directionally at what can be put forward as an answer in order for the question to make any sense as a question. All questions, just as much as all assertions, must come from a place of being-in-the-world, and thus carry with them the world as it has been already experienced by our Being as Dasein: being *there* (*da)* in the world. But if the question 'What is truth' is intrinsic and grounding to all other questions concerning the reality of this world, then we have one more fore-structure, the 'fore-question', which disturbingly does not take us to a place of assertion, but to the open interrogative which anticipates something that we may not in fact find in-the-world (hence the question). For what is it that we have pre-grasped or pre-conceived in the fundamental question about truth? Or we could ask anew: what does it mean to be 'from the truth' (ἐκ τῆς ἀληθείας)? The question arises from something that is not there, from something that does not meet our eye directly, but comes to us only through a witness. And yet this something that is absent, this nothing, must be somehow prior in our grasp, if we are able to ask the question with any accepted sense. But truth is never something 'at hand', which is why we ask the question. What is this nothing then which we have had prior in our grasp? It can only be another question, or *questioning itself*, the *question* of truth. Our shift in understanding then is that truth, if it has a 'locus' anywhere, does not lie in that which is being asserted but in that which is being interrogated. Is this not what Pilate shows us? Truth lies somewhere in the question 'What is truth?'. Truth is in the question.

Heidegger saw clearly that the 'phenomenon of truth is so thoroughly coupled with the problem of Being that our investigation, as it proceeds further, will necessarily come up against the problem of truth'.[7] The question of ἀλήθεια carries no assertion, no facticity even, but only the inquisitive, open-ended nature of an interrogative quest whose lack of closure, even in its most rhetorical form, cuts to the very core of our Being. But if this fore-question carries nothing at its center, what does it say for the structure of our Being? Is there a nothing which helps constitute our being-in-the-world, a silence that follows – and now we could say that *precedes* – our question of truth? In Heidegger's reappraisal and attempted

---

[4] Martin Heidegger, *Being and Time*, trans. John Macquarrie and Edward Robinson (Oxford: Basil Blackwell, 1962), p. 196.

[5] '*Vorhabe*', '*Vorsicht*', and '*Vorgriff*'. *Ibid.*, pp. 188ff.

[6] *Ibid.*, p. 199.

[7] *Ibid.*, p. 196.

overturning of traditional ontology, the Being of the Self finds its existential structure not only as Being-in-the-world, the Dasein thrown into the light of worldly existence, but, we also learn, as Being-towards-death, the Dasein cast within the anxiety and against the reality of its pending non-existence. The nothingness of death, then, is for Heidegger built into the very structural mode of Being.

This nothingness raises itself now in connection with Heidegger's famous rendering of ἀλήθεια as 'unconcealedness', ἀ-λήθεια, in which the prefix discloses the privative nature of truth (a 'not' forgetting or an 'un'- concealing). As uncovering is a way of Being for Being-in-the-world, the Dasein becomes 'true' or 'truth' in the sense of Being-uncovered.[8] But the truth of Dasein, Heidegger tells us, also carries the privative side of its structure, so that Being-in-the-world is characterized by both the positive and the negative: 'The goddess of Truth who guides Parmenides, puts two pathways before him, one of uncovering, one of hiding; but this signifies nothing else than that Dasein is already both in the truth and in untruth.'[9] The existential condition of Being is thus predicated upon the dichotomy of concealment and disclosure, and the movement from the one to other is for Heidegger what constitutes ἀλήθεια. But indeed this movement cannot conceal its point of departure, for it is the very lacuna of John's Gospel, which, in the very nature of ἀλήθεια questioned by Pilate, conceals and discloses at the same time: conceals the answer of the question, and discloses the answer as the question. Herein lies its rhetorical force – exposing the answer as the question.

Of course Heidegger also deepens the issue, for now the gap is not merely textual, but existential. Our Being itself holds a lacuna, a cavity which, though it may contain possibility, is in essence a lack or a privation, an opening to our non-existence. Heidegger's marking of this space has continued to be redrawn and extended in the course of our postmodern advance, and with bolder lines, so that all structures of the Self become unstable and collapsible bridges over an indefinable yet ultimately unavoidable space. As Pilate's question is never directly answered, so too at the innermost part of our Being and Selfhood we find no direct answers. All that we can call direct is a primordial, and abiding, nothingness – a silent ringing before and between question and answer. In this prior and intervallic place, at the heart of the dehiscent force of asking (interrogative) and of the occlusive force of response (assertion), there is no speech, no language. It is 'the rest' of Hamlet's final words: 'the rest is silence'. This space is inarticulable, ineffable, beyond anything we can conceptualize or formulate. It is why John sends Pilate immediately out into the courtyard after the question: an answer is not available.

We might say then that Pilate also represents the crisis of our times, the crisis of our postmodern predicament, in that we no longer have available a ready and consensual answer for this question of truth. All answers and all bridges crumble under their own weight and disappear into the chasm. We can no longer ignore the disquieting fact that this question of truth involves a nothingness, that the question

---

8 *Ibid.*, p. 263.

9 *Ibid.*, p. 265. Cf. also Martin Heidegger *Parmenides*, trans. André Schuwer and Richard Rojcewicz (Bloomington: Indiana University Press, 1992), particularly, though not exclusively, pp. 1–16.

is party to the gap. Nor can we elude the fact that this gap stands at the center of who we are as beings, that an ontological stability of the self is no longer available in this post-Heideggerean world, that this caesura in John is nothing more than the caesura we now discover as an inexorable feature of our essential interiority, that the ὁ ὢν, the "one being" of Jesus' ὁ ὢν ἐκ τῆς ἀληθείας, is, contrary to our persistent and arrogant beliefs, no longer us, and that we no longer hear the voice of truth, at least as once conceived.

But perhaps this 'as once conceived' is our problem, as we show great reluctance to give up our prior assertions of truth. The question for us now is how we might reposition ourselves to accept a new conception. In light of John's Gospel, some might still say this is a question for theology alone. In light of Heidegger, others might say it is still a question for philosophy alone. But each of these disciplines has employed a discourse that, both in the traditional rendering and in the traditional deciphering of truth, no longer supplies us with any sufficiency for the task. The question of truth is too much implicated in the silence of the gap. The 'one being' is also, ontologically, too much implicated. And the very structures of our cultural speech and logic, under the severe charge of a postmodern critique (in whatever form – poststructuralist, and others), are perhaps the most implicated of all. Thus, we need a new approach, a new language, one that can carry better the weight of the gap's existence, one that will furnish us, not with the means to eliminate or bypass the gap, nor with the words to explain it – the gap is, we remember, inexplicable – but rather with the assumptions and formalizations that will allow the gap its proper and abiding place among our future interrogations and investigations into truth.

By language, of course, we do not mean a *lingua*, but rather a *grammar*, with all its economies of logic, and their necessary conceptualizations and symbolizations. We mean, in fact, a λόγος. A new Logos is necessary, one that takes the entire Greek heritage of this complex term, and even John's christianizing of it, and reposits them within the precipitous vicinity of the gap. We realize now that the one voice in John 18:37 we struggle so hard to hear is that of the λόγος of John 1:1, the Word who was there from the beginning. Is this because that voice is now dead, as Nietzsche announced? It is, if by that voice we mean, as Nietzsche surely did, and Kierkegaard foresaw, the logocentric *Sprache* constructed to fill later the silence in the middle of John 18:38, and personified in a religious system of dogmatic theology and institutionalization. If that λόγος is no longer available as a solvent economy, as a sustainable logic, as a comprehensible and comprehensive tongue, as an absolute and unwavering metaphysics, then we need to find a new manner of speaking. We need to reconstitute and re-fund λόγος.

Is this possible? How are we to do this, and not cast ourselves wholly and irretrievably into the gap of nothingness itself? How can anything survive by means of the postmetaphysical, if λόγος itself is not an assured ground, not the solid mass that once formed the *terra firma* either side of the gap? What would we be left to say at the 'post-'?

Heidegger may still offer us a clue. Following the above passage in *Sein and Zeit* concerning Parmenides' duplicitous goddess of Truth, he says that the way to truth or 'uncovering' is 'achieved only in κρίνειν λόγῳ – in distinguishing between these [truth and untruth] understandingly, and making one's decision for the one rather than the other.'[10] In this κρίνειν λόγῳ, 'to judge by the word', 'to distinguish logically', 'to select or decide with reason', we may discover the possibility of a refunded language, a language which receives back a voice capable of speaking towards truth. This language becomes, once again, *critical*, as suggested by the verb κρίνειν, its etymological root. But despite the shadow of Heidegger's own and much criticized decision for one politics and one ideology rather than another, critique ought not to bring closure. Critique here is what we have already seen employed earlier by Kant, for whom *Kritik* is not principally a metaphysics of metaphysics,[11] but first and foremost, as Jaspers describes of Kant, with an existential emphasis that Heidegger himself had seized upon, 'a means of elucidating our consciousness of the phenomenality of existence and examining the limits of what is being for us'.[12]

Standing before Jesus, Pilate comes up to the limit of his being, as he tries to judge the Word. His limit is the wrong jurisdiction of judgment, as it remains bound to legalistic and pragmatic authority. But he cannot see this, his consciousness has not been elucidated, and thus in the end he assumes his 'judgment seat' (John 19:13) and hands over Jesus to the chief priests. Closure comes with great consequence. So how do we maintain a critique of limits without resorting to the kind of closure which, in assuming the wrong jurisdiction or in bearing the wrong judgment, leads to the catastrophe present if not in John's overall scheme of the passion narrative then certainly in the early Heidegger's Germany?

Kant can offer a clue. What is too often forgotten about the great Kantian philosophy, grounded upon its three monumental Critiques, is that fundamentally it is a philosophy about limits, about drawing limits on what is possible within our consciousness and its phenomenality. *Kritik* begins with differentiation, and proceeds by delimitation. It first selects material to be considered, separating out one from among a store of experiences or possibilities that are to be examined, and then makes further judgment upon what it has differentiated. Judgment, in fact, is at the heart of the process. Judgment makes distinctions through division, and then assesses or even places value upon not simply what has been divided, but the divisions themselves. To be critical, in this sense, is to make discrete – that is, *contra* any totalitarianism, to make non-continuous or non-uniform. And this requires an imposition of limits. Such delimiting stems in a significant sense from a negative impetus: 'The greatest and perhaps the sole use of all philosophy of pure reason is therefore only negative; since it serves not as an organon for the extension but as a discipline for the limitation of pure reason, and, instead of discovering truth, has only the modest merit of guarding against error.'[13] *Kritik*, then, is not a decision or assertion of positive content, but rather a mode or method of setting boundaries to our inquiry and to our possibilities. By the Third Critique,

---

[10] Heidegger, *Being and Time*, p. 265.

[11] See for example Kant, *Critique of Pure Reason*, pp. 659–660, for Kant's own understanding of the term 'metaphysics', which, when properly understood, he was not averse to employing.

[12] Karl Jaspers, *Kant* [from *The Great Philosophers, Vol. 1*], trans. Ralph Mannheim (NY: Harvest/ Harcourt, Brace and Company, 1957/1962), p. 141.

[13] Kant, *Critique of Pure Reason*, p. 629.

the Critique of Judgment, this *Kritik* will become in effect a supreme critique of itself: judgments are made of the very faculty of judgment.[14]

This move of radical reflexivity will come to mark the late twentieth century in defining ways, even if the contemporary critical stance has now included, quite rightly, a critique of Kant's own judgment on judgment. But here we see where postmodernity has a deep debt to Kant: not in critique as employment of hegemonic reason towards a metaphysics of metaphysics, but in critique as an open-ended inquiry which imposes limits without closure. Closure implies that the critical move will at some stage find a resting point, that even in critiquing the critique, a decisive and sovereign position of authority is reached by which all other decisions must adhere. This point, of course, emerges for Kant in the *a priori*, that ground, preceding all experience, upon which is based all our possibilities of knowing, and which provides a universality and a corresponding final authority. And Kant's subsequent move towards the transcendental is made to confirm this authority: transcendental deduction, the longest pole in the massive Kantian tent, is posited to justify and validate this *a priori* claim to unity and universality by objectifying the scope and the limits of its ground. But even Kant himself acknowledges that one can never truly be 'transcendental' to the limits, that one must always work *within* the limits to mark out (or objectify) the limits. His critique is always operative, and never transcends itself, so that even deduction, required to grant the right to decisive authority, is nothing other than a limitation. In this sense, and beyond Kant's original intentions,[15] critique closes only by delimiting, and yet delimitation is not properly a closure, at least in terms of authoritative finality, but a marking out of the places beyond which, ultimately, we can go no further in our articulations or conceptualizations. These places, in their greatest extent, are coterminous with the lacuna of John's Gospel situated behind the question 'What is truth?', and thus are, in effect, places of great openings, places without closure or finality. Radical judgment of judgment never allows the system – any system, Kantian or otherwise – to be hermetically sealed. Critique does not cast judgment, but makes judgment, and keeps making judgment. '[P]hilosophy can never be learned ... we can at most learn to *philosophise*'.[16] Here, at this limitation and provisionality, the postmodern turn is in accord with Kant.

Here we may also bring on the charge, directed at all the concomitant 'post-' designations – post-metaphysical, post-Christian, post-secular, and most

[14] 'A Critique of pure reason, i.e. of our faculty of judging on *a priori* principles, would be incomplete if the critical examination of judgment, which is a faculty of knowledge, and, as such, lays claim to independent principles, were not dealt with separately.' Kant's Preface to *The Critique of Judgement*, trans. James Creed Meredith (Oxford: Clarendon Press, 1952), p. 4.

[15] 'As to *certainty*, I have prescribed to myself the maxim, that in this kind of investigation it is in no wise permissible to hold *opinions*. Everything, therefore, which bears any manner of resemblance to a hypothesis is to be treated as contraband; it is not to be put up for sale even at the lowest price, but forthwith confiscated, immediately upon detection. Any knowledge that professes to hold *a priori* lays claim to be regarded as absolutely necessary. This applies still more to any *determination* of all pure *a priori*, since such determination has to serve as the measure, and therefore as the [supreme] example, of all apodeictic (philosophical) certainty.' Kant, *Critique of Pure Reason*, p. 11.

[16] *Ibid.*, p. 657.

significantly post-critical – of an 'undecidability'. But we need not fear this charge if by the term 'undecidability' we mean demarcations of authority that have no claims to finality. Decisions are made within critique, but as Kant admits, these are not decisions of truth, neither as knowledge of things in themselves or as anything else we might describe beyond the objects of our experience. The 'apodeictic certainty' Kant so often invokes is never towards anything that is *in itself*. Critical decisions are thus decisions to *keep deciding*, beyond unity and universality, decisions of an all-important *as if*,[17] whose conditionality is always open to further critique. In Kantian terms, we know an object not in regard to its existence but to its form, and forms can never hold immaculately or unassailably against existence. This is the point Heidegger will make so forcefully, even as he sees it inherent in Kant.[18] All forms weaken in proximity to the gap; a certain, inevitable undecidability is inherent in any of our formations, formulations and formalities. This is the postmodern dilemma, adumbrated by Kant, even in the face of his own formalism.

Had Pilate remained undecided, things would have been very different. This goes without saying. But of course Pilate was in no position to remain undecided. He was forced to act. Nevertheless, for one brief moment he was called out of his duty and his jurisdiction to consider a judgment of a very different kind, a judgment, we might say, of his own Being. The closest he came to making this judgment was to ask the primordial question that stands behind all questions. And in doing so he opened up a space that we are all called upon to face, if only for a brief textual and rhetorical moment. This is a critical space of openness, of openness to a new judgment, a new way of speaking, a new κρίνειν λόγῳ, a new truth. Even if the language of this truth is predicated on a question, on silence, on nothing.

We need then to admit a profound respect for this space. And precisely because it is an opening, a gap, that reveals the silence of nothing. We are not, however, accustomed to allowing truth to linger in nothing, as nothing. We have invented disciplines of inquiry and knowledge precisely so that truth will have *something*, will contain *something*. Truth is about content, not about lack of content. How do we pay our respects to something that is not there, a caesura in our continuity of accumulated knowledge and fact, a deep fissure in our carapace of consciousness? Our disciplines have had varying success.

Theology has paid its respects, to be sure, but in the West it has done so in a manner that at times we must say has been all too disrespectful. More often, Western theology has either tried to fill the gap, a move it quickly discovers to be

---

17 'But reason cannot think this systematic unity otherwise than by giving to the idea of this unity an object; and since experience can never give an example of complete systematic unity, the object which we have to assign to the idea is not such as experience can ever supply. This object, as thus entertained by reason (*ens rationis ratiocinatae*), is a mere idea; it is not assumed as a something that is real absolutely and *in itself*, but is postulated only problematically (since we cannot reach it through any of the concepts of the understanding) in order that we may view all connection of the things of the world of sense *as if* they had their ground in such a being.' *Ibid.*, p. 556.

18 See Martin Heidegger, *Kant and the Problem of Metaphysics*, 5th edn., trans. Richard Taft (Bloomington: Indiana University Press, 1990, rpt. 1997).

utterly futile, or tried to bridge the gap, with its sometimes wide, often stiff structures of systematic and fundamentalist doctrine. Yet increasingly, it now finds these structures crack and break under the slightest movement, either from below – the hollow, silent reverberations from the deep – or more usually from either side of the gap – secular skepticism on the one side and religious sectarianism on the other. Mysticism has always kept a keen eye on this space, and promoted silence and solitude as the ruling response. But its writers have never been allowed into the fold of accepted disciplines set up by the institutions of Church and University. 'Mystical discipline' is a creature unto itself, one usually chastised by the establishment, and one that has thus remained, even to this day, a movement of individual and isolated spirituality. In this respect, Blanchot is a mystic. As for theology proper, it has carried its own fears and betrayed its own vertigo as, by definition, it goes out of its way to rid the silence with words of assurance.

Philosophy too has given its respect, as we have just seen with Kant and Heidegger, though increasingly in the modern era it does so irrespective of its former partner in theology. Philosophical respect has at times run deep, with its tenacious regard for the intellectual possibilities and discursive intricacies open to the human mind. But as a discipline it too has overbuilt its structures, often well beyond the confines of the gap, and in the direction of its own classical heritage. Under the question of truth it has been guilty of its own catholicism, but like theology, that catholicism has always been susceptible to the historical and cultural contingencies that threaten abiding consensus. Philosophers have never been able to agree, but they nevertheless have worked consistently under the assumption or presupposition of agreement. Indeed, the predominant philosophical understanding of truth is one of agreement. But of course the very nature of Pilate's question – its very *existence* as a question – dictates against agreement.

The discipline of art, for its part, has been far more innovative and pliable with its respect. Art loves to dally along the borders of the 'caverns measureless to man',[19] to steal a quick peek over the precipice, and, in its greatest moments, to leap with great passion and élan over the gaping canyon. It is never definitive with what it sees ('close your eyes with holy dread'), nor lingering in its regard, but it has provided us with some of the most impressive and extravagant crossings, as it yields to that great interrogative which drives all great art. Art has always been able to see what neither theology nor philosophy has been willing to readily accept: that first and foremost, all language is predicated upon silence. Art has seen this because art is never far away from rhetoric, whose potency, we have just seen, trades as much on what is *not* said as on what is said. And though rhetoric may become a discipline, as it did with the ancient Greeks, it is a discipline that is always in close relation to subversion, even against its own structures, which is why great art will always, as Nietzsche preached, subvert what has been established.

Science has paid the least respect. In fact, it tends to ignore the existence of any kind of gap altogether. In its endless quantifications and positivity, it pretends that the nothingness is not there. In its greatest hubris, it will claim that, through a

[19] Samuel Taylor Coleridge, 'Kubla Khan', in *The Major Works*, ed. H.J. Jackson (Oxford: Oxford University Press, 2000), p. 103.

continental shift of its own devising, it has closed the gap irreversibly and given us a flat and solid terrain upon which we can all firmly plant our inductive feet. In effect, it turns the gap into a sign of equation, so that if on the one side lay the grand question, its interrogative force now becomes emasculated by a rationality that sends it to the other side in the form of a verifiable and thoroughly quantifiable predicate. There is little or no respect here, except insofar as the gap is a historical reality which once marked out the territory science was eventually to overcome and master. And although modern science, natural and social, has now shown that we can *function* without explicit or implicit acknowledgment of a still existing gap (it in fact suggests continually that we function *better*), the twentieth century must cause us (and has caused us) to question seriously the nature of this functioning. We may function, admittedly, but do we not function more out of a deep-seated malaise that keeps us to mere function? Can we, in good conscience, assert that we in any way thrive in our once-celebrated humanity, either spiritually, psychically, socially, ethically, or even – and this is perhaps most significant – cynically? Is there not rather an overriding discontent, which breeds apathetic indifference – one century-long winter of discontent and indifference? If we could be thoroughgoing in our cynicism, we could at least be content in an assured state of unknowing, with its Rabelaisian passion for levity and its Cervantean passion for come-what-may.[20] But we cannot be thoroughly cynical in this way, for science will not allow it: there is nothing more antithetical to science than cynicism. We do not seek a cure for cancer nor to put men on Mars out of cynicism, of any kind or to any degree. Science and its results make sure that we can never be content with unknowing, that we will never consent, in the face of electric light and heat on command, to live in an urn with Diogenes. Yet science has also proven to fall short of our desires. In diminishing the interrogative and eradicating the imperative from our total experience, science asks only one set of questions and brackets out any ethical demand. As Kant says, mathematics and empirical science may have created an island for itself, but the island is only so big:

> This domain is an island, enclosed by nature itself within unalterable limits. It is the land of truth – enchanting name! – surrounded by a wide and stormy ocean, the native home of illusion, where many a cloud bank and many a swiftly melting iceberg give the deceptive appearance of farther shores, deluding the adventurous seafarer ever anew with empty hopes, and engaging him in enterprises which he can never abandon and yet is unable to carry to completion.[21]

We have become formidable discontents as castaways, and increasingly indifferent before the illusions and deceptions parading around our limited and isolated land.

If we find ourselves turning back again to the theologians, to the philosophers, to the artists, and to their respective disciplines, it is not because any one of them has

[20] Friedrich Nietzsche: 'Of greatness one must either be silent or speak with greatness. With greatness – that means cynically and with innocence.' – 'Preface (November 1887–March 1888), 1', *The Will to Power* ed. Walter Kaufmann, trans. Walter Kaufmann and R.J. Hollingdale (New York: Vintage/ Random House, 1967), p. 3.

[21] Jaspers, *Kant*, pp. 52–53.

succeeded in relieving us of our illusions, but on the contrary because each has contributed to the illusions in important ways. For it is from these illusions that we, both guided and misguided towards what is truth, can ask the question anew. Their approaches and methods may never fully satisfy, but at least they have taught us, out of their own peculiarities, to anticipate the question, and in rare moments to anticipate *in* the question.

Let us keep respecting the gap, then. The Latin root of this verb 'respect' might help us: let us *see it again*, and again. Like Pilate, let us return to it with repeated questions. Let us stop on any overpass we might have constructed, and let us gaze into it repeatedly. For such re-seeing and re-visioning is what theology, philosophy and art can offer, even if, in each of their disciplines, the glimpse is only ever fleeting, and to the systematicians who mark their fields, a deep embarrassment.

And in this respect, let us try to elucidate a new consciousness, one that stands in John's Gospel between the ambiguous inquisition of Pilate's Τί ἐστιν ἀλήθεια; ('What is truth?') and the assertive conviction of the following verse, 'Εγὼ οὐδεμίαν εὑρίσκω ἐν αὐτῷ αἰτίαν ('I find no crime in him.'). What can possibly stand 'between' here, in these uncertain and obscure regions of our existence and our experience, besides the profound realization of a chasm of nothingness dwelling underneath? What, with respect to this chasm, is left open for us to build?

In the shadows of our critical heritage, we can now make a new judgment: a new judgment, and yet by no means a new concept. What if we suggest, as this new judgment, an old term all too familiar?:

Imagination

2 Bulgakov

'Why should a tramp like you upset the crowds in the bazaar by talking about truth, something of which you have no conception? What is truth?'

The question comes again with respect to authority.

At this the Procurator thought: 'Ye gods! This is a court of law, and I am asking him an irrelevant question ... my mind no longer obeys me ....' Once more he had a vision of a goblet of dark liquid. 'Poison, I need poison ....'

The question of truth – asked here out of the disobedience of the mind, a mind struggling with pain, a mind visionary, with visions of death. In the forbidden and forbidding call of self-annihilation comes the question. In the fore-bidding call of death comes, unbidden, the question of truth. And irrelevant – irrelevant before the law, the mind is poisoned with this irrelevance; the mind is poisoned with irrelevant existence. Poison it out of existence. Salve it with poison. And eschew the truth. What possibly could its relevance be here?

'At this point the truth is chiefly that your head is aching and aching so hard that you are having cowardly thoughts about death.'

Ah, the truth of the moment. Nothing grand, nothing sweeping. Just truth as it emerges, not *from*, but *as* the pain of the head, that vision, cowardly or noble, of non-existence.

'You cannot even think and you can only long for your dog, who is clearly the only creature for whom you have any affection.'

Long only for a dog? The cynical way out: amid the pain of thinking, or non-thinking, one longs for the carefree indifference of a dog. But Kyniks like Diogenes are rare. And the pain, and the truth, is momentary.

'But the pain will stop soon and your headache will go.'

And the head will be free once again to make something of the situation.

'Your trouble is,' went on the unstoppable prisoner, 'that your mind is too closed and you have finally lost your faith in human beings. You must admit that no one ought to lavish all their devotion on a dog. Your life is a cramped one, hegemon.'

Uncramp the mind, and the head, released from the moment of painful truth, can be cleared enough to make a judgment. But a new judgment. One not in the court of law.

'So you are a physician?
'No, no,' was the prisoner's eager reply. 'Believe me I am not.'
'Very well, if you wish to keep it a secret, do so. It has no direct bearing on the case.'

A new judgment, made but not cast. Made outside the bounds of the formal structures of logic and arbitration, outside the jurisdiction of set principle and law –

where it has no bearing. And no longer on official record, lost to binding inscription.

> The secretary picked up his scroll, decided to take no more notes for a while and to be astonished at nothing he might hear.

Here, in this space, the 'hegemon' sets aside his rule and in a moment of personal clarity sees past the truth of his pain to something other. What is this strange other?

The strange other becomes *The Master and Margarita* by the Russian dramatist and novelist Mikhail Bulgakov.[1] This novel, written in 1938, two years before the author's death, becomes the author's own imaginative reflex under the force of the question. Or one might say his judgment. It is a celebrated work of strange events and preposterous characters: a black cat, a naked woman, a seven-foot ex-choirmaster with a pince-nez, and the Devil himself, who calls himself Woland. A whirlwind of bewildering and bewitching occurrences, of reckless activity, of wizardry and conjuration. An irreverent story of shameless carousal, burlesque devilry and caustic ridicule. And yet amid all this, there arises the story of Pontius Pilate. At first as a separate narrative, a story within a story, set back from the crazy flights of diabolical prankishness and Muscovite decadence. A return to ancient Jerusalem, early 'in the morning on the fourteenth of the spring month of Nisan', to be precise. An exchange between a pensive and distraught Procurator, a head pounding with pain, and a sorry-looking Yeshua Ha-Notsri, bound at the wrists and whipped at the back. Pilate and Jesus, face to face in the praetorium, or rather on a balcony in the palace of Herod the Great. In private, away from the disturbance of the crowds. And what transpires in this one chapter, Chapter 2, is first a profound rewriting, a twist of the context in which this famous confrontation was supposed to have taken place. And then, with a respect that one at first can barely discern, this rewriting becomes the confrontation itself, that hidden, concealed, blank aftermath to a question which, once posed, becomes in this altered context irrelevant, and yet at the same time is the most relevant question to the matter at hand, relevant to both text and context. For what should truth be doing within such an offbeat tale, such a wild and scandalous vaudeville as *The Master and Margarita*? And yet, in the second chapter already, and in three subsequent chapters (16, 25, 26), we find the relative sobriety of an ancient world and its revered history, which, in extreme counterpoint to the sorcery and necromancy happening about the streets and rooms of twentieth-century Russia, belong, as we know, to the persisting question of religious and theological truth. What really happened at that decisive moment when the die was cast for Jesus, and the politics of the day sent him to the excruciation of a Roman cross? What led Pilate to say what he did, and what led Jesus *not* to say what he might have said? Is this not a question of truth, and more, a truth of the most pressing kind, insofar as these events were to have a piercing effect on the course of the next two thousand years?

---

[1] The above quotes are taken from Mikhail Bulgakov, *The Master and Margarita*, trans. Michael Glenny (London: Harvill Press/Harper and Row, 1967), Chapter 2, pp. 33–35.

Were this juxtaposition – between the black magic of a contemporary and devilish entourage and the 'kingdom of truth' of the historical Jesus – to remain only a juxtaposition, we might see the hand of a clever author who wants to expose in the exaggerations of contrasting narratives the moral dilapidation of his own times. And one could say that, under such a satirical force, 'truth' would befit the scene. But the narratives are not in juxtaposition. The narratives are fused organically together. What might have been an isolated rendering of a momentous yet mysterious encounter, one that works to the very heart of a sacred history and tradition, is in fact a fabulous account of supplementary figures whose unseemly lives intersect, in varying ways but to substantial degrees, with a criminal who was crucified under Roman law for, in the end, treason, and who was known mockingly as the 'King of the Jews'. And this account is not in sacred counterpoint – it is merged, even from the outset, with the profane story of Woland the Devil, who prowls about Moscow creating havoc and madness. For it is from this Devil, disguised as a professor of black magic, that we first hear the story of Pontius Pilate. The affront then is double: not only does the story's rendering take great liberties with the original text and its following tradition, but it emerges from the larger story of demonic drollery, and is in fact taken over by its outrageous affairs and characters. How can truth remain an issue, retain any force, even the issue and the force of an interrogative, in such discreditable and antithetical company?

It cannot, of course, if it is *historical* truth we mean. Or even *religious* truth, truth pertaining to the grounds of religious orthodoxy. But Bulgakov never claims or even feigns to be writing historical or religious truth. Nor does he claim to be rewriting religious history. Jesus is Yeshua Ha-Notsri (Jesus' name in Hebrew). He is clearly not the Jesus of the common Christian tradition. Bulgakov does not offer a theological interpretation with pretensions, however muted or subtle, to binding truth. He is far craftier than this. If he offers any truth, it is a *theatrical truth*, albeit one caught up in a highly complex hermeneutic.

Opening tableau, Chapter One. Two men sit on a park bench. Literati: editor and poet. They argue about the existence of God. The editor, having commissioned the poet to write an anti-religious poem, does not like the results: the poem's main topic, Jesus Christ, though drawn in 'very black colours', is still off the mark. To the poet's mind his Jesus is 'completely alive, a Jesus who had completely existed', but the main object was not supposed to be a well-wrought Jesus, even if he had every possible fault. The main object was rather a denial of the very existence of a historical person called Jesus in the first place. Jesus as mere invention, as pure myth. The editor tries to drive home this point: the birth of Jesus from a virgin is not unique to Christianity; Christianity is simply one with all the other mythical, and hence false, religions. The nativity myth ought to be dismissed outright, not, as in the poem, assumed a reality, however colored that reality might be.

Enter the Devil. Intrusively, in disguise, and suspiciously odd. Amid the question of Jesus' truth – between the rendering of Jesus 'completely alive' and the adamant refutation of an historical existence, between Jesus all-too-real and Jesus all-too-fictitious – the Devil slides into the conversation. As always, emerging from the thick swirling smoke of factions carried too far. In order to confuse: he neither denies the reality nor supports the orthodoxy.

A strange turn. But what of the *proofs* of God's existence, the Devil asks? The two confessed atheists, editor and poet, dismiss such proofs, all 'five' of them. And the Devil is impressed, seeing that they have just repeated the views of Kant, the 'immortal Emmanuel', as the Devil calls him (by no means unaware of the irony of that Hebraic/Christian name). But Kant, says the Devil, demolishes all five proofs only to formulate a sixth proof of his own (God *is* with us). Kant belongs in an asylum, say the atheists, as does anyone who should claim to prove the existence of God. The 'truth' of God is sheer madness. (But as the reader soon learns, madness follows everyone around in this novel. Madness and schizophrenia.) The Devil agrees about Kant, and he was trying to tell the famed philosopher as much only that very morning over breakfast: 'People will think you're mad' with such abstruse proof, the Devil told him. Kant and the Devil, now named Woland, together for breakfast, that very morning? What is going on here? It is not Kant who is mad, think the editor and poet, but this strange individual ranting before them. Breakfast with Kant! Madness! And the Devil only confirms their worst fears when he predicts the editor's death by decapitation under the wheels of a tram. Madness getting out of hand. But not madness at all, says the Devil, handing them his card. He is a professor himself like Kant. But a professor of black magic. German idealism and the occult sipping morning tea together. And as if this madness is not enough, think the two, as if truth could somehow find its way into all this imaginary prattle, as if the question of the reality of Jesus was somehow still relevant amid their atheistic confidence and its mounting suspicions towards this absurd prognosticator, the Devil tells them in a whisper: 'Jesus did exist, you know'. Madness in league with both Kant and God. God with us through insanity. And as corroboration, this lunatic begins a story: the story of Pontius Pilate. Pilate before Christ. Bulgakov's Chapter 2. *The tableau ends.*

This opening scene, that will give way to, and reveal, a new narrative valence in Pilate's interrogation, is itself an interrogation, a ludic inversion or prelude of the ancient story which it precedes. The Devil interrogates two atheists, who have claims to the question of truth. But what *is* the truth, he asks them? Who or what governs human life and the world's order? 'Man rules himself', is their reply. And for this claim to self-mastery, one is sentenced to a gruesome death under the wheels of a tram. Proof that the dogmatism of self-mastery is as perilous as the dogmatism of religious orthodoxy. Truth is fixed neither by adamant denial of God nor by adamant assertion. Truth is not fixed. This is the point – truth cannot be fixed, unless 'fixed' by fraud. And it is the Devil who must make clear this point, not Christ. The Devil has always been the great master of *duplicity.* Whereas Christ remains silent before the question of truth, the Devil takes up the charge and runs, only to come to the point, through duplicity, that truth is itself duplicitous. Hidden and uncovered, uncovered and yet hidden. And this is precisely what is offered in the second chapter: a new reading of a truth which is not a truth. An imaginative uncovering of what remains hidden, a pretend history. A made-up reality: Jesus *did* exist, and here's the proof – a Jesus who is not Jesus. At least, not the traditional Jesus.

How are we to read this Jesus, in light of Pilate? But how are we to read this Pilate? As the one who poses the great question, and crawls into himself to find the answer, outside the jurisdiction of the court of law, which he nevertheless returns to and upholds, against himself. And where is this 'outside' that is 'inside', this private balcony of the soul? What is this duplicitous place which goes one way and another at the same time – pity and admiration, dismissal and acceptance, condemnation and absolution? It is a place of judgment. Of judgment made through discernment, not cast in accusation, a judgment outside binding legality, a judgment that will not conform to the grounding conviction of a unified self or system. Like a question posed by a mind that no longer obeys, this judgment splits apart, and confutes itself. Before this Jesus, the self divides in self-judgment, the arbiter going one way, the invalid going the other. The Procurator is left a deeply divided man.

Such a split has its counterpart in the chapters which immediately surround it: the preludic Chapter 1 ('Never Talk to a Stranger') and Chapter 3 ('The Seventh Proof'). Before the Devil, the atheists are divided, the editor going one way, the poet the other. That is, the editor is sent to his death, the poet allowed to live on. The editor, the arbiter of literary decision, the arch-atheist, becomes the seventh proof of God's existence by dying a death prescribed in detail by the Devil, while the poet is left to pursue the Devil's fleeing specter, only to be later committed to an asylum. Here both the editorial and the poetic within Pilate are prefigured, the adjudicator and the aching, imaginative soul. As the Devil confounds disbelief by forcing editor and poet, who represent censor and creator, to part company, so Yeshua as Jesus confounds belief by forcing the judiciary and the existential to part company. And here Yeshua and Woland come together, 'truth' and 'untruth' in league with one another. The question of the existence of God will be dealt with *outside* the bounds of traditional systems, traditional logics, traditional hermeneutics, traditional sanity. And yet *inside* the imagination of the one, Pilate, who seeks relief beyond the dogged pain of experience. And so follows the Devil's story of Pilate, Chapter 2, which is not simply a concocted tale, but a 'history' which the Devil himself has witnessed. He was in fact *there* on the balcony – the balcony, that place which is both part of the structure and outside of the structure. He was there in person, but incognito, in secret. Watching the exchange between Pilate and Yeshua. Like the writer of John's Gospel. And as proof of this witness – the Devil, witness to the truth! – as proof to the disbelieving editor and poet who are about to part company, the Devil realizes his mad prediction: the editor slips under an oncoming tram, and loses his head. Truth emerging from madness, a familiar refrain – 'matter and impertinency mixed'[2]. Such is the Devil's duplicity. And so the story of Pilate emerges from the nonsense of mad events, from the black magic of Woland, and we are left wondering how to negotiate (with) the duplicitous truth that is thus being invoked. We as readers are as much confounded by this truth as the characters.

The confounding is of a hermeneutical nature. We have been tutored by centuries of historical-criticism and millennia of impermeable logocentrism to locate meaning and truth in the trustworthy fixity of our textual and narrative apparatuses. *Even* if that location is provisional within the artifice of fiction, where the meaning or 'truth' is adjusted under the pretense of the 'possible' and the

---

[2] Shakespeare, *King Lear*, Act IV, Scene vi.

'probable' (Aristotle), or of the 'imaginable'. But Bulgakov frustrates such location. It is not simply that the contemporary events in his story are improbable; we have learned to overcome such 'improbabilities' long ago, while still rescuing a sense or meaning. It is more that what should pass as legitimate meaning, perhaps even 'truth', if not in a historical sense then in a moral or spiritual sense – the rendering of a story invested with truth from both within and without its own frame, the 'sacred' and yet incomplete story of Pilate before Jesus, in which lies the fundamental question of truth – is given the wrong authority, the wrong source of legitimation. This is the primary offense of Bulgakov's novel: the traditional authority for truth, both religious and textual truth, is here taken away, and replaced by (and with) a duplicity. That the Devil should bear witness to the truth, and furnish the real story of Jesus, is not the central problem. It is rather that the Devil's 'real' story subverts both the original authority – in this case only Matthew's written version of the Gospel (the other Synoptic writers do not exist here, nor interestingly does John) – and *its own* authority. In the story of Pilate's world, Matthew, the sole chronicler of Yeshua's mission, is discredited by Yeshua himself: 'But once I caught a glimpse of that parchment and I was horrified. I had said not a word of what was written there.'[3] When the story returns to Moscow, we learn that the older story is *not* the Devil's after all. It is part of a novel being written by another character, the Master of Bulgakov's title. And this inner novel merges with the outer novel when we meet its author, the 'hero', and learn of his plight, whereby his novel, his crowning achievement and *tour de force*, has remained both unfinished and unpublished (yet all the while on Woland's tongue). The Devil's version then is in fact someone else's version – an incomplete version at that – which in turn becomes part of the entire 'version' being wickedly played out on the streets of Moscow, and which receives its finishing touches only when all the versions have merged completely and indistinguishably together. The end of the inner story becomes the end of the outer story, in a finale played out on a balcony. And yet when the Devil had said he was *there* on the balcony, witness to the truth, we now have to ask 'what balcony?'. The balcony was only ever a novelist's construct. And in the larger picture, a novelist's construct of a novelist's construct. Wherein lies any authority now?

The witness becomes the witness of an imagination. Imaginary witness. If the Devil was truly *there* (but where is *there* exactly?), he must have been party to the imagination of the Master. We are reminded of the Devil of Blake. Truth as conjured by devilish inspiration. The truth of a new Evangelist, the 'Perfect Hermeneut',[4] yet one of the Devil's party, like Milton. But the characters of this imagination break into the wider, outer novel, the story of the Devil and his entourage playing rakish havoc with Moscow, so that both Matthew and Pilate come to inhabit the 'reality' outside the Master's imagination as much as inside. Outside and inside confused again. Authority – who writes what? who legitimates what? – does not fit neatly, or

[3] Bulgakov, *The Master and Margarita*, p. 31.

[4] Veronika Spira, 'God, Evil and the Saviour: Hermeneutics and the Reconstruction of Character in Bulgakov's *The Master and Margarita*', in *Literary Theory and Biblical Hermeneutics*, ed. Tibor Fabiny (Szeged, Hungary: Department of English, Attila József University, 1992), p. 217.

fixedly, within such confusion. And with Pilate's question of truth still in the air, this constitutes a serious violation of authority, surely.

Who should we charge with such violation? Bulgakov himself, who in a rare intrusion into the narrative at the end of the novel's first half, Book One, has the audacity to call his tale a 'true story'?[5] Or when, at the beginning of the second half, he calls himself, or his narrator, 'the truthful narrator'?[6] But can we charge the author with a violation of his own authority? This is a profound and complex question which any imaginative text asks. If there is a satisfactory resolution to this question, it only begs the larger question, what is truth? And lest we be guilty of Bulgakov's own self-described 'Pilatism', let us not judge Bulgakov on these grounds prematurely. Let us not sentence him only to want to recant our sentence later.

The arbiter and editor require a tidy resolution, and cast judgment accordingly. But in Bulgakov's two stories, the arbiter, Pilate, rues his judicial decision, while the editor loses his head. The invalid and poet on the other hand come to a different fate. The invalid, again Pilate, seeks release from his pain, manifested in a heartfelt yearning to extend his conversation with Yeshua, the only person who ever granted him temporary relief. And in the end his desire is fulfilled. The Muscovite poet Ivan, for his part, undergoes reform. Committed to a psychiatric hospital, he regains his own head: through conversation between his two split selves (Chapter 11, 'The Two Ivans'); through conversation with the Master, the patient next door (Chapter 13, 'Enter the Hero'); and through a dream about Matthew the Levite, his alter ego, the false chronicler of the Master's story who witnesses the crucifixion and rescues the dead body of Yeshua from the cross (Chapter 16, 'The Execution'). As a part of the Master's novel, this dream brings Master and poet together at the center point of a crossing chiastic structure. Where the Master begins as an historian in a research institute, and becomes an immortal writer, the poet begins as a self-aggrandizing writer, and becomes a professor at the Institute for History and Philosophy.

The dream of Chapter 16 is the crucial point of intersection, the inferior hermeneut (Matthew) and the inferior poet (Ivan) becoming mirror images of each other. Bulgakov is here trying to tell us to suspend judgment on authority, to avoid the improper judgment of the editor, and to judge like the poet – not the old poet, the 'old Ivan', but the 'new Ivan' who is open to future possibility, even the possibility of belief (in the Devil, in the Master's version of the story, in Yeshua). For it is an editor, we remember, who first rejects out of hand the Master's manuscript of Pilate's story; it is an editor who deprecates this novel publicly, and sends the Master into despair and incapability. The arbiter/editor judges from a decisive court of law with final authority and closure. But the invalid/poet judges from the open-ended position of the divided self with the duplicity of an authoritative *as-if.* Towards a split-decision, a decision of undecidability. The invalid is given a chance to redeem himself, to retract his first decision. The entire novel concludes as the Master, guided by Woland the Devil, grants a now living Pilate freedom to reunite with Yeshua, to leave the inner text and seek on a

---

[5] Bulgakov, *The Master and Margarita*, p. 245.

[6] *Ibid.*, p. 250. 'Even I, the truthful narrator, yet a mere onlooker, feel a pain when I think what Margarita went through. . . .'.

moonbeam his salvation in the outer text. To leave 'text' altogether, in fact, as the inner and outer become one: 'His hero had now vanished irretrievably into the abyss; on the night of Sunday, the day of the Resurrection, pardon had been granted to the astrologer's son, fifth Procurator of Judaea, the cruel Pontius Pilate'.[7] The poet too is given a chance to redeem himself, to retract his first decision. Ivan is freed from the poverty of his weak atheistic writing, freed from the outer text, freed even from his new position as professor of History and Philosophy, to seek on a moonbeam his salvation in the inner text: 'Then the moon goes mad, deluges Ivan with streams of light, sprays light everywhere, a moonlight flood invades the room, the light sways, rises, drowns the bed. It is then that Ivan sleeps with a look of happiness on his face.'[8] The Master becomes the conflation of these two: invalid and poet, interior and exterior, the visitor on the balcony. And what transpires under the Master's hand? In the end the poet has become a 'disciple', while Pilate marches on as a *fait accompli* to the one who calls him, to the one who had called him from the cross with his last dying words – 'Hegemon'.[9] Hegemon, it is finished, completed 'with a single sentence'.[10]

As a new creation, a new limit, a new judgment, a new language, the character of Pilate becomes the ultimate authority for Bulgakov. Amid his multi-valent and open-ended hermeneutics, Pilate is the only seeking individual (seeking has hegemonic roots[11]) who reaches across the chasm to the truth of Jesus. Not even the Master is allowed to enter this kingdom. Pilate becomes a new authority for the critical question of truth. And this is just as we may have suspected, for were we to span the gap following the question in John's Gospel, must not Pilate be present in that crossing? Does not Pilate indicate the means of that crossing? Is Pilate not *crucial*, in every sense of the term? Has not Bulgakov pointed us in the only direction we could have gone, and given the imaginative Pilate the final word on the matter?

What is truth then? What does the imaginative Pilate tell us? What is the verdict of his case? Let us quote Bulgakov, the Devil, the Master – they are all one and the same here. Let us use their figure of authority. As the last word, the final judgment, *vis-à-vis* Jesus, at the very moment in which it was discussed, in its totality, to its fullest extent, with no remainder, this is what Pilate reveals, and only reveals, concerning the question of truth:

> No one knows what passed through the mind of the Procurator of Judaea, but he permitted himself to raise his hand as though shading himself from a ray of sunlight and, shielded by that hand, to throw the prisoner a glance that conveyed a hint.[12]

---

[7] *Ibid.*, p. 432.

[8] *Ibid.*, p. 445.

[9] *Ibid.*, p. 206.

[10] *Ibid.*, p. 429.

[11] Etymologically, the Oxford English Dictionary tells us, the verb 'to seek' can be traced back, through Latin, to the Greek verb *hegeisthai*, 'to lead', from which the word 'hegemon' is also derived.

[12] Bulgakov, *The Master and Margarita*, p. 39.

3 Kant

The question, famed of old, by which logicians were supposed to be driven into a corner, obliged either to have recourse to a pitiful sophism, or to confess their ignorance and consequently the emptiness of their whole art, is the question: What is truth? The nominal definition of truth, that it is the agreement of knowledge with its object, is assumed as granted; the question asked is as to what is the general and sure criterion of the truth of any and every knowledge.

Immanuel Kant, *Critique of Pure Reason*[1]

The truth of 'any and every knowledge', which Kant here seeks at the outset of his entire critical philosophy, is a quest seemingly more immodest than even that of the old logicians to which he refers. It is a quest more at risk of outright failure, more liable itself to drive one into a corner of ignorance or emptiness. Why does Kant, the great German thinker, who set out to give Western philosophy a new agenda, though one entirely indebted to and dependent upon that philosophy, invoke such a grand and dangerous question – not only to be asked, but also to be answered – when he is so fully aware of the risks? Finding a 'general and sure' criterion of the truth seems, in light of the West's own history, an impossible task. Why this question of truth here again, and why in such inflated terms? Kant even expounds upon the possible perils of the question:

> To know what questions may reasonably [*vernünftiger*] be asked is already a great and necessary proof of sagacity and insight. For if a question is absurd in itself and calls for an answer where none is required, it not only brings shame on the propounder of the question, but may betray an incautious listener into absurd answers, thus presenting, as the ancients said, the ludicrous spectacle of one man milking a he-goat and the other holding a sieve underneath.[2]

Was it reasonable of Kant to ask not simply about the nature of truth but about a 'general and sure' criterion of it, then? How does he avoid his own ludicrous image, and not sit beneath a refractory billy goat waiting for milk? Yet if he does escape such comedy, it is because he posits a very clear and limited definition of truth at the outset. Truth, he says, and takes as granted, is nothing other than 'the agreement of knowledge with its object'. Can this limitation be of help to us in making any inquiry into truth, even of the most modest kind? Kant provides an important starting point not because of the answers he finds to this cautiously posed question, reached through an unprecedented systematic philosophical analysis, but because of his mode of dealing with the question under *limitation*. If we return once again to this limitation, and now specifically to the critical apparatus under which it operates, we may find in turn a new reasonableness [*Vernünftigkeit*] to the question at large.

---

[1] Kant, *Critique of Pure Reason*, A 58, B 82, p. 97. In Norman Kemp Smith's edition, 'A' refers to Kant's first edition of the Critique in 1781, while 'B' refers to Kant's second edition in 1787. See 'Translator's Preface', p. vi, for further details.

[2] *Ibid.*, A 58, B 82, p. 97.

Transcendental Mode

Kant had said, one cannot learn 'philosophy' but only 'how to philosophize'.[3] This redirection to the 'how' is of crucial importance, for the first great limit is already imposed here. One does not learn substantive *facta* of knowledge which in their totality constitute or produce *a* philosophy. One does not arrive, through the correct disciplinary and logical means, at a comprehensive body of philosophical understanding which is then *possessed* as a unified and substantial whole. One cannot possess philosophy; one can only go about the business of *doing* philosophy. And this *doing* must be self-aware, must always be conscious of *how* it is proceeding, and at what its procedure is aimed. It requires a self-reflexivity which makes its mode, its *modus operandi*, the principal object of inquiry. This, we have already said, is a decisive shift.

Such a shift could not have been made much before Kant's time. It demands an understanding of reflection which only modern philosophy in its Cartesian roots could supply. This is not to say that the ancients did not have a sense of the manner in which philosophy was conducted. Plato himself was all too aware of the uniqueness of his own mode of inquiry, of the inventions of Socratic philosophy by means of a certain dialectical approach and its subsequent written form in dialogue. And it is in the tension between *how* one philosophizes and what one philosophizes *about* – the *Protagoras* dialogue provides here a supreme example –where Plato's currency, even amid radical schools of contemporary philosophy, continues to lie. One might say that Plato was forced to keep that tension in tacit abeyance as much as possible, in order for the services of the λόγοι (*logoi*) to remain paramount – that is, for λόγος (*logos*) to remain an end in itself. But even if this were not the case for Plato, the very structure of λόγος became, in its later Neoplatonic versions of an absolute teleological understanding, something which could not allow its own mechanism to turn on itself. The λόγος, as the underlying principle of the construction or *organon* of the world, would cease to be an absolute, would lose all its teleological force, were it to expose its own internal operations to the scrutiny of that same operative mechanism itself. But this specific threat is ameliorated when the 'self' comes into its own, when the notion of a self-conscious being, who can turn its own ability to cogitate – and to doubt – on itself, and can find new ground and certainty in this very *ability*, is introduced into the philosophical procedure. From Descartes' inaugural self-reflexivity is born a philosophy of reflection by which the reflexive *mode* comes into being as a determining feature. It is left to someone of Kant's intellectual capacity to make this reflexive mode, in his own terms, constitutive and not merely regulative.

But *how* does Kant make mode constitutive? Herein lies the important departure point not for a future metaphysics, but for a future understanding of the critical method as a vital transgression of disciplinary boundaries, including, indeed culminating in, a transgression of metaphysics' own boundaries.

Kant uses the 'nominal' definition of truth as his own starting point: the agreement of knowledge with its object. This question of agreement very quickly

[3] See above, p. 25, n. 16. See also Ernst Cassirer, *Kant's Life and Thought*, trans. James Haden (New Haven: Yale University Press, 1981), p. 52.

modulates into a question of the relation between subject and object, *the* problem in modern philosophy since Descartes. How does the knower stand in relation to what is purportedly known? Or to redirect the question from epistemology to ontology, how does the world out there *in itself* precisely relate to the world inside the self-conscious and observing Being? Does the subject have any access to an object *as such*, or does the subject simply mediate an object through its own internal devices, without ever reaching or experiencing the object's essential nature as a separate and self-sufficient entity? We know this question of subject/object agreement has been the defining issue that has marked out the territory of modern philosophy in all its 'rationalist' and 'empiricist' divisions, and in its metaphysical orientation overall. But Kant could not accept the notion of objectivity as the primordial ground from which all subsequent notions pertaining to subjectivity find their basis. Such ground always necessitated, he felt, some irrational leap between the object and its representation, and turned for its explanations either to the ill-defined region of traditional metaphysics, or, when the problem seemed no longer soluble, to the inexplicable realm of the divine. The *deus ex machina* is what Kant called such explanations – a resort to the gods to bridge the gap between, and in turn to validate, an object and our knowledge of it through its representation. But to Kant this move 'encourages all sorts of wild notions and every pious and speculative brainstorm',[4] and provides us with no more utility than would a sieve as a container for milk. Rather than beginning with the object *in itself*, the 'what' of the object, Kant begins instead with the way one accesses that object, with the 'how' of judgment about the object.[5] And he posits in the opening of the First Critique a new term (or a newly conceived term) to define this 'how', transcendental philosophy: 'I entitle *transcendental* all knowledge which is occupied not so much with the objects as with the mode of our knowledge of objects in so far as this mode of knowledge is possible *a priori*.'[6] The transcendental then becomes a reflexive move: the inquiry transcends itself to look at itself, thus making an analysis of method, of *modus cognescendi*, the foundation of any philosophical procedure.

We need to be clear at this point, because this move is more than simply a prolegomenon. The First Critique, which all Kant's pre-critical writing had been leading towards, as Cassirer has shown us,[7] becomes, in Kant's words, a treatise on method. Inquiry into method, not just as a preliminary but as a sustained and comprehensive operation guiding all philosophical endeavor, has already made the decisive shift away from traditional metaphysics. For such a shift recalibrates the nature of the quest, under the assumption that what is being sought cannot in any way be divorced from how it is sought, and more, that how it is sought controls in fact what is sought. In the syntax of this last postulate, the 'in fact' here loses its old sense, its old ontological force of an actuality distinct from the seeker and the seeking, and now instead joins forces with the 'control' of the how. Thus we should rather render the sentence: how it is being sought *in fact* controls what is being

[4] Cassirer, *Kant's Life and Thought*, p. 129.
[5] *Ibid.*, p. 131.
[6] Kant, *Critique of Pure Reason*, A 11–12, B 25, p. 59.
[7] Cassirer, *Kant's Life and Thought*, pp. 39–138.

sought, where now the 'in fact' has the adverbial force directed unequivocally upon the main verb 'controls', extending even to the 'how' or the 'being sought', and not upon the relative pronoun 'what'. That is, grammatically, the 'in fact' loses its predicative allegiance and sides with the subject. This is no mere linguistic finessing, for this reappraisal of the 'in fact' goes precisely to the heart of the Kantian project, and shows us that at the grammatological level of the subject/predicate economy there is a restructuring that corresponds to the subject/object agreement under review in Kant's employed definition of truth.

This restructuring, which amounts to a reversal, finds its most potent expression in Kant's self-described Copernican revolution, which turns around the initial question of agreement completely: what if subjectivity did not conform to objectivity in the acquiring of knowledge, but objectivity conformed to subjectivity?[8] What if any 'in fact' could only ever apply to that which can be offered within, and by, the subject? We indeed seem pressed into an idealism here, if not a solipsism, though of course Kant's understanding of idealism has very clear limits, and in no way means that the 'in fact' is only ever in reference to something illusory, but rather that it is only ever in reference to appearance, which is governed subjectively. We know that appearance for Kant has little to do with an object *in itself*. How we then arrive at an appearance becomes the transcendental question, with the shift in concern (which both Husserl and Heidegger will later pick up) that moves from what lies behind the appearance, which is not accessible to us, to what allows that appearance to arise and stand before us in the first place. This is a question of method, of mode, and if a reasonable answer can be supplied, then the general question of agreement is so reconstituted that it borders on irrelevancy. If we retain any sense of 'agreement' within Kant's Copernican revolution, it is not an agreement *with*, as such, where two separate entities must accord with one another. It is more an agreement *among*, where accord is a purely intrinsic matter, and in accordance to (with) itself. This brings us again to a defining reflexivity, where we seek out the parameters of this accordance as it functions under and upon its own devices. In a way, then, transcendental philosophy becomes a self-actualizing, even self-creating, pursuit.

Why self-creating? Because if what is actually sought becomes the *way* in which it (what is actually sought) is sought, then there is a kind of circularity or self-referentiality here, and philosophy proper, at least in the transcendental sense, takes as its subject the process of philosophiz*ing*. A philosophy of philosophizing. But why even start? Why even begin the process of philosophizing if it only ever leads back upon itself? Because, Kant would say, as much as philosophy (or philosophizing) is about seeking what we know, it is also about, and maybe even more about, seeking what we do not know, and we start philosophizing in order to know where our knowledge cannot extend. To know that we do not in fact know returns us, of course, to the very roots of Western philosophy – Socrates' axiom. There is, then, as we have already seen, a kind of negative impulse at the heart of the Kantian method, which had already guided Kant in his earlier essay '*Träume eines Geistersehers, erläutert durch Träume der Metaphysick*' ('Dreams of a

[8] Kant, *Critique of Pure Reason*, B xxvii, p. 22.

Visionary, Explained by Dreams of a Metaphysics', 1766), and which Kant directly addresses in the Preface to the Second Edition of the *Critique of Pure Reason*: 'On a cursory view of the present work it may seem that its results are merely *negative*, warning us that we must never venture with speculative reason beyond the limits of experience. Such is in fact its primary use.' And only a few sentences later: 'So far, therefore, as Critique limits speculative reason, it is indeed *negative* ...'.[9] This negativity is quickly countered with a positive value, but this positive value is only ever established by the beneficial results of the negative force, so that to question the positive value 'would thus be like saying that the police are of no positive benefit, inasmuch as their main business is merely to prevent the violence of which citizens stand in mutual fear, in order that each may pursue his vocation in peace and security.'[10] So the negative impetus remains 'primary' by keeping us within the bounds of where we ought, as philosophers, to be employing our reason. The *method* of this employment, then, carries a double role: it first delineates what we can and cannot do, and then in that very delineation provides us with the material by which and for which our reason is employed. Thus the method is a *deployment*, a setting into action of philosophy. And it is therefore a creative deployment, as it sets into action itself. Transcendental philosophy manifests this deployment as it marks its method.

Critical Judgment

This focus on method becomes itself a method, and it is to this *meta*-method that Kant gives the name *critical*. The critical method, *Kritik*, looks at its own operations as the 'how' of the 'what', so that if it (this critical method and the subject who employs/deploys it) knows anything of the 'what', it knows it only as that which has come about through the 'how'. It knows only, *in fact*, what it has *created*. The 'fact' here has been appropriated by creation. This Kant says in his famous description of 'what we are adopting as our new method of thought' still only in the Preface to the Second Edition: 'namely, that we can know *a priori* of things only what we ourselves put into them.'[11] Despite the many qualifications necessary for this famous assertion, one 'fact' is nevertheless implied – the critical has entered the realm of the creative.

To understand fully this merging of the critical into the creative, we need to penetrate more deeply into the Kantian Critique and its uncompromising critical nature. Let us remind ourselves again of the κρίνειν at the root of the word 'critical', and the judging upon which all critical activity of the Kantian kind relies. Again, the judging here is the selection or determination of limits, as we have seen clearly at the embarkation of the project. 'Philosophy consists in knowing our limits'.[12] But more than limiting reason simply to the realm of experience, what

[9] *Ibid.*, B xxiv–xxv, p. 26. See also above, p. 24.
[10] *Ibid.*, B xxv, p. 27.
[11] *Ibid.*, B xviii, p. 23.
[12] Jaspers, *Kant*, p. 97.

Kant means further is the ability, and in a practical sense the requirement, of the faculty of judgment to take in an array of possibilities, whether before we have experienced them as manifested realities or after, select from these possibilities some and not others, differentiate those that we have selected from those we have not, and, in the final analysis, or what Kant will call synthesis, unify them into some principled whole. Thus we can repeat what we have said earlier, that limiting is not only a placing of borders to mark out the general purview, but a defining *within* those borders. In both cases, judgment is predominant.

In the First Critique, the faculty of judgment, which drives any act of thinking, is divided into two well-known and much discussed parts: the analytic and the synthetic. It is important that we remind ourselves of these basics again. Analytic judgments, we recall, are those that clarify, while synthetic judgments are those that amplify. As Kant puts it: 'In all judgments in which the relation of a subject to the predicate is thought . . ., this relation is possible in two different ways. Either the predicate B belongs to the subject A, as something which is (covertly) contained in this concept A; or B lies outside the concept A, although it does indeed stand in connection with it.'[13] As the etymologies suggest, analysis takes things apart, while synthesis puts things together. The taking apart assumes a given wholeness from the start; thus the subject and predicate, as part of this same whole, belong to one another, and to describe one is in effect to describe the other. The one is 'contained' in the other – though, as Kant feels compelled to add, 'covertly'. Analysis adds nothing to what is given, but is simply a breaking up 'into those constituent concepts that have all along been thought in it'.[14] Here, subject and predicate are established, as Kant says, through 'identity'. That is, the conceptual identity of the predicate B is to be found in the subject A, and the judgment is only ever a clarification of that which was already in hand, so to speak. Synthesis, conversely, assumes a lack of wholeness from the start, and requires a putting together of one thing with another extraneous to the first. The predicate has no conceptual identity with the subject, and thus expands, extends or amplifies that which is given in the subject. Synthetic judgments invite extrinsic elements that add something new. For the purposes of knowledge, then, synthetic judgments are the far more important of the two.

Where do these new, extrinsic elements come from, exactly? From experience, for one. Indeed, what may be thought about subject A may be added to by any number of predicative possibilities in experience: predicates B, C, D, E, and so on, as the empirical world supplies them. These predicates are found to be connected in some observed and requisite way with the concept of the subject, and our judgment places them under that concept as parts of a whole. Kant uses the example of the weight of a body: though the predicate 'weight' does not intrinsically lie with the concept of body (as say the predicate 'extension' does – to define 'body' requires the use of the term 'extension', though not the term 'weight'), it is nevertheless attached synthetically to the concept through experience, because it is found to be 'invariably connected' with it.[15] We drop the body of a sizable stone on our foot,

---

[13] Kant, *Critique of Pure Reason*, A 6, B 10, p. 48.

[14] *Ibid.*, A7, B 11, p. 48.

[15] *Ibid.*, B 12, p. 50.

and we feel its weight every time, though we could never have conceived of this weight prior to experiencing this stone in the physical world. And since this world is continually supplying us with predicates to our conceptual subjects, 'Judgments of experience, as such, are one and all synthetic.'[16]

But what of synthetic judgments *prior* to experience – that is, *a priori*? Where do extrinsic predicates come from when not from experience, when we think, for example, mathematically or geometrically? Are *a priori* synthetic judgments possible at all? We know that this question is the main propelling force behind the First Critique, and sets the agenda for its entire treatment of *pure* reason (that is, reason untrammeled by experience). Outside of experience, outside of picking up a stone and dropping it on our foot, or of setting down a bucket under a male goat to see if it will yield any milk, how is a predicate connected to a subject? 'Upon what, then, am I to rely, when I seek to go beyond concept A, and to know that another concept B is connected with it? Through what is the synthesis made possible?' Here Kant introduces the variable 'X': 'What', he asks, 'is here the unknown = X which gives the support to the understanding when it believes that it can discover outside the concept A a predicate B foreign to this concept, which it yet at the same time considers to be connected with it?'[17] This 'X' is not in any way connected with experience – ultimately susceptible as it would be to Hume's skepticism – but is constituted instead in synthetic principles of judgment themselves, the same principles which form the very conditions for the possibility of experience. The task is to uncover these synthetic principles, to disclose the nature and the identity of this mysterious 'X', and in doing so thus lay out the method or mode by which we come to any such agreement of the object with the subject – by which we come, that is, to 'truth'.

As the place, then, between two distinct and self-subsisting realms, the X becomes the crucial factor within the region of truth, as it allows passage from the subject to the object and vice versa. But we need to be careful with using the analogy of 'place', for this X cannot in itself be a 'what' with spatial properties and coordinates, an isolable locality within a larger determinable district, a third term which concretely spans and unites two separate entities. The X is rather a 'how', a structural mode which does not merely 'give support', as Kant first says, but which provides the very conditions for the possibility of moving from subject A to a foreign predicate B. The provision of such conditions, we see, is a kind of generating and originary structure which furnishes something from nothing through the very grounds of possibility. In both long-standing traditions of theology and philosophy prior to Kant, this provisionary structure had been customarily associated with creation in its most primordial sense, and hence with divinity. God becomes that to which all acts of generation are traced back, until the very conditions of generation are reached. In Greek terms, this originary point was termed λόγος; in later Christian terms it becomes the personal Creator who constructs the worlds found in the Hebrew and Christian scriptures respectively. But even amid such deifications, the element of mystery in the precise act of

[16] *Ibid.*, B 12, p. 49.

[17] *Ibid.*, A 9, B 13, pp. 50–51.

creation was never fully done away with or accounted for. And Kant himself was aware of the great 'unknown' which traditionally marked this mystery, *das Unbekannte* = *X*, as he calls it. At the end of the section on the distinction between the two judgments, Kant concludes with reference to a 'requisite for such a sure and wide synthesis as will lead to a genuinely new addition [*wirklich neuen Unbau*] to all previous knowledge.'[18] In the First Edition of the Critique Kant added, directly after this, a further thought he later excised from the Second Edition:

> A certain mystery lies here concealed; and only upon its solution can the advance into the limitless field of the knowledge yielded by pure understanding be made sure and trustworthy. What we must do is to discover, in all its proper universality, the ground of the possibility of *a priori* synthetic judgments, to obtain insight into the conditions which make each kind of such judgments possible, and to mark out all this knowledge, which forms a genus by itself, not in any cursory outline, but in a system, with completeness and in a manner sufficient for any use, according to its original sources, divisions, extent, and limits. So much, meantime, as regards what is peculiar in synthetic judgments.[19]

Within this reiteration of the task, Kant admits that a 'certain mystery lies here concealed', the very mystery which has accompanied any 'genuinely new addition to all previous knowledge' in ages past.[20] But Kant's own footnote after the original opening clause suggests that if past philosophers and theologians had been aware of what they might discover in this 'genuinely new addition', they would not have made recourse so quickly and so futilely to the *deus ex machina*: 'If it had occurred to any of the ancients even to raise this question, this by itself would, up to our own time, have been a powerful influence against all systems of pure reason, and would have saved us so many of those vain attempts, which have been blindly undertaken without knowledge of what it is that requires to be done.'[21] Does the fact that Kant in the Second Edition excised this reference to a concealed 'mystery' indicate that he, who felt *he* knew very well what was required to be done, was about to lay bare that mystery in his analysis to follow, revealing that the critical nature of the X, hitherto unknown, is the very thing which we not only ought to disclose in all its conceivable determinations, but *can* disclose? But if we *can* disclose it, it is only because the disclosure itself is constituted by limitation. The unknown is known by the very limits which make up its disclosure, so that in the determining 'how', what is generated are the limits (conditions) of the possibility of generation. Kant's creative force, then, becomes the mode by which conditions are provided. Beyond that mode, that *machina*, we cannot know anything. It is best then to leave the *deus* out of it.

Is this possible? Is it possible to leave the *deus* out of the machine altogether?

---

[18] *Ibid.*, A 10, B 14, p. 51.

[19] *Ibid.*, A 10, pp. 51–52.

[20] It can be assumed that the 'here' [*hier*] of 'A certain mystery lies here concealed' [*Es liegt also hier ein gewißes Geheimnis verborgen*] refers to the 'genuinely new addition' [*wirklich neuen Unbau*] of the preceding sentence. But it is by no means clear and unequivocal, and perhaps Kant's best option in addressing the confusion was to discard the paragraph altogether.

[21] Kant, *Critique of Pure Reason*, A 10, pp. 51–52.

This is a question that would be hurled at Kant by many subsequent thinkers. But we get ahead of ourselves if we try to address the question at this juncture. We will heed, at least for now, Kant's own warnings.

In Search of 'X'

As the 'X' is the crux of the Kantian matter, and of *Kritik's* creativity, we need to pursue more fully the way it is rigorously worked out in the body of the first part of the Critique, 'The Transcendental Doctrine of Elements', and, in particular, in the matter's most detailed exposition within the section on 'Transcendental Deduction'. First, under the inherited categories of *aesthesis* and *noesis*, Kant draws a correlated distinction between sensibility and understanding. Sensibility concerns the elements given to us in intuition (*aesthesis*) which we simply receive without any noetic processing, or thinking as such. According to this definition, when a given object affects us, what we actually receive is not the object in itself, but only rather an appearance of the object, which Kant qualifies later as a representation. The capacity to receive these representations is sensibility. Intuition, understood as a corollary to sensibility, allows a mode of knowledge to relate immediately to these representations. When sensibility *receives* a representation, then, it is only ever derivative, and not original.[22] The two purest forms of sensible intuition are, of course, space and time, though in addition we are constantly receiving empirical representations as a result of our engagement, through sensations, with the sensate world. Were we simply to receive these representations, one upon the other, without any unifying sense of how they relate to one another or to the manifold of experience, we would not understand or know them in any real sense. Understanding, then, has to do with the method by which the given objects, as representations, are processed by our thoughts (*noesis*), and by which we can claim a knowledge of them. Understanding is 'the mind's power of producing representations from itself, the *spontaneity* of knowledge'[23], or as is later qualified (since the object as first represented is only ever given to us, or intuited, as representation), of producing a 'representation of a representation' of the object.[24] This 'representation of a representation' is a mediate knowledge, mediating the intuited representation with a larger whole or unified representation. This reduplication of representations relies on concepts: those functions which lay out the unifying principles or connections within any manifold. The working out of all these relations within understanding, then, comes under the 'Analytic of Concepts'. Here concepts, along with their fourfold categories,[25] bear the same relation to understanding as intuitions bear towards sensibility: they become that which allows the mode of knowledge to relate to representations at all, mediately in the case of concepts and immediately in the case of intuitions. Combined, concepts and

---

[22] *Ibid.*, B 72, p. 90.
[23] *Ibid.*, A 51, B 75, p. 93.
[24] *Ibid.*, A 68, B 93, p. 105.
[25] Of quantity, quality, relation and modality – see *Ibid.*, A 77ff, B 102ff, pp. 111ff.

intuitions constitute all our knowledge. But whereas intuitions help supply the elements (sensibility), concepts help supply the method (understanding) by unifying or connecting the many into the one. Such connecting is clearly dependent upon a synthesis, or presumes a synthesis, so that to understand anything requires the services of synthetic judgment to bring the various and otherwise indeterminate representations of objects to a place where they can be apprehended as a single representation amid the entire manifold of representations. This *limiting* shares the same structural framework as the subject/predicate relation in the faculty of judgment just discussed above, for indeed synthesis is always a judgment. Thus the question remains, how does one bridge the gap from the sensibility of intuition to the concepts of understanding? Here again the same variable 'X' presents itself as a mystery to be solved.

Imagination

Early in the 'Analytic of Concepts', Kant gives us a clue to the nature of this new modulation of the 'X'. 'Synthesis in general, as we shall hereafter see, is the mere result of the power of imagination [*Einbildungskraft*], a blind but indispensable function of the soul, without which we should have no knowledge whatsoever, but of which we are scarcely ever conscious.'[26] Here is the first real mention of the 'power of imagination' which comes into play with such significance not only in the Critiques as a whole, but in subsequent Western thinking and Western culture. At this early stage Kant calls it a 'blind' function of the soul, of which 'we are scarcely ever conscious'. In post-Kantian thinking, we have become more than conscious of imagination's power, to the point where we have valorized, even deified, the notion. Whether this aggrandizement is justified remains an open question at this stage. Here with Kant we are alerted to the more anthropological question of why imagination had remained a 'blind function' for so long, and if for Kant it still continues to remain 'blind' in some way.

A closer examination of the 'Transcendental Deduction' may help us. In this pivotal section, Kant places the following question before us: what proof of *right* (that is deduction, in the legal sense) do we have to employ any concept *a priori*, where experience is not available for ratification, or where available, is insufficient for the task? We might ask the question yet another way: what right does understanding have to add something *new* to sensibility? On what grounds, ultimately, does *a priori* synthesis, the connecting of pure subject with a pure foreign predicate, lie? We know now that in the Kantian scheme there is first a manifold of pure intuition, rooted in space and time, which operate *a priori*. There are then concepts which give unity through a representation of intuited representations. This unified representation is none other than a representation of the synthetic unity – a re-presentation of itself as the giver of unity. This is why Kant speaks of 'the mind's power of producing representations from itself'. But what right, we may ask, does understanding have to represent itself, like a

[26] *Ibid.*, A 78, B 103, p. 112.

defendant standing as judge in its own trial? What justification is there for this self-defense and its corresponding self-productivity? Kant puts the problem his own way: it is a question of 'how *subjective conditions of thought* can have *objective validity*.'[27]

What is to be discovered in all these permutations of the question are the *a priori* conditions upon which the possibility of experience rests. For in establishing and ratifying those conditions, which must pertain *both* to subjectivity and to objectivity, the bridge across all the various 'polarities' discussed so far – subject/predicate, aesthetic/noetic, sensibility/understanding, intuition/concept, and even *a priori/a posteriori* – is, and must be, established. The Transcendental Deduction attempts to lay out this crossing, or better, this 'X', as a means of final proof, and it does so by introducing the mediating power of imagination. But in Kant, imagination comes to us in two ways, because the Deduction is presented to us in two ways. There is the explication of the Deduction in the First Edition of 1781 (Transcendental Deduction A) and a completely reworked explication in the Second Edition of 1787 (Transcendental Deduction B). Two versions: as if the imaginary power could not be contained in one version alone. Yet what we find is that the second version actually retreats from the emphasis on imagination put forward in the first. Ultimately, a proper assessment of the complexities of Kant's strange and uneven treatment of this imagination requires an examination of both versions of the Deduction in their order.

In the first version, the two sides requiring mediation – mediation towards that agreement between knowledge and its object which Kant had set forth at the outset in his definition of truth, and which we have been discussing all along in various appropriations – are now determined even more specifically. In the synthetic movement from intuition to concept, we are given representations *sensibly* to represent in turn *cognitively*. The intuited representations come to us in a manifold, but from the manifold a unity must arise, in order for us to grasp the representation *as* a representation. Kant calls the synthesizing of the various parts of the manifold into a unity the *synthesis of apprehension*, 'because it is directed immediately upon intuition, which does indeed offer a manifold, but a manifold which can never be represented as a manifold, and as contained *in a single representation*, save in virtue of such a synthesis.'[28] This synthesis is 'pure' in that it must first and foremost be exercised *a priori*. But in the apprehension of a unified representation, we may ask what it is that allows us the synthetic unity. For simply to observe things in succession to one another does not in itself produce unity. One could merely have a disconnected string of separate and distinct entities or representations, which have no more relation to one another than a random set of numbers pulled from a lottery machine. In order to establish a relation or an association, the distinct entities must be bound together by some 'rule' or 'law'. This rule or law not only unifies them, and brings them under one structure, but allows us to 'reproduce' one from another within the calculus of the structure, even when a representation might not be present before us. Without this reproduction,

[27] *Ibid.*, A 89, B 122, p. 124.

[28] *Ibid.*, A 99, pp. 131–132.

we could never associate anything in a structural sense. We could only take things at random and indeterminately: a dinner plate would never be associated with a circle, for example, nor then associated with food, and thus we could never reproduce a plate in our mind as something of a certain size and a certain shape which functions as the receptacle for our food. But whence these reproductive capabilities? What makes the reproduction (of a circle, of a plate, of food, and so on) possible in the first place, to furnish in turn the ground for any synthetic unity of appearances or representations? For Kant it is *imagination*. Through imagination, the synthesis of reproduction is possible. And again, this synthesis is possible *a priori*, for

> experience as such necessarily presupposes the reproducibility of appearances. When I seek to draw a line in thought, or to think of the time from one noon to another, or even to represent to myself some particular number, obviously the various manifold representations that are involved must be apprehended by me in thought one after the other. But if I were always to drop out of thought the preceding representations (the first parts of the line, the antecedent parts of the time period, or the units in the order represented), and did not reproduce them while advancing to those that follow, a complete representation would never be obtained: none of the above-mentioned thoughts, not even the purest and most elementary representations of space and time, could arise.[29]

A pure transcendental synthesis of imagination, then, conditions the very possibility of all experience, and provides, in the form of a transcendental mode, the passage to the conceptual side of knowledge in the final synthesis.

But merely to reproduce representations in association does not yet bring us to knowledge. For if 'we were not conscious that what we think is the same as what we thought a moment before, all reproduction in the series of representations would be useless.'[30] The last step, knowledge, requires the formation of all the associated representations into a unified whole, or concept. But such a formation must take place first within our consciousness, so that we can become aware that what we are associating is in fact part of a unity of synthesis. This consciousness of the unity of synthesis – a transcendental condition – Kant calls *apperception*, or the synthesis of recognition in a concept. The *transcendental apperception* then is that pure original unified consciousness (*self*-consciousness) which precedes all representational data brought by intuitions and makes the unity of the synthesis of all these data, and hence their recognition, possible according to concepts.

Thus Kant sums up these difficult ideas: 'There are three subjective sources of knowledge upon which rests the possibility of experience in general and of knowledge of its objects – *sense*, *imagination*, and *apperception* ... *Sense* represents appearances empirically in *perception*, *imagination* in *association* (and reproduction), *apperception* in the *empirical consciousness* of the identity of the reproduced representations with the appearances whereby they were given, that is, in recognition.'[31] But Kant now needs to makes one more crucial distinction. For

---

[29] *Ibid.*, A 101–102, p. 133.

[30] *Ibid.*, A. 103, p. 133.

[31] *Ibid.*, A 115, p. 141.

the foregoing triad of sources – sense, imagination and apperception – are presented here within an empirical context, but we know that each of them must be grounded in a corresponding *a priori purity* – pure intuition, pure synthesis of imagination, and pure apperception respectively. Pure intuition (space and time) and pure apperception (self-identity in original unified consciousness) have been accounted for. But the *pure* synthesis of imagination needs a further qualification. In the above description of the synthesis of reproduction in terms of association, Kant says 'experience as such necessarily presupposes the reproducibility of appearances', for if, in thinking a series of representations necessary for a concept, the preceding representation always dropped out, one would never be able to retain each gathered representation long enough to place within a whole. Like slippery, wriggling fish, they would keep springing from our grasp the moment we reached for another, and we would only ever be in possession of one representation at a time. Reproduction acts as a kind of gaff hook: it allows us to retrieve the fish, even though it may have escaped from our hand. It allows us to retain the preceding representation. Imagination is the faculty which supplies this gaff. But if this faculty is to function in the pure *a priori*, before anything is at hand from experience, is it right to say it 'reproduces'? For what is there available to reproduce *a priori*, except itself and its reproducing capabilities, that is, the continuing possibility of the *functioning* itself? Imagination is not the reproduction *per se* (the regaffed), but the *synthesis* of the reproduction (the *regaffing*). What allows this *synthesis* then must be a productive source, not a reproductive source. It *produces* the gaff hook before there is anything to be gaffed, and is thus transcendental. Hence: 'But only the *productive* synthesis of the imagination can take place *a priori*; the reproductive rests upon empirical conditions. Thus the principle of the necessary unity of pure (productive) synthesis of imagination, prior to apperception, is the ground of the possibility of knowledge, especially of experience.'[32]

With this distinction between productive and reproductive synthesis in imagination, Kant has provided the keystone of the First Deduction. '*The unity of the apperception in relation to the synthesis of imagination* is the *understanding*; and this same unity, with reference to the *transcendental synthesis* of the imagination, the *pure understanding*.'[33] The productive nature of the imagination becomes then the single most reduced feature that supports and unites the two sides of sensibility and understanding. Although Kant is unwilling to call this feature the keystone of the Deduction as a whole, and in fact admits it is 'indeed strange' that everything in knowledge should depend upon *this*, the transcendental function of imagination,[34] nevertheless he does point toward this centrality in the following summary:

> A pure imagination, which conditions all *a priori* knowledge, is thus one of the fundamental faculties of the human soul. By its means we bring the manifold of intuition on the one side, into connection with the condition of the necessary unity of pure apperception on the other. The extremes, namely sensibility and understanding, must

[32] *Ibid.*, A 118, pp. 142–143.

[33] *Ibid.*, A 119, p. 143.

[34] *Ibid.*, A 123, p. 146.

> stand in necessary connection with each other through the mediation of this transcendental function of imagination, because otherwise the former, though indeed yielding appearances, would supply no objects of empirical knowledge, and consequently no experience.[35]

Experience, then, is not possible without pure imagination conditioning all *a priori* knowledge. Pure, productive imagination, in turn, becomes the 'X', the filled-in blank, that missing variable which sits at the core of all agreement with knowledge and its object.

Now this is in the First Edition of the Deduction. In the Second Edition Kant backs away from the formidable centrality of this result, almost as if it had surprised even him. Why? What is so 'strange' about this faculty of imagination as the very condition of all possible knowledge? Is it because its productive nature, at its most primordial moment, is synonymous with 'creation', so that in one sense (though a highly qualified sense) we can say that we in fact *create* the world, or at least we create that world which is knowable to us?

In the Second Deduction, Kant shifts the emphasis from the threefold sources of sense, imagination and apperception, with imagination as the crucial condition for the outer terms, to the outer term of apperception by itself, and to the transcendental unity of apperception as self-consciousness. In this shift, imagination is no longer the mediating 'ground' between sensibility and understanding, but becomes associated with the synthetic function of the understanding. The term 'imagination' appears only briefly in the middle of the Second Deduction as a further explication of synthesis, where synthesis combines the manifold found in representations in relation to the unity of apperception. These representations, we have seen, can come either from sensible intuitions, or, as representation of representations, from the concepts and their categories as informed by those intuitions. Either way, their own unity is required and supplied through *a priori* synthesis. The synthesis of the manifold in the former, the sensible intuitions, here Kant now entitles 'figurative synthesis' (*synthesis speciosa*), while that of the manifold in the latter, the concept and their categories, he entitles 'combination through the understanding' (*synthesis intellectualis*).[36] But in order for figurative synthesis to correlate with intellectual synthesis, something must bring them together as a whole: a transcendental synthesis. This something he now calls imagination. As similar as this definition appears to be to the mediating function of imagination in the First Deduction, the following passage in the second version shows how imagination no longer acts as a 'ground' for either side, but struggles to find a home *amid* one side or the other:

> *Imagination* is the faculty of representing in intuition an object that is *not in itself present*. Now since all our intuition is sensible, the imagination, owing to the subjective condition under which alone it can give to the concepts of understanding a corresponding intuition, belongs to *sensibility*. But inasmuch as its synthesis is an expression of spontaneity, which is determinative and not, like sense, determinable merely, and which is therefore able to determine sense *a priori* in respect of its form in accordance with the unity of

---

[35] *Ibid.*, A 124, p. 146.
[36] *Ibid.*, B 151, p. 164.

> apperception, imagination is to that extent a faculty which determines the sensibility *a priori*; and its synthesis of intuitions, conforming as it does to the *categories*, must be the transcendental synthesis of *imagination*. This synthesis is an action of the understanding on the sensibility ...[37]

In this redescription, Kant admits that imagination belongs to sensibility insofar as it *subjectively* provides through synthesis an intuition to the concepts. But insofar as this synthesis is 'an expression of spontaneity' – coming not from any extraneous source, but from within itself and by its own powers – imagination belongs to understanding and its concepts, which Kant, even as far back as the opening sentence of the 'Transcendental Logic', has said always operate through spontaneity.[38] The idea of spontaneity is important here, for that which is spontaneous is not determined by other outside forces ('determinable'), but in fact does the determining itself ('determinative'). Thus imagination 'determines' sense or the sensibility *a priori*, is thus called *productive* imagination as distinguished from *reproductive* imagination ('whose synthesis is entirely subject to empirical laws ... of association'[39]), and is therefore rightly better understood as 'an action of understanding on the sensibility', and not the other way around, as it may first appear. Gone then is imagination as a structural ground for both sides, and in its place is an imagination as a subordinate function of understanding.

Why this appropriation of imagination by understanding? Why did Kant feel compelled to rewrite the productive power of imagination not as the 'X' that supplies the *a priori* conditions which allow the two sides of sensibility and understanding to come together, but as an instrument of one of those sides as it interacts with, and upon, the other? Why this retreat into the confines of a known (or knowing) entity? We have held back the voice of Heidegger amid all this discussion and all these questions so far, but we can hold back no longer, since Heidegger's particular insight into this matter of imagination helps us to see the immensity of the issues at stake here.

Heidegger and Interpretation

In his decidedly individual reading of Kant in *Kant and the Problem of Metaphysics* (1929), which, despite its provocative and 'violent' interpretation of the Kantian scheme, to which many have taken exception, has received general neglect for too long now, Heidegger has brought the 'creative' implications of Kant's Critique to center stage.[40] In the all-important Part Three ('The Laying of the Ground for

---

37 *Ibid.*, B 152–153, p. 165.

38 *Ibid.*, A 50–51, B 74–75, pp. 92–93.

39 *Ibid.*, B 152, p. 165.

40 Heidegger, *Kant and the Problem of Metaphysics*, p. 175. Among the thinkers who *have* treated this work recently, particularly in its reading of Kant's imagination, are Slavoj Žižek and, as Žižek himself draws upon, Cornelius Castoriadis. Cf. Slavoj Žižek's *The Ticklish Subject* (New York: Verso, 1999), and Cornelius Castoriadis' 'The Discovery of the Imagination' in *Constellations*, vol. 1, no. 2 (October 1994).

Metaphysics in its Originality') Heidegger focuses on the transcendental power of imagination almost exclusively. Here he too seizes upon the curious disjunction between the 'two versions' of imagination in the two Deductions. After showing, with an interpretation that seems intent on validating the thoughts just completed in his own magnum opus *Sein und Zeit*,[41] how the power of imagination acts as what he calls the 'formative center of ontological knowledge' and its ground of possibility, or as the root of the 'two stems' of pure intuition and pure thinking, Heidegger remarks on Kant's 'shrinking-back' from the transcendental power of imagination in the second version:

> [The] original, essential constitution of humankind, 'rooted' in the transcendental power of imagination, is the 'unknown' into which Kant must have looked if he spoke of the 'root unknown to us', for the unknown is not that of which we simply know nothing. Rather, it is what pushes against us as something disquieting in what is known. And yet, Kant did not carry through with the more original interpretation of the transcendental power of imagination; indeed, he did not even make the attempt in spite of the clear, initial sketching-out of such an analytic which he himself recognized for the first time. On the contrary:
>
> Kant shrank back [*zurückgewichen*] from this unknown root.[42]

The 'unknown', the 'X', is that disquieting feature of, or indeed within, what is known, but which we cannot face squarely. It is the unknown that remains prior to knowledge and its determining grasp, but an unknown which, according to Heidegger, Kant was all too willing to give over to knowledge (understanding), or to the knowing of Reason and Logic. Here we see Heidegger's attempt, as inaugurated just a year or two before in the publication of *Sein und Zeit*, to move beyond not merely the traditional metaphysics of his forefathers, but the very ground for that metaphysics in the primacy of Logic, as he sees that attempt initiated and then aborted in Kant. In the long-standing contention between sensibility and reason, between Aesthetic and Logic, even as Kant has understood and employed these terms, has imagination now become the great leveler, supplanting any claims to the throne by the queen of all sciences, pure reason herself? So Heidegger asks:

> How is the baser faculty of sensibility also to be able to constitute the essence of reason? Does not everything fall into confusion if the lowest takes the place of the highest? What is to happen with the venerable tradition, according to which Ratio and Logic have claimed the central function in the history of metaphysics? Can the primacy of Logic fall? Can the architectonic of the laying of the ground for metaphysics in general, the division into the Transcendental Aesthetic and Logic, still be upheld if what it has for its theme is basically to be the transcendental power of imagination?

---

[41] Žižek suggests *Kant and the Problem of Metaphysics* is a direct extension of the unfinished *Sein und Zeit*, so that, together with the 1927 lectures at Marburg, published later as *The Basics Problems of Phenomenology*, we get a trilogy that is 'a rough realized version of the entire *Being and Time* project' (*The Ticklish Subject*, p. 22).

[42] Heidegger, *Kant and the Problem of Metaphysics*, p. 112.

> Will not the *Critique of Pure Reason* have deprived itself of its own theme if pure reason reverts to the transcendental power of imagination? Does this ground-laying not lead us to an abyss?[43]

This 'abyss' is the very same abyss we have seen earlier in Pilate's question to Jesus, and Bulgakov's corresponding 'hint'. It is an abyss from which even the most intrepid among us, in the desperate need for the known and the reasonable, shrink back. Heidegger's reading of Kant, in all its 'violence' to the traditional understanding of the 'Reason' of Kant's title, in all its emphasis on a fundamental ontology as opposed to a fundamental epistemology, shows us in its appraisal of the power of imagination this power's very centrality within the First Critique despite itself and despite the author:

> In the radicalism of the questions, Kant brought the 'possibility' of metaphysics to this abyss. He saw the unknown. He had to shrink back. It was not just that the transcendental power of imagination frightened him, but rather that in between [the two Editions] pure reason as reason drew him increasingly under its spell.[44]

Kant saw the unknown, the 'X', yet could not abide there, could not abide *it*. Nevertheless, his initial seeing is what we must retain, Heidegger radically asserts:

> However, because the transcendental power of imagination, on the grounds of its indissoluble, original structure, opens up the possibility of the laying of the ground for ontological knowledge, and thereby for metaphysics, then for this reason the first edition remains closer to the innermost thrust of the problematic of a laying of the ground for metaphysics. With reference to this most central question of the whole work, therefore, it [the First Edition] deserves a fundamental priority over the second. All reinterpretation [*Umdeutung*] of the pure power of imagination as a function of pure thinking – a re-interpretation which 'German Idealism' even accentuated subsequent to the second edition of the *Critique of Pure Reason* – misunderstands its specific essence.[45]

Presumably, it is Kant's own 'reinterpretation' that is under principal indictment here. In shrinking back, Kant has missed his argument's own essence. And yet, how can Heidegger overstep Kant's own re-evaluation with a later, 'ontological' interpretation, and claim that Kant has missed his own point? Is this not the height of textual violence?

Slavoj Žižek argues, with his typical meandering rigor, that violence is already built into the Kantian scheme of transcendental imagination. He too refers to the scheme's two versions, and to Heidegger's charge of 'shrinking-back' in the second, but then draws upon Hegel (read, as always, through a Lacanian lens) to reconsider the essence of imagination as one that begins in a fundamental negativity. Hegel in various places suggests that imagination, far from synthesizing disparate manifolds into unified representations as with Kant, actually disrupts, decomposes, breaks apart what it first receives from a Whole. This 'activity of

[43] *Ibid.*, p. 117.
[44] *Ibid.*, p. 118.
[45] *Ibid.*, p. 138.

dissolution' carries with it an inherent violence that marks the very constitution of the Subject in its most elemental power. Žižek wonders, what if

> Hegel is indicating a kind of even more mysterious *obverse* of the synthetic imagination, an even more primordial power of 'pre-synthetic imagination', of *tearing apart* sensible elements out of their context, of *dismembering* the immediate experience of the organic Whole? It would therefore be too hasty to identify this 'night of the world' with the Void of the mystic experience: it designates, rather, its exact opposite, that is, the primordial Big Bang, the violent self-contrast by means of which the balance and inner peace of the Void of which mystics speak are perturbed, thrown out of joint.

He concludes:

> What Kant neglects is the fact that the primordial form of imagination is the exact opposite of this synthetic activity: imagination enables us to tear the texture of reality apart, to treat as effectively existing something that is merely a component of the living Whole.[46]

At the real heart of imagination then is a 'monstrous' chaos, which Žižek equates with the Lacanian 'Real', that 'black hole in reality' so much referred to in all of his writings.[47] But what Žižek forgets in this admittedly bold reading, as a result perhaps of too cursory an analysis of Kant's two versions of the Transcendental Deduction, is the fact that the transcendental function of imagination for Kant, particularly in the abandoned First Edition (but really in both editions), is principally, before anything else, a *mode*. As mode, it is a productive source that first allows synthesis its very potency to synthesize. The transcendental function of imagination then is conceivably a productive source for the obverse as well, namely, for analysis, even analysis in its most destructive or violent form as a dissecting or dismembering impetus, which Žižek is drawing from Hegel here. That is, as mode, it is already in one sense 'pre-synthetic', since it provides the conditions for any synthesis (or, if we wanted, its opposite) to arise at all. Nevertheless, we could agree to at least this much: what Kant recoils from are the violent possibilities inherent in this mode, the threatening potential and disruptive potentiality of its abyss that, whether in positive synthesis or negative analysis, forces one into the unknown.

Žižek in fact goes even further in his argument to claim, along with Castoriadis, that Heidegger *himself* shrinks back from embracing the full consequences of such an unknown, 'since it indicates a gap in the very ontological edifice of Being' as it tries to situate itself against the horizon of time and temporality. Žižek's contention here needs much further development to be clear, but it appears he wants to claim in general that an imagination of this radical a nature even disturbs our temporal understanding, so that the abyss of imagination 'cannot be properly placed ontologically' in the same way, and to the same extent, as it cannot be properly

[46] Žižek, *The Ticklish Subject*, pp. 31–32.

[47] See especially Slavoj Žižek, *Looking Awry: An Introduction to Jacques Lacan Through Popular Culture* (Cambridge, Mass.: MIT Press, 1991), and the first section 'How Real is Reality?'.

placed epistemologically. And he borrows Castoriadis' assertion that Heidegger, like Kant, effectively abandons this very question of imagination in all his subsequent writings.[48] Whether this latter claim is supportable is questionable. But the emphasis Žižek wants to make is that the violence runs deep, disturbing and even militating against those whose one-time political allegiances, like Heidegger's, might have otherwise indicated they had embraced such a violence.

Heidegger supplies his own response to the question of violence, at least in regards to the text. At the end of his Part Three on imagination's power in *Kant and the Problem of Metaphysics*, Heidegger makes no apology for the 'violence' he had imposed on Kant, as he tries to force his way, as he says, to the very essence of 'what Kant "had wanted to say" '.

> Certainly, in order to wring from what the words say, what it is they want to say, every interpretation [*Interpretation*] must necessarily use violence. Such violence, however, cannot be roving arbitrariness. The power of an idea which shines forth must drive and guide the laying-out [*Auslegung*]. Only in the power of this idea can an interpretation risk what is always audacious, namely, entrusting itself to the concealed inner passion of a work in order to be able, through this, to place itself within the unsaid and force it into speech. That is one way, however, by which the guiding idea, in its power to illuminate, comes to light.[49]

Despite the hermeneutical difficulties with a phrase like the 'power of an idea which shines forth', and the great dangers in the politicization of such an espousal of violence (dangers of course Heidegger himself fell prey to in his links with German Nazism[50]), this passage at the very least points to that high risk and audacity of giving oneself over to the 'concealed inner passion', that is, to that unknown 'X', the power of imagination, which Kant first laid bare, and then subsequently covered over by a safe reversion to 'pure reason', and which Žižek claims Heidegger himself fled. This inner passion, this 'unsaid', which Heidegger at least tries to force into speech, becomes for Heidegger the grounding moment for all metaphysics, even as, or *by virtue of the fact that*, it carries us beyond metaphysics to face a daunting but unavoidable abyss.

Instead of Heidegger's claim about what words want to say in spite of what the author of the words want them to say (of course, there is still a metaphysics at work in this claim), perhaps we are better off saying that the words of Kant's Second Deduction, the second version of imagination, the second 'interpretation', are less acceptable because they are less *critical*. The reinterpretation does not allow its own powers – the power of imagination under the sovereignty of understanding, and thus of Logic – to be laid bare. We may say that the power that drives the ability to reinterpret is primordially the very power of imagination about which we have been speaking, either productively or reproductively: it is either that power to imagine (or re-imagine) what we have already received determinably, or, as with Heidegger's more 'violent' reading, it is that power to imagine determinatively

[48] Žižek, *The Ticklish Subject*, p. 24.
[49] Heidegger, *Kant and the Problem of Metaphysics*, p. 141.
[50] Cf. Žižek, *The Ticklish Subject*, pp. 11ff.

what has not been received, but what lays possible in the words, concealed and unsaid. Kant's reinterpretation of himself was not violent enough, then. It was, conversely, too tame, domesticating the unknown to a known and knowable site (understanding). It is this domestication which Heidegger wants to expose as lacking the promise first held out by imagination in its initial (and 'blind') manifestation, and which we might expose as not taking the critical turn fiercely enough to keep its eye on its own constitutive mode (as Žižek himself fails to do). That this mode – imagination in its transcendency – should lead back on itself to a still as yet unvoiced and unarticulated power of imagination, in other words to a faculty for which we would have no other words, since it precedes, and indeed provides the conditions for, the power of logic and λόγος in the first place, should not inhibit us. Truth, Heidegger reminds us in his definition, is ἀ-λήθεια, an un-concealing or an un-forgetting. Or we might now say: an un-forgetting the unsaid, an un-forgetting the 'X'. If we insisted on retaining at least to some degree Kant's definition of truth and its idea of agreement, truth here would now become an agreement to and with the unsaid. The unsaid and hence the unknown. But such an agreement, under critique (*Kritik*), could not itself remain unsaid. Thus, in imagination, we must plunge into, and navigate, its depths.

4 Goethe

I clearly remembered how I often stood there, following the river with my eyes, with strange presentiments in my heart; how colorfully my imagination painted the countries through which the river flowed, and how soon I discovered that my imagination had limits. Still I knew that the river ran on and on, and I completely lost myself in the vision of an unseen far country.

Goethe's Werther in *The Sorrows of Young Werther*[1]

One of the great human curiosities: that someone should feel compelled to write about themselves. Not write just for themselves, in the singular privacy of a diary or journal. But write expressly for others, *about* themselves. (But of course we know that even in the most private of personal writing, which one 'wouldn't dare' show another, one always, covertly, with some admixture of hope and betrayal, has another set of eyes in mind.) Autobiography becomes the strange merging of life and work, of βίος (*bios*) and τέχνη (*techne*), a marriage between one's productive life and the producing, or reproducing, of that life. By definition, writers of autobiography must feel that they have produced something worthy in their life, and that such productivity justifies, in a proportionate manner, its reproduction. But why then have two of the most influential figures in our history – Socrates and Jesus – not only offered no autobiography, but avoided (and in Socrates' case explicitly abjured) writing altogether? Are not their lives most worthy of reproduction? Perhaps. But *self*-reproduction? The curiosity is with this 'self-', this 'auto'. If Socrates and Jesus, these great masters of self-denial and literary silence, allowed the authority of their words to be claimed and transcribed by other authors (and let us be mindful of the 'author' built in to the term 'authority', as surely as both Plato and the Gospel writers were mindful), why should anyone who follows them presume and claim an authority to define their own particular life?

Augustine's authority for autobiographical reproduction lay in *confession*. The confessional makes one worthy, and most of all worthy to write, and to write about oneself as confessor. Confession is an act of conversion: 'Augustine confesses his God and confesses himself not because he is converted: he becomes converted or tries to become converted while making confession.'[2] He remakes himself. So too, in a way, Rousseau in his *Confessions*, who tries to become worthy (before himself, before his detractors, before his God) through the act of writing. And in this sense the later *Reveries of the Solitary Walker* out-confess the *Confessions*, and become Rousseau's 'true' confessions: the conversion of the self in the self's reproduction. But what then of Goethe? What are the 'true' confessions of the quintessential German author who called his autobiography *Aus meinem Leben: Dichtung und Wahrheit* (*From My Life: Poetry and Truth*)? Where is the truth in this reproduction of a most productive life, in which the author too has famously written, 'Therefore

---

1 Johann Wolfgang von Goethe, *The Sorrows of Young Werther*, trans. Elizabeth Mayer and Louise Bogan; poems trans. W.H. Auden (New York: Random House, 1971), pp. 96–97, hereafter referred to as *Werther*. Or Johann Wolfgang von Goethe, *Sämtliche Werke, Vol. 2.2*, p. 415. The German edition hereafter referred to as Goethe, *SW*.

2 Jean-François Lyotard, *The Confession of Augustine*, trans. Richard Beardsworth (Stanford: Stanford University Press, 2000), p. 49.

all my published works are but fragments of one great confession, which this little book is a bold attempt to complete'?[3]

That Goethe should entitle this attempt 'Poetry and Truth' halts us in our tracks. As with any biography or autobiography, we are confronted yet again with that pressing question of truth. Does the sheer fact that one writes a biography of oneself act as the guarantor of truth for the account? But of course this depends on what kind of truth we look for in a biography. If we look simply for factual details of dates, times and places, we usually trust the autobiographical self as more accurate than any other. If we look for psychological veracity, here too we often assume this self has more to reveal. But is there still another kind of truth, a larger truth that goes beyond the specific compass of the *bios* in question? What is the *Wahrheit* to which Goethe refers in his title? Is it the truth of his life's particular details, or is it a more abstracted notion of Truth which emerges from those details? What is this *Wahrheit's* relation to *Dichtung*? Is it set off against poetry as a rival or competing reality, or is it paired with poetry through some inveterate kinship?

Goethe's life is one of the most chronicled of any great figure. His work is one of the most extensive (41 volumes), most studied, most influential of European thinkers and writers. Goethe 'confesses' that his work is his life – fragments of a 'great confession' working into a completed whole. But what is the truth of that confessed life? What is the truth of that confessed work? Is the truth that which binds the life and the work together? Or perhaps we should ask, what does Goethe confess *to*?

There is a man who sells his soul to the Devil, and there is a 'genius' who spends the better part of his life (almost sixty years) re-telling that story. Is this not worthy of some confession, great or small?

Goethe has much to confess, not least because, from the beginning of his career, he let his life be the material for this work – and the material not merely for biographical truth, but for poetic and imaginative creation. Thus we have the great sensation *The Sorrows of Young Werther*, which first appeared in 1774 when Goethe was 24 years old. The artistic and social response which this story provoked, from caricatures to operas, may seem surprising to our late modern sensibility, which gives little credence now to a tale of high-flown sentimental passion, in which a romantic 'hero' cannot contain his implacable love for the idealized perfections of a married woman, and resorts to suicide as his only recourse and restitution. And yet this story became such a literary success in its day that, as we know, troubled Werthers began appearing everywhere, with reports, however apocryphal, of the discovery of young corpses in riverbeds with copies of *Werther* in their pocket. Incredulous or not, we nevertheless must admit the powerful allegory such an image becomes for the conflation of fiction and reality, a

3 Johann Wolfgang von Goethe, *Goethe's Collected Works, Vol. 4, From My Own Life: Poetry and Truth, Parts One to Three*, trans. Robert R. Heitner, eds Thomas P. Saine and Jeffrey L. Sammons (New York: Suhrkamp Publishers, 1997), p. 214. Or Goethe, *SW, Vol. 16, Aus meinem Leben: Dichtung und Wahrheit*, ed. Peter Sprengel (Munich: Carl Hanser, 1985), p. 306. '*Alles was daher von mir bekannt geworden, sind nur Bruchstücke einer großen Konfession, welche vollständig zu machen dieses Büchlein ein gewagter Versuch ist.*'

conflation the likes of which we have not seen until our recent obsession with cinema and Hollywood, though even then seldom accomplished with such flare. The inspiration of an extreme and unrequited passion which compels one to an extreme and wholly profane act, the intense emotional force that drives its readers to imitate a most severe and irrevocable consummation, the deliberate fusion of fiction with fact – are these not grounds for a deep confession from Goethe? We might think so all the more when the story itself is not a pure invention, a creation *ex nihilo*, but borrowed from a particular and traceable experience in the author's own life. Thus Goethe would later confess, in the first version of his 'Second Roman Elegy':

> Ask whom you will, I am safe from you now, you fair ladies and fine society gentlemen! 'But did Werther really live? Did it all really happen like that? Which town has the right to boast of the lovely Lotte as its citizen?' Oh, how often I have cursed those foolish pages of mine which made my youthful sufferings public property! If Werther had been my brother and I had killed him, I could scarcely have been so persecuted by his avenging sorrowful ghost.[4]

Werther's object of unmitigated affection, Lotte, is, we know, based on the actual person of Charlotte Kestner, née Buff, for whom the young Goethe had a short-lived and ill-advised passion while in Wetzlar during the period from 1772–74. Aware of his imprudence, Goethe left the company of this 'new Héloïse' and her husband before any indiscretions could take place, and obviously before any drastic act of self-annihilation. And yet the reproduction of this experience in the inflated pages of *Werther* the novel, which also drew on an actual event in Wetzlar in which a fellow student, for reasons of unrequited love, took his own life, becomes a kind of indiscretion that Goethe himself would later rue. To expose one's life and one's improper intimacies to the public eye, and in such exaggerated and bold dress, is certainly a risky enterprise, and one which the immature Goethe had not fully calculated. Yet it is common knowledge (we could even say axiomatic) that artists steal from their own experiences and personal surroundings for the stuff of their fictions. Perhaps more indiscreet in Goethe's case – that is, more radical for the understanding of his day – is the manner in which life and work, truth and poetry, were made to share the same imaginative space. For here, in *Werther*, the imaginative space is no longer governed simply by the literary form or genre in which the life, both the protagonist's and the author's, is subsumed. This imaginative space becomes, with a simultaneity that engulfs both figures, the autonomous self of the individual. So Werther writes to his friend early in the account:

> That the life of man is but a dream is a thought which has occurred to many people, and I myself am constantly haunted by it. When I see the limitations which imprison the active and speculative faculties of man; when I see how all human activity is directed toward procuring satisfaction for needs that have no other purpose than prolonging our miserable existence; when I see, moreover, how any comfort we may derive from certain points of inquiry is merely a dream-like kind of resignation, in which we paint our prison walls

[4] As quoted by W.H. Auden in his Foreword to Goethe, *Werther*, p. vii.

> with gaily colored figures and luminous prospects – all this, Wilhelm, leaves me speechless. I withdraw into my inner self and there discover a world – a world, it is true, rather of vague perceptions and dim desires than of creative power and vital force. And then everything swims before my senses, and I go on smiling at the outer world like someone in a dream.[5]

This Romantic notion of a self-contained world, a world contained by the self, however unsatisfactorily, had already been prefigured by Rousseau, though its best expression comes two years after *Werther* was written, when in 1776 Rousseau began his last work, his ten walks described in *The Reveries of the Solitary Walker*. How can we not see this following passage from the climactic Fifth Walk of those *Reveries* as a homology of the lines just quoted from Werther?:

> Upon emerging from a long and sweet reverie, upon seeing myself surrounded by greenery, flowers, and birds, and letting my eyes wander in the distance on the romantic shores which bordered a vast stretch of crystal-clear water, I assimilated all these lovely objects to my fictions; and finally finding myself brought back by degrees to myself and to what surrounded me, I could not mark out the point separating the fictions from the realities; it was this thorough conjunction of everything which made the absorbed and solitary life I led during this beautiful sojourn so dear to me. If it could only occur again! ... I know men will be careful not to give me back such a sweet refuge when they did not want to leave me there. But at least they will not prevent me from transporting myself there each day on the wings of my imagination and from enjoying for a few hours the same pleasure as if I were still living there. The sweetest thing I would do would be to dream there at my ease. In dreaming that I am there, do I not do the same thing? I do even more: to the allure of an abstract and monotonous reverie, I join charming images which make it more intense. In my ecstasies, their objects often eluded my senses. Now the deeper my reverie is, the more intensely it depicts them to me. I am often more in the midst of them and even more pleasantly so than when I was really there.[6]

Where Werther's inner world is a haunting prison of 'vague perceptions' and 'dim desires', Rousseau's inner world, his reverie, more real in some sense than the original it is trying to conjure, is a transportation of pleasure. Nevertheless, the impulse of both, though leading in opposite directions, one to melancholy, one to ecstasy, is the same. The inner self and its imaginative powers produce a world distinct from that which is outside it, a self-created world where the boundary between subjective and objective, imagination and reality, blurs. The outer world becomes a dream, and the inner world, whether blissful or dark, a self-contained reality. Self-contained, because the world and self have become one. Life and work fuse utterly: for Rousseau it is only through the writing of the reverie, the reproduction of the ecstatic moment in imagination, that he can remake himself, can convert himself into a human being happy again with his existence. This 'sentiment of existence' is a moment of pure autonomy, autonomy from the outer encroachments and dictates of the world, yes, but autonomy also from the strict

---

5 Goethe, *Werther*, pp. 11–12. Goethe, *SW, Vol. 2.2*, pp. 355–356.

6 Jean-Jacques Rousseau, *The Reveries of the Solitary Walker*, trans. Charles E. Butterworth (Indianapolis: Hackett, 1992), pp. 70–71.

division of what one experiences and what one produces from that experience: 'What do we enjoy in such a situation? Nothing external to ourselves, nothing if not ourselves and our own existence. As long as this state lasts, we are sufficient unto ourselves, like God.'[7]

The literary theorist Hans Robert Jauss, in comparing Rousseau's *Nouvelle Héloïse* with Goethe's *Werther*, writes:

> The formal innovation introduced by Goethe's *Werther* (the one-sidedness produced by moving from the dialogic principle underlying the epistolary novel to a monologue in the form of letters) 'to which we can no longer imagine fitting responses', ... and the abandonment of moral commentary led to more than the postulate that the work and the reader were aesthetically autonomous. The change in horizon introduced by these events also produced a new understanding and legitimation of the individual: through the return of the self, the *homme sensible* is supposed to rediscover the lost wholeness of the *homme naturel*, and reestablish in his inner world the original form of that outer world on which he has turned his back.[8]

A *self-legitimation*, 'sufficient unto ourselves'. If Rousseau must confess this solitary moment – which in the Fifth Walk takes place on an isolated island, let us not forget – and confess it through the written letter, as if issuing a written confession for the apostate nature of this pure autonomy ('like God'!), how much more must Goethe's Werther confess, whose autonomy leads to the apostasy of self-inflicted death.

So Jauss can read this story as a profane transformation of the Christian Gospel: 'Goethe's *Werther*, with its reprise of the parable of the prodigal son, and its worldly contrafact to the Gospel of John, had to strike one as a provocative secularization of the story of Christ's Passion.'[9] Self-deliverance through self-annihilation, an inverted kenosis through *Weltschmerz*. And the 'worldly contrafact to the Gospel of John'? Jauss refers here to Christ's farewell discourse and prayer in John 14–17. But we might also see Werther's total self-absorption in light of the next two chapters in John, Jesus before Pilate, Werther not only as an accuser, but also as the accused and as arbiter of his fate – all three merged into one. As Jesus may have stood before Pilate as the answer to his rhetorical question (but as a tacit, 'rhetorical' answer), so Werther stands before himself in pure autonomy, accused of and by his own law, to be self-sacrificed:

> And what does it mean that Albert is your husband? Husband! That may be for this world – and in this world it is sin that I love you, that I should like to snatch you from his arms into mine. Sin? Very well, and I am punishing myself for it; for this sin, which I have tasted in all its rapture, which gave me life-giving balm and strength. From now on you are mine! mine Lotte! I go before you. I go to my Father, to your Father. I shall put my sorrow before Him, and He will comfort me until you come; and I shall fly to meet you and clasp you and stay with you before the Infinite Being in an eternal embrace.

---

[7] *Ibid.*, p. 69.

[8] Hans Robert Jauss, *Question and Answer: Forms of Dialogic Understanding*, trans. Michael Hays (Minneapolis: University of Minnesota Press, 1989), pp. 185–186.

[9] *Ibid.*, p. 191.

> I do not dream; I am not deluded! So near the grave, I see everything with great clearness.[10]

A great self-deluded clarity, in which the truth of the self is unable to shine forth. For Werther's inner world is so completely self-absorbed it obfuscates its own demise – '*Not* be! [*Vergehen!*] What does this mean? It is only a word, a mere sound, and stirs nothing in me.'[11] And thus this inner world is divided against itself, as it plunges itself into the nothingness of the grave, with no redemption, not even self-redemption.

Must not Goethe the author also confess to this self-division? Goethe makes clear that Werther does not find redemption, makes clear that the grave is the grave, that the apparent calmness of the soul which Werther in his last remarks confesses and attributes to God, 'who gives these last moments such warmth, such strength!',[12] is a blind confession and an empty attribution. Thus Goethe says in the very last line of the novel, as Werther's coffin is being carried away: 'No clergymen attended.' The bell of secularity fades into a pervading silence. But there is more than a thoroughly desacralized Passion here. As the mockery of self-truth, Werther, Goethe's *doppelgänger*, also mocks the truth of Goethe's own self. In his act of suicide, Werther rends that fabric which unites the life of Goethe with the work of Goethe. Werther cannot stand before Goethe as the truth, even the truth of a confession. For what is confessed in *Werther* is clearly not a truth. As others ask, 'But did Werther really live? Did it all really happen like that?', Goethe, if he were to be truthful, would have to confess: 'Of course not, and I am living proof.'

What Goethe actually says in *Dichtung und Wahrheit* about such proof is very little. Surprisingly little, for one who admits to a confession.

Goethe brings us to his time with Lotte in Wetzlar through a brief commentary on the classical rhetoricians. This transition is worth considering. A good rhetorician, Aristotle informs us, must first know the audience, for it is they the rhetoric must persuade. In order to know an audience, one must have lived with them, not simply studied them or read about them. So Goethe says of 'the most celebrated orators, that these men had educated [*gebildet*] themselves in the very midst of life. One could never speak about their characteristic qualities as artists without simultaneously mentioning their personal characteristics.' Is this why Goethe writes his autobiography, so that his own artistic peculiarities can be better understood in light of his personal characteristics? He goes on: 'This seemed to be less the case with poets, but everywhere nature and art came in contact only through life, and so the sum of all my thinking and contemplation remained my old resolution to study the inner and outer nature, and just to let it lead the way [*walten zu lassen*] as I lovingly imitated it.'[13] This is a remarkable admission, for here Goethe deliberately pursues the artistic power of the rhetorician and orator. This pursuit takes a peculiar form, for if Nature and Art only come in contact through

---

10 Goethe, *Werther*, p. 157. Goethe, *SW, Vol. 2.2*, p. 458.

11 Goethe, *Werther*, p. 156. Goethe, *SW, Vol. 2.2*, p. 457.

12 Goethe, *Werther*, pp. 163–164. Goethe, *SW, Vol. 2.2*, p. 463.

13 Goethe, *Poetry and Truth*, p. 399. Goethe, *SW, Vol. 16*, p. 574.

life, it is to life then, his *own* life, where Goethe will go. The fusion of the internal with the external Nature here justifies this decision, as he takes his two separate experiences – of Lotte (internal) and the suicide of his fellow-student (external) – and brings them into the same aesthetic space in a 'loving' imitation. What is this loving imitation that allows Nature to have everywhere its way, its sway (*walten zu lassen*)? How can imitation allow the imitated its freedom to sway? Freedom of Nature seems at fundamental odds with its aesthetic imitation. Any sway within Nature does not seem possible through imitation – unless it, Nature, is made rhetorical. That is, unless it somehow comes into direct contact with its audience, with life. But what does it mean to come into contact with life other than to understand and experience both internal and external Nature as they come together in any one individual? If Nature is to lead the way and have its sway, it must then be self-reflexive, it must *imitate itself*, persuade itself, make its audience itself. It must become Art. Goethe's own striving here is for a rhetorical self-reflection, in which he becomes his own audience, known and persuaded, a loving imitation of himself by which this self – Werther – can have its own sway. Its autonomy.

In his very next lines Goethe, under the current of his own rhetoric, takes us to this Werther: 'These influences, which gave me no rest by day or night, were supplemented by two large, indeed enormous topics of a richness I only had to appreciate to a certain extent in order to produce something of significance. These were the older era, when Götz von Berlichingen lived, and modern times, whose sad flowering is depicted in *Werther*.' What we might expect to follow here is a full disclosure of the 'Nature' behind the 'Art', the truth behind the poetry, the reality or 'ethical grounds', as Goethe calls them, of his obsession with Lotte. But what we get is something quite different. The next sentence follows: 'That resolution, to let my inner nature follow its own course and to let my outer nature influence me in its own capacity brought me to the strange circumstances under which *Werther* was conceived and written.' This fine piece of rhetoric, which, however persuasively articulated, says very little, and offers very little in the way of confession, serves as a prelude to Goethe's version of Romantic harmony between on the one hand Nature, a vital living organism with unbounded influence, and on the other Spirit, or the individual soul:

> I was trying to free myself inwardly of everything alien, to observe external things lovingly, and to let all beings, from the human down to those barely perceptible, have their effect on me, each in its own way. Thus there arose a marvelous feeling of kinship with individual objects in nature, and a heartfelt accord or harmony with the whole, so that every alteration affected me deeply, whether it was of places and regions, or of times of day and seasons, or whatever else might occur. The artist's gaze joined the poet's, while the beautiful rural landscape, brightened by its friendly river, inclined me even more to solitude and fostered my quiet but wide-ranging contemplations.
>
> But ever since I had left that family circle in Sesenheim, and then my circle of friends in Frankfurt and Darmstadt, there had been an emptiness [*Leere*] in my bosom that I could not fill. Consequently I found myself in a state where, in order to take us unawares and bring all good resolutions to naught, an affection only needs to approach in a light disguise.[14]

[14] Goethe, *Poetry and Truth*, p. 399. Goethe, *SW*, *Vol. 16*, p. 575.

Such a Romanticism, important in its own right, does not, however, carry us into the heart of the matter. Even its pseudo-confessional language by which it concludes, the 'disguise', the taking 'unawares', the 'resolutions' rendered vain, does not reveal anything other than a rhetorical striving intended to fill an emptiness even Nature in all her harmonizing between the inner and the outer could not avoid. To get to the truth of any confession here, we must understand that this striving, rhetoric's contact 'through life', its intimacy with its audience, must manifest itself, not through Nature, but through Art, or through the aestheticization of Nature, both inner and outer, subjective and objective – that is, through the constructs of the imagination and its reproductions – so that what is to follow can only be a rhetorical reproduction of Nature (Nature as either the self or the external world internalized within the self) in its most affected form. In this regard we would understand the character of Werther as the rhetoricization of the 'confessed' emptiness in the author's soul, and the character of Lotte as the rhetoricization of that which overcomes the emptiness, however incompletely and against all the author's better intentions.

Does the author himself make this connection? Does he turn his own rhetoric on itself, to expose it for what it is, and so let the disguise of the affections lose its opacity, that we might see through to the truth of the inner soul? The subsequent paragraph in Goethe's account shows clearly the way autobiography here confesses to the unconfessed:

> And since the writer has now arrived at this stage of his undertaking, this book will become what it is really supposed to be. It was not declared to be an independent entity, but was meant to fill the gaps in an author's life, to complete many fragments, and to preserve the memory of bold enterprises [*Wagnisse*] lost and forgotten. What is already done, however, cannot, and should not, be repeated. Also, it would now be in vain for the poet to try to summon up his dim mental powers [*verdüsterten Seelenkräfte*], useless for him to ask them to revive the sweet attachment that so greatly enriched his sojourn in the Lahn valley. Fortunately his guiding genius provided for that earlier by prompting him, in his capable youth, to capture and describe the recent past, and to be bold enough to set it before the public at a favorable moment. It probably needs no further explanation that I am referring here to the little book *Werther*. However, I shall by and by reveal a few things about the persons depicted in it, and about the sentiments portrayed.[15]

The autobiographical Goethe here confesses that, in becoming finally 'what it is really supposed to be', his autobiography will not and can not repeat the original event. It will, as in Bulgakov, simply 'fill the gaps'. It will preserve the memories, especially of the '*Wagnisse*', the risks. But it will *not* re-present those risks. That, he says, has already been done, thanks to the 'guiding genius' which prompted the initial writing of *Werther*. The original event then can only ever be seen through the lens of the artifice, the rhetoric of the reproduction, the genius of Art. The autobiography can only ever hint; and it must make its hints by an unshakable and inevitable dependency on Art. As for the original, it is forever lost in the '*verdüsterten Seelenkräfte*', literally, in the darkened powers of the soul.

[15] Goethe, *Poetry and Truth*, pp. 399-400. Goethe, *SW*, *Vol. 16*, pp. 575–576.

Yet amidst this pseudo-confession, this masked revelation – a veiled attempt at discretion to cover an original outpouring of indiscretion – Goethe still holds out promise to 'reveal a few things'. And for the next two paragraphs he endeavors to give us a scant background to his time with Lotte and her '*Bräutigam*' ('bridegroom'). But his portraiture reveals nothing of consequence. And to put even more padding between his autobiographical self and the original event about which everyone knows and everyone wonders, the author describes his own entry into the lives of his two betrothed friends in the third person:

> The new arrival, quite free from any ties, felt unconcerned in the presence of a girl who, since she was already spoken for, would not interpret his most agreeable services as wooing, and thus could take the more delight in them. He calmly let matters proceed, but was soon so entangled and enchained, yet also treated so trustingly and amicably by the young couple, that he no longer recognized himself [*er sich selbst nicht mehr kannte*].[16]

Only later, in the 'objectivity' of autobiographical distance, can Goethe now say he no longer recognized or knew himself. And here rhetoric does not bring us any closer to Goethe's life, as Goethe had hoped; rather, it masks, veils, erases the identity of the truth of himself. So amidst all the costume and disguise of the '*deutsches Idylle*' ('German idyll') called *Werther*, this 'Ur-text of German sentimentality', as Jauss calls it,[17] where can Goethe leave us autobiographically but back with Art, with the imaginative space that fills the gap between the original and the present, even as he concludes his two meager paragraphs on *Werther* with a quote from Rousseau: 'I will be understood by anyone who remembers what was predicted for the happy-unhappy lover of the new Héloïse: "And, sitting at the feet of his beloved, he will card hemp, and he will wish to continue carding hemp, today, tomorrow, and next day, indeed for his whole life." '[18] All Goethe can reveal, as once himself the 'happy-unhappy' paramour, is a reappropriation of an already inhabited imaginative world – his own as much as any other.

In the end Poetry and Truth cannot be differentiated. This conclusion may seem nothing more than a classical truism accepted long ago, except for the fact that the *Wahrheit* of Goethe can by no means refer only to some abstract universal Truth which permeates the spirit of all great art, and binds together every civilized culture with the celebratory greatness of a homogeneous, if infinitely permutable, human nature. The *Wahrheit* must be *his* truth, Goethe's individual self as it unfolds under veil, *sotte voce*, aestheticized in the poetry of his imagination and in the rhetoric of his autobiographical utterance. The *Wahrheit* must be his work. His *Dichtung*.

This the later Goethe saw. In the last lines of the first poem of 'Trilogie der Leidenschaft' ('Trilogy of Passion', 1823–4), subtitled '*An Werther*' ('To Werther'), he writes:

---

[16] Goethe, *Poetry and Truth*, p. 400. Goethe, *SW, Vol. 16*, p. 577.

[17] Jauss, *Question and Answer*, p. 169.

[18] Goethe, *Poetry and Truth*, pp. 401–402, quoting from Rousseau, *La nouvelle Héloïse* (1761). Goethe, *SW, Vol. 16*, 578. See also Jauss, *Question and Answer*, pp. 175–176.

Wie klingt es rührend wenn der Dichter singt,
Den Tod zu meiden den das Scheiden bringt!
Verstrickt in solche Qualen halbverschuldert,
Geb' ihm ein Gott zu sagen was er duldet.[19]

[How stirring the sound when the poet sings,
To avoid the death which parting brings.
Ensnared in such agonies, half-guilty,
Give him a god to speak what he suffers.]

A decade after the *Dichtung und Wahrheit* of 1811–14, the two sides of Poetry and Truth merge in Goethe's admission that the poet is '*halbverschuldert*', 'half-guilty'. He, Goethe, shares in the guilt of Werther, as the *ihm* here holds a double force: it ostensibly refers to *der Dichter*, the poet, including Goethe himself, but it also can, and even should, include Werther as well, whose sufferings need the aid of a god to be voiced. A shared suffering – creation, creator, god. A triune of passion. The poet both god-like and half-guilty. A quasi-confession.

'Only one single word, Frau Councillor,' he begged; 'one single question, quickly answered; Frau Councillor must perceive, when one stands, all unexpected, before the original, when it is vouchsafed one to inquire at the very source, one cannot refrain ...

We have seen this before: someone standing before the original with one single question, unexpectedly, inquiring at the very source, unable to refrain.

Frau Councillor, that very last scene before Werther takes his leave; that heart-rendering scene between the three of you, where you speak of the dear, departed mother and the final parting and Werther grasps Lotte's hand and cries: 'We shall meet again, in all the world we shall know each other's forms again!' – that was real, was it not, it actually happened, the Herr Privy Councillor did not make it up?
'Yes and no, my friend, yes and no,' she good-naturedly answered ....

Yes and no. A quasi-confession. Truth hidden between affirmation and denial.

We have said that, aesthetically, Werther has enjoyed a long period of influence upon subsequent imaginations. Thomas Mann, over a century and a half later, brings 'Werther' alive again in his novel *Lotte in Weimar* (1939), though now, with a remarkable aesthetic reversal, in the figure of Goethe himself. Mann asks the question we have been asking all along: what might be the truth of any *bios* that spawns a work of art, in this case *Werther*? But here Mann approaches the question from the perspective of Lotte – not the Lotte of the novel *Werther*, but Charlotte Kestner, with whom the real Goethe had had his dalliance, and about whom he

[19] Goethe, *SW, Vol. 13.1. Die Jahret, 1820–1826*, eds. Gisela Henckmann and Irmela Schneider (Munich: Carl Hanser, 1992), p. 135.

writes briefly in *Dichtung und Wahrheit*. Extant letters reveal that this Lotte visited Goethe late in his years while he was living in Weimar, after her own husband had passed on and her eleven children had reached adulthood. What, Mann wonders, might have transpired in this meeting between the two old 'lovers'? What might have been? – a question Lotte herself is continually plagued with throughout the story. Mann constructs for us a picture of Lotte's arrival in Weimar, the adopted town of the great celebrity, where she too becomes a celebrity in the eyes of its inquisitive citizens.[20] Mann's picture culminates in a furtive encounter between Goethe and Lotte in the closing pages of the book, where the old Goethe, now reinstated as the young 'Werther', that is, as the rhetorical confession to a youthful emptiness, confronts his old passion, the rhetorical idealization which filled that emptiness. What Mann does in this imaginative re-creation is trade on the very conflation of *bios* and *techne* which Goethe had initiated, and in effect re-aestheticize Werther back into the Goethe who first created him. This reversal is significant not from any purely biographical or autobiographical point of view, which serves to further or complete the picture of a famous man's life, but because it exposes the embeddedness in Art by which that life must now be made manifest. *Lotte in Weimar* is fascinating because, more than anything else, it plays Goethe at his own game, and rather than posit a truth or a plausibility about two well-known figures and their lesser-known encounter, it renders memory as a self-legitimation of its own aesthetic reproduction.

Memory is, as we have seen with Rousseau, never far from imagination, and hence modernism's great obsession with memory becomes not simply a recovery of things past, but a re-creation that stands as its own reality. We recall that Rousseau, in later re-imaging his moments of pleasure on his solitary island, claims he was more in possession of those moments, was more 'present', than when he was actually there on the island originally. And in his memory's re-imaging, he becomes more in possession of himself, becomes 'himself' for perhaps the first time as a totally self-conscious and autonomous being. But this re-imaging is not a purely mental act, a recollection that remains noetically abstracted, but is *written down*, is made concrete by its commitment to script. This compulsion to autobiography, this sentiment of existence turned from a pure private interiority to a public exteriority in the manifested form of a journal, a written confession, makes of Rousseau's memory an aesthetic faculty, even an aesthetic creation, in whose imaginative space fictions and realities become indistinguishable. So too in Goethe's *Werther*, the author and the protagonist become so intertwined in the rhetorical inflation of the author's creative memory, that the public is left thereafter to ask, 'Did it really happen that way?' Again, such a question does not betray the public's general ignorance of the workings of the creative mind, which we have said has always drawn on personal experience. Rather, it is a response to the self-proclamation of the work of art itself, whose self-involvement – 'I withdraw into my inner self and there discover a world ...' – can no longer offer, in its aestheticization of memory, the sharp distinction between poetry and truth. The

[20] Thomas Mann, *Lotte in Weimar*, trans. H.T. Lowe-Porter (London: Minerva, 1997). The above quotations are from p. 11.

public has every right to ask, 'Did it really happen that way?', and to pose the question as much to Goethe's 'fiction' in *Werther* as to Rousseau's 'reality' in his *Reveries*.

In Mann's story Lotte does not escape this conflation of the fiction with the real. She too is caught up in Goethe's memory. And thus Mann crafts a narrative in which the memory of one person, Goethe, both real and fictional, is rememorialized in and through the memory of another, Charlotte Kestner, who is both real and fictional. Here memory itself becomes part of the conflation of poetry and truth – a poetic truth, and a truthful poetry. Through the character of Goethe's son August in conversation with Lotte, Mann writes:

> But the happiest means to resolve and to banish all one's own personal problems is of course the gift of poesy. In that confessional lies power to spiritualize our memories, to convert them into terms of universal humanity and make them issue enduring works of art.

This highly Rousseauean sentiment is a memorial to Goethe himself, spoken by the obeisant son, the offspring of genius. But Mann creates through this offspring of Goethe his own offspring as a work of art, his own novel about Goethe, which itself memorializes genius. And thus, with a kind of self-referentiality whereby form and content completely merge, memory holding memory, memory begetting memory, in an unabashed aesthetic procreation, the offspring continues his thought:

> 'Memory,' he went on, 'is certainly a strange thing. I have often thought about it; my life with a man like my father gives rise to many varied reflections, some of them quite natural and proper, some not so much so. Memory must play an important part in the poet's life and work, the two being so interwoven that one may properly call them one, and speak of the poet's work as his life, his life as his work.'[21]

Memory as *poesis* here unites *bios* and *techne*, so that poetry and truth merge into one. Mann, in writing about memory, in memorializing Lotte and Goethe as he does, is able to raise the form of the novel to a place where poetry and truth become identical. We read *Lotte in Weimar*, as eighteenth-century Europeans once read *Werther*, and we are compelled to ask, 'Did it really happen that way?' We do not ask this because we believe that the words of Mann mirror some spatio-temporal actuality of an event in the past, however vaguely or accurately, but because Mann asks us to rethink our notion of memory, to shift its definition from one of recollection to one of imagination. In this rethinking lies a 'spiritualizing' that begets a work of art. And in this begetting, the 'really' of 'Did it really happen that way?' is transmuted in the same way as the 'in fact' was transmuted earlier in Kant. For we now know that the answer to our question 'Did it really happen that way?' cannot come in a definitive form of a strict affirmation or a strict denial, but that in the 'really' must reside both a 'yes' and a 'no'. ''Yes and no, my friend, yes and no'', Lotte had replied. And so too in both Mann's and Goethe's memorializations, the 'yes' and the 'no' are drawn together into the same imaginative space, and forever alter our ability to attribute an exact and fixed domain to either assertion.

---

[21] *Ibid.*, p. 175.

We may still maintain that *Werther* and *Lotte in Weimar* are 'fictions', and most of us will, but when we say this we no longer understand 'fiction' in any classical sense, as a pure creation separate from anything we call 'fact'. If 'fact' now is part of our memory, or in Kantian terms, is part of our judgment, or part of our imagination, then fiction also becomes part of 'fact', part of the real in 'really'. Along with Goethe's son, we say life has become work just as work has become life. And so the son extends his thought yet one stage further:

> It is not alone that the poetry is conditioned by the memories of the past; not alone that in Faust . . . the memories recur as an *idée fixe*. No, as I see it, memory becomes an *idée fixe* for life as well.[22]

In the final confrontation between Goethe and Lotte, a passage of great literary craftsmanship, Mann's own *idée fixe* with what might have happened is offered in the same aesthetic register as that of Jesus and Pilate in Bulgakov's *The Master and Margarita*. In the darkness of a coach, Goethe's past passions, to this point only a repressed undercurrent of the novel, now resurface in a frank conversation guided by all the careful maturity and social experience that Goethe and Lotte have acquired since they were young. In the candidness of old age, we again might expect a full disclosure from Goethe, a deep confession. And indeed the entire story, throughout which the 'yes and no' of Lotte's initial reply has resonated imploringly, has forced upon us a desire for resolution one way or another. Mann offers us a kind of confession, but a resolution remains ambiguous. Goethe says to his old friend and 'love':

> Dear soul, let me answer you from my heart, in expiation and farewell. You speak of sacrifice. But it is a mystery, indivisible, like all else in the world and one's person, one's life, one's work. Conversion, transformation, is all.'[23]

Goethe's answer from the heart here, this quasi-confession, then proceeds into a rhapsody on artistic sacrifice, on spiritual transformation, on the unity of nature and culture, and of time, and ultimately on the Werther-like visions of harmony in death and of the 'All-in-One' that overcomes all separation, where the ripeness of *Lear*'s Edgar gives way to conversion. It is a splendid piece of rhetoric, better read in context than quoted, a sublime elegy on an immortalized passion, in which the life and work of Goethe fuse wonderfully: 'Then once more the hour of Werther and Tasso will strike, as at midnight already midday strikes, and God give me to say what I suffer . . .'. But what in all this does Goethe confess *to?* To *what* exactly is he converted? Goethe will only say:

> Wouldst thou ask of me repentance? Only wait. I see her riding towards me, in a mantle grey.[24]

---

22 *Ibid.*
23 *Ibid.*, p. 320.
24 *Ibid.*, p. 321.

Amid all the color of his rhetoric, a grey mantle still conceals the specific meaning of Goethe's confession. The 'yes and no' continue to resonate without resolution, keeping repentance at bay, and blurring the definition in Goethe's life between poetry and truth, as Goethe's last lines to Charlotte Kestner echo Werther's last sentiments to his beloved Lotte: 'In my heart, dear visions, may you rest – and what a pleasant moment that will be, when we anon wake together!'[25]

If confession is an act of conversion, as it is for Augustine, then Goethe, both the Goethe of *Dichtung und Wahrheit* and the Goethe here of *Lotte in Weimar*, undergoes a partial conversion, but a conversion not, as we can see, to some doctrinaire faith. He converts himself rather to a spiritualized memory, a memory that is both content and form, both 'the sacrifice and he that offers it', as he himself describes. It is a memory of godlikeness, of a creator who creates as he memorializes, creates and memorializes himself. And thus, he also converts himself towards an understanding of truth that is bound inextricably with the imaginative space his own genius must configure. Goethe is recorded as saying late in his life: 'If God had intended people to live and act in truth, then he would have had to arrange things differently.'[26] Goethe throughout his prodigious career had taken it upon himself to assist in the rearrangement of truth in his own life, not necessarily as some usurpation of the divine office, but as part of humanity's most noble task:

> Der edle Mensch
> Sei hilfreich und gut!
> Unermüdet schaff' er
> Das Nutzliche, Rechte,
> Sei uns en Vorbild
> Jener geahneten Wesen!
>
> [Let the noble Man
> Be helpful and good!
> Untiring let him do
> The useful, the right,
> And be for us a model
> Of those sensed immortal beings!]
> ('*Das Göttliche*' ['The Divine'], 1783)[27]

But this noble task entails both risks and dangers, not least of which is the concern that the conflation of poetry and truth can bring one to the edges or borders of what is known and understood, and in rearranging those borders, can take us beyond the simple divisions of 'yes' and 'no', of 'fiction' and 'real', and beyond even what is normally conceived of as the good, the useful and the right. Hence

---

[25] *Ibid.*

[26] Johan Wolfgang von Goethe, *Maxims and Reflections*, trans. Elisabeth Stopp (London: Penguin, 1998), p. 112.

[27] Johan Wolfgang von Goethe, *Selected Poems*, trans. John Whaley (London: J.M. Dent, 1998), pp. 46–47. Goethe, *SW, Vol. 2.1. Erstes Weimare Jahrzehnt, 1775–1786*, ed. Hartmut Reinhardt (Munich: Carl Hanser, 1987), p. 91.

Werther, the passionate, unrequited lover who shoots himself dead, and leaves a legacy of torment for those who live beyond his deed (Goethe especially), and of ambiguity about what, in the end, is noble and divine. The risk is that the model [*Vorbild*] may not prefigure either, on the one hand, the sense or truth of oneself, or, on the other, the sense, the prefigured [*geahneten*] notions, of those exalted beings associated with the divine. The model may lead towards apostasy – Werther, the unredeemed.

Or worse, it may lead towards a zone of darkness.

> It follows that it is wrong to conceive of God and the Devil as opposed principles; more correctly, the diabolic is only one side – the wrong side, if you like – of the divine. If God is All, then He is also the Devil; and one cannot approach to the godlike without at the same time approaching to the diabolic – so that, in a manner of speaking, heaven looks at you out of one eye, and the hell of the iciest negation and most destructive neutrality out of the other. But whether they lie close together or far apart, it is two eyes, my dear lady, that make up one gaze. So now I ask you: what sort of gaze is that wherein the horrifying contradiction of the eyes is united? I will tell you, tell you and myself: it is the gaze of absolute art, which is at once absolute love and absolute nihilism and indifference, and implies that horrifying approach to the godlike-diabolic which we call genius.[28]

If we have had our one eye on the passions of Werther, our other eye must inevitably cast its gaze upon the passions of Goethe's Faust. Let us not forget that the figure of Faust was a real historical character, Dr. Johan Faust, or Faustus, and that the original source for Marlowe, for Goethe, and for Mann (and countless lesser writers) was a written 'biography' of this man's life, the *Historia von D. Iohan Fausten* (1587), or its English translation, *The Historie of the damnable life, and deserved death of Doctor Iahn Faustus, ... 1592.* According to these biographical accounts, admonitory more than documentary (for biography had at that point still only moral purpose, following on from Augustine), the actual Dr. Faustus, born in the old province of Weimar, and dying around the late 1530s, had obtained his doctorate in Divinity. The notorious Faustian pact, in which the Christian theologian sells his soul to the Devil, becomes all the more sinister for the religious authority Faust represents. Nor should we forget that in all the Doctor's insatiable inquisitiveness into the nature of the world and beyond, which leads him to discard theology and turn to the realms of the diabolical, the threefold request to Mephostophiles ends with the demand that, in all Faust's interrogations, the spirit 'should tell him nothing but that which is true.'[29] Significantly, the pact which is

[28] Mann, *Lotte in Weimar*, p. 57.

[29] From *The History of the Damnable Life and Deserved Death of Doctor John Faustus*, in 'The Source of Doctor Faustus', *Christopher Marlowe, Doctor Faustus*, ed. Sylvan Barnet (New York: Signet, 1969, 2001), p. 97.

later agreed upon and signed in blood does not include this provision – dropped out, so to speak, at the time of commitment in blood to script. This pivotal moment of contract, in which the signature is made out of the life-blood of the one who signs, should not be lost on us, given all we have said so far. For here, in the irrevocable signing over of oneself, we have the great fusion of life and work once again, though this time, in the early retellings of the story, the self is damnably lost, not gained, and the quest for truth forgotten. It is also significant that when Marlowe's Faustus moves to write his deed, his blood congeals, and he cannot complete the writing of the contract, until Mephostophiles brings fire to melt his blood and let it flow freely again from the body to the page.

> Faustus: What might the staying of my blood portend?
> Is it unwilling I should write this bill?
> Why streams it not that I may write afresh:
> 'Faustus gives to thee his soul?' O there it stayed.
> Why shouldst thou not? Is not thy soul thine own?
> Then write again: 'Faustus gives to thee his soul.'[30]

The image of demonic fire heating and inciting the blood of the reprobate is one that rings familiar enough, but we should observe that the image, in the context of all that we have been suggesting above, may also serve as an allegory for the life, the *bios*, which inevitably congeals outside of its historical particularity in time if not heated again by the flames of some kind of reproduction, of some kind of biography. The melting of this blood becomes, we could say, an allegory of the written self. But does such an allegory turn the Devil into the main afflatus behind the artistic endeavor? Is the Devil always complicit with the artist, and especially the artistic genius? Why then did the Devil not incite the real Faust to write his own story, his autobiography?

We might say the self-reproduction of autobiographical confession was not available to the historical Faustus of the Renaissance. Confession is not possible when the rights to conversion has been sold away. Faust, theologically, had no self to write about in confession, having sold it to God's chief adversary. Even the fictional Faustus was unable, despite many efforts, to bring himself to repent, even though he leaves this earth in regret, cursing himself and Lucifer. But this inability to convert himself, and convert himself to script, does not prevent a long and rich Faustian heritage from emerging out of the ashes of his death, does not, that is, prevent a biographical Faustus from taking shape, even one poetically charged and animated in a character on the stage. The Devil may not have permitted Faust to write his confessions, since the Augustinian kind of self-reproduction is antithetical to the Devil's cause (though Rousseau would certainly reformulate the genre in his confessions centuries later). But the Devil would gladly suffer a theatrical Faustus, since on the stage the self is always, in some sense, concealed.

The theatrical stage, in its earliest incarnation, was concerned with masks, concealments through which, paradoxically, great revelations appear. This strange marriage of duplicity and truth, of concealment and disclosure, has been one of

---

[30] *Ibid.*, 2, i, lns 65–70 (p. 20).

the most enduring features of theater, above all the other arts, for unlike literature, the plastic arts, and to a large extent music, the living actors of the stage, and the unpredictable nature of their performance, connect us, through their play-acting, with *bios* most directly, most immediately, and, in terms of its passions and responses, most 'realistically'. Theater has always been about blood and pen coming together. The masks of the early stage were a constant reminder of the artificiality of the script, but an artificiality brought to life through the flowing blood of the performance, as it flows through, and in some sense past, the costume and the script. It is in this flowing of human blood that we find revelation and truth. Thus the conflictual nature, the tension between artifice and flesh-and-blood, which makes tragedy in particular (where blood so often flows out) so powerful.

This inherent conflict between artifice and life also makes the stage especially ripe for the Faustian story. That the character of Faust was grounded upon an actual historical person certainly provided a moral gravity to the theater-going audience of Marlowe's day, more so even than the legendary Don Juan, or the *dramma giocoso* of Mozart's *Don Giovanni* centuries later. But like Don Juan, the Faustian character also wore masks: the Divinity student turned magician and necromancer, who fools even his students and colleagues. And in this willingness to adopt that one mask considered unthinkable in his day, the mask of perdition freely chosen and signed for with one's own blood, there emerges a Promethean-like spirit who takes matters into his own hands, defying the gods, asserting self and soul in the face of cosmic forces. More than anything, this defiance, this self-bloodletting, is what makes the stage the perfect point of entry for the Faustian character to emerge into popular awareness. The risks, the uncertainties, the self-experiment of putting on a new and unknown mask, of parading a new and unknown persona, however diabolical, is what Faust through his defiance, tragically and heroically, enacts for us. And this undaunted spirit is what certainly must have attracted the young Marlowe of the sixteenth century, whose own renegade reputation and dramatically abbreviated life would seem an uncanny echo of this Promethean archetype.

This defiance is also what attracted Goethe, though now in an age of such intellectual, philosophical and spiritual reorientation that this defiance could manifest itself as something more than deviance from a given morality: that is, as the assertion of an unprecedented autonomous self. The conflicts and tension involved in this self-assertion attracted and fascinated Goethe for the majority of his artistic life. For in Faust he discovered a figure whose self-struggle for autonomy arises from a pact in which ultimately that autonomy is to be given away. Herein lies the stuff of tragedy. Bloodletting that both cures and kills, like Socrates' *pharmakon*, though exuded, not ingested. (The ingested is philosophy; the exuded theater.)

Goethe knew this. Which is why he begins his play *Faust* with a Prelude in the Theater. There, playwright, director and clown converse as representatives of the artistic process: creator, enabler and common audience, respectively. The blood and the pen seek unity at the outset. Before the curtain rises, the director desires to please the crowd; the clown, for his part, wants to see the whole business come off as a love affair; while the poet and playwright yearns for peace and quiet, for retreat from the noise of the unruly world:

Verhülle mir das wogende Gedränge,
Das wider Willen uns zum Strudel zieht!
Nein, führe mich zur stillen Himmelsenge,
Wo nur dem Dichter reine Freude blüht ...[31]

[Veil me from the surging crowd,
That against our will draws us to the whirl!
No, lead me to the quiet confines of heaven,
Where only for the poet pure joy blooms ...]

But even the poet must admit the theatrical paradox of life and illusion, of the everyday crowd and masks, or masking (*Verhüllung*), for he himself seeks to be veiled or masked in order to carry on his task. And so he longs to return to '*Der Drang nach Wahrheit und die Lust am Trug*'[32] – the yearning for truth and the pleasure in illusion, that combination which has characterized all great art, though brought most palpably to us by the stage. Thus, even before the prologue in heaven, where the stage opens upon the celestial sphere, and the deities begin by making their own bargain in the unmistakable manner of Job's prologue, Goethe gives us a *meta*-scene, a proscenium of the proscenium, a *skene* before the *skene*, accomplishing precisely what he did in *Werther*, inserting himself into the action of the drama, as the creator and playwright conveniently, if thinly, veiled.

What can we say then about the Faust that follows this Prelude, who, unlike Goethe's Tasso, is in no sense a Werther, about whose infamy so much has been written, so much imitated, so much lauded, so much debated, so much analyzed – this transfigured character who, despite his initial evocation of the godly Job, acts independently of any religious piety, doctrine, morality, or dogmatism, who takes on the Mephisto with shameless confidence and arrogance, who strives for striving, and who, in this version of the play, takes us to some of the greatest heights of German Romanticism, self-expression, culture and critique? How much of this Faust can we say is Goethe? Where in the tragedy does work and life, *Dichtung und Wahrheit*, fiction and reality come together?

Was ich besitze, seh ich wie im Weiten,
Und was verschwand, wird mir zu Wirklichkeiten.[33]

[What I possess, I see as at a distance,
And what has vanished, becomes for me realities.]

These words conclude the tragedy's opening Dedication, which precedes even the Prelude in the Theater. Before the curtain has been raised, we are set into that aesthetic space where the present fades, and the once-faded past now becomes present, more present and more real than when first experienced, as in Rousseau's *Reveries*. This is the modern world of Romantic art, or the Romantic world of

[31] Goethe, *Faust*, lns. 61–64, in *SW, Vol. 6.1. Weimarer Klassik, 1798–1806*, ed. Victor Lange (Munich: Carl Hanser, 1992), p. 536.

[32] Goethe, *Faust*, ln. 193. *SW*, *Vol. 6.1*, p. 540.

[33] Goethe, *Faust*, lns. 31–32. *SW*, *Vol. 6.1*, p. 536.

modern art, where the imagined and the real do not simply coexist, but conjoin. We are led into this world as part of the Dedication, but who leads us? To whom do these opening words better belong? To Goethe? Or to Faust?

In the play itself, Faust's relation to words, to *logoi,* provides us with the necessary limits for the question of poetry and truth in *Faust* overall. (For Goethe's *Faust* is all about the coupling of illusion with truth, the damnable with the heavenly, the created with the creator, the wretched with the pure. In the Prologue even Mephisto and God get along affably, as Mann's character had suggested.) Faust begins his opening speech by dismissing his studies and scholarly pursuits, all the logocentric disciplines of philosophy, jurisprudence, medicine and theology. He charges himself:

> Schau alle Wirkenskraft und Samen
> Und tu nicht mehr in Worten kramen.[34]
>
> [Behold all creativity and things seminal
> And rummage no more among words.]

But his subsequent foray into the dark secrets of the occult must be through books and signs, and he conjures up spirits only by invocation of their written symbols. In a later moment of contemplation and of yearning for some greater revelation, he turns back to the New Testament, and offers his famous rendering of John's Prologue, Ἐν ἀρχῇ ἦν ὁ λόγος, 'In the beginning was the Word' ('*Im Anfang war das Wort*'). In his dissatisfaction with the translation, he transforms the word 'Word' [*Wort*] first into 'Mind' [*Sinn*], then 'Force' [*Kraft*], and finally 'Deed' or 'Act' – '*Im Anfang war die Tat!*'.[35] In all that has been made of this Faustian exegesis, we here simply point out that, during this entire move from the inscribed *logos* to the vitality of the act, Faust sits poised with a pen, and in the end *writes out* his translation ('*Und schreibe getrost* [And write confidently]*: Im Anfang war die Tat!*'). He no more escapes the word here than in the end he escapes the Word, or the Word escapes him. Despite everything, despite even the assertion of the last lines of the entire drama ('*Das Unbeschreibliche/Hier ist's getan* [The indescribable/Here was enacted]'[36]), his immortal body rises heavenward. And it rises on the wings of a chorus of words, his action having been played out in words, his body now being borne by words, even if words about the 'indescribable'. 'The play's the thing ...', whose fusion of word and action contains all characters, whether Faust or the Word. Faust's converting of the Word to the Act is simply the theatrical process, where the 'word', human or divine, is played out on the stage. This process is already set in motion for us at the beginning of *Faust*, where the Prologue in Heaven follows upon the Prelude in the Theater. 'In the beginning was the Word' is already part of the stage.

---

[34] Goethe, *Faust*, lns. 384–385. *SW, Vol. 6.1*, p. 545.

[35] Goethe, *Faust*, ln. 1237. *SW, Vol. 6.1*, p. 568.

[36] Goethe, *Faust*, lns. 12108–12109. *SW, Vol. 18.1. Letzte Jahre, 1827–1832*, eds. Gisela Henckmann, and Dorothea Hölscher-Lohmeyer (Munich: Carl Hanser, 1987), p. 351.

In Faust's study when the bargain is struck with Mephisto, as the details of the contract are finalized, the Spirit asks, 'for the sake of life or death', that the agreement be set in writing. Faust bristles at this request, and disparages writing in favor of the spoken word, especially in matters eternal:

> Allein ein Pergament, beschreiben und beprägt,
> Ist ein Gespenst, vor dem sich alle scheuen.
> Das Wort erstirbt schon in der Feder
> Die Herrschaft führen Wachs und Leder.[37]
>
> [And yet a parchment, written on and sealed,
> Is but a phantom, from which all shrink back.
> The word dies already in the quill,
> While wax and leather take over rule.]

True to his earlier translation of 'Word' to 'Act', Faust here gives no credence to inscription. He considers words dead as soon as the pen begins to write, and thus utterly meaningless before the ink can dry. Faust will sign anything, with any person, concerning any matter, in any medium, because ultimately it all means nothing. His signature will be merely '*der Fratze*', he says ('*So mag es bei der Fratze bleiben*'), a caricature of the real, like a mask, a drawn face. But in the very next line Mephisto asks for this *Fratze* to be drawn in blood, '*ein ganz besondrer Saft*' ['a very special juice'].[38] Mephisto sees the humor here, the blood that seeps through the mask, the necessary commingling of life and artifice. And as much as Faust dismisses writing as empty artificiality, *der Fratze*, and seeks a self-attainment through pure striving and excess of human spirit – '*Und was der ganzen Menscheit zugeteilt ist/Will ich in meinem innern Selbst genießen*' ['And what all humankind is apportioned with/I shall enjoy in my inner self'][39] – Mephisto knows this noble goal is futile, and must admonish, '*Der Zeit ist kurz, die Kunst ist lang*' ['Time is short, Art is lasting'].[40] Rather let the poet, he says, fulfill your dreams. As for you, '*Du bist am Ende – was du bist*' ['You are in the end just what you are'].[41] He tells Faust to forget all speculations, all striving of the mind and all striving of the spirit, and plunge into the world headlong with abandon. Artifice will act a worthy substitute. And indeed Mephisto illustrates this immediately when, upon the interruption of a student, he masks himself in the scholarly robes of Faust, and pretends that he is the master, giving us a wonderful charade – a *Fratze* – of the tutor with his disciple.

---

[37] Goethe, *Faust*, lns. 1726–1729. *SW, Vol. 6.1*, pp. 581–582.

[38] Goethe, *Faust*, lns. 1739–1740. *SW, Vol. 6.1*, p. 582.

[39] Goethe, *Faust*, lns. 1770–1771. *SW, Vol. 6.1*, p. 583.

[40] Goethe, *Faust*, ln. 1787. *SW, Vol. 6.1*, p. 583. Cf. Chaucer: 'The lyf so short, the craft so longe to lerne.' – opening line to 'Parliament of Fowls' in *The Complete Poetry and Prose of Geoffrey Chaucer*, ed. John H. Fisher (New York: Holt, Rinehart and Winston, 1977, rpt. 1989), p. 566.

[41] Goethe, *Faust*, ln. 1806. *SW, Vol. 6.1*, p. 584.

Mephisto: ... Doch Euch des Schreibens ja befließt.
Als diktiert Euch der Heilig Geist.
Schüler: Das sollt Ihr mir nicht zweimal sagen!
Ich denke mir, wieviel es nützt;
Denn, was man Schwarz auf Weis besitzt,
Kann man getrost nach Hause tragen.[42]

[Mephisto: ... But become an enthusiast of writing,
As if the Holy Spirit dictates to you!
Student: That you need not tell me twice!
I understand how useful writing is;
For what one possesses black on white,
One can take home with assurance.]

With the Devil's irony, Mephisto sends the student away with a fresh inscription in his book, an autograph, a signature: '*Eritis sicut Deus, scientes bonum et malum*' ('Then you will become like God, knowing good and evil').[43]

And so in his exchange with Faust, at the moment of decisive contract, and in his exchange *as* Faust, at the moment of discipleship and discipline which parodies that contract, Mephisto articulates a 'truth' which the heroic Faust himself cannot seem to perceive: that the blood is never divorced from the word, that every drop of blood shed becomes an inkwell for the story of good and evil in this world, and that the commingling of the one humor (blood) with the other humor (parody and masks) becomes a metaphor for that commingling which has frightened theologians throughout the ages – the commingling of God and Devil, as well as of God and Human. Of course, the commingling of God and Human, which frightened even the God of the Garden of Eden, is the very commingling which John is able to comprehend and reevaluate in his Prologue, where the God who becomes blood is the God who was always, and already, the Word. But this truth has implications even John must conceal, or fall silent before. For in this truth, artifice and the real, writing and lifeblood, interchange, in the same way that *Faust's* Prelude in the Theater interchanges with the Prologue in Heaven, and theatrical characters give way to divine characters. In this interchange between Word and Act, between the theological and the theatrical, God and the Devil come together, as God converses '*So menschlich mit dem Teufel selbst*' ['so humanely with the Devil himself'].[44] And in this interchange we are not far away from Blake's marriage of Heaven and Hell. Or from Bulgakov's *The Master and Margarita*. Or from Nietzsche's reexamination of good and evil.

---

[42] Goethe, *Faust*, lns. 1962–1967. *SW, Vol. 6.1*, p. 588.
[43] Goethe, *Faust*, ln. 2048. *SW, Vol. 6.1*, p. 590.
[44] Goethe, *Faust*, ln. 353. *SW, Vol. 6.1*, p. 544.

Interlude

[*Room in a sanatorium in Germany. Sparsely furnished, with a bed and a couch. In one corner sits a coat rack, on which hangs a long housecoat. Friedrich Nietzsche sits on the side of the bed, his hair tousled, and his head in his hands. Manuscripts lie strewn at his feet. A separately bound selection by Kierkegaard on Mozart's* Don Giovanni *sits spread down beside him. Enter a small figure, with a carriage much larger than his diminutive size should allow. He is dressed in a tight-fitting, gaudy-colored suit with a waist-coat. He affects an air of refinement, but with a sense of mockery, like a circus ringmaster. He assumes the couch with an easy manner and familiarity, and with lissome gestures, and fingernails that are abnormally long, strokes a long, pointy goatee, before addressing the occupant on the bed.*]

Figure: So you call yourself the Antichrist.

Nietzsche [*startled*]: Hmph?

Figure: The Antichrist. This self-appellation. You've written it and written about it often. Much to the horror of your detractors, naturally. But perfectly delightful to those in my circles, I can assure you.

Nietzsche [*gruffly*]: I wasn't expecting visitors, especially those unannounced.

Figure: No, I suspect not. You've lived an uncommonly solitary life, and I should think there are few, with the exception of your lovely but, I must say, overly devoted sister, who would deign to visit now.

Nietzsche: Well, then, I've already taken my medicine. You can leave now.

Figure: Come now, so ornery. Another splitting migraine? They've been your nemesis, haven't they? Though, I suspect, they've also helped to focus the brain. Suffering, in its most intense forms, can do that, you know.

Nietzsche: It is piercingly cold in here suddenly. Could you close the door tightly as you leave?

Figure: When I leave, yes, when I leave, though I've only just arrived. We have much to discuss, you and I. Put on your coat and hat – that should brace you from the cold.

Nietzsche: And exactly who is it who speaks so familiarly with me?

Figure: Who? You feign you don't know me? How mortifying! You know me like you know your own psyche, my dear boy. Maybe better. Now go fetch something warm to put around yourself, or your clattering teeth will bring the nurses in a running panic.

[*Nietzsche moves to the coat rack and puts on his housecoat. He turns around warily.*]

Nietzsche: You're still here.

Figure: Why shouldn't I be?

Nietzsche: Because my mind tells me you're not here. You seem to have appeared out of nowhere, speaking a familiar German and bringing a frigidity of Arctic extreme, and you claim we have much to discuss. About what, I do not know. All sense tells me that this experience cannot be real. It is more likely my illness is causing me to see what is really not there.

Figure: Well here is a paradox! Nietzsche speaking of sense! Listen, dear boy, you may be suffering from mental disturbances as of late, and your presence here at this hospital for the deranged may have some justification, medically speaking, but I can assure you, you can trust your five senses now, those senses in which you have put so much stock for all that supposed 'philosophical biologism' of yours. I am no more the result of your infirmities than are your philosophical writings.

Nietzsche: So you know me by my writings, is that it? My work was never intended to stimulate the masses, and least of all to generate devotees. If you are here for some sort of philosophical camaraderie, or to bask in what may now be perceived as a fashionable iconoclasm, you can take your sycophantic ways back to the pathetic herd from which they came. I am not about to be entertainment for hangers-on, even in this degenerate state. Pshaw! Get out of here!

Figure: Bravo! Bravo! Just the kind of caustic, misanthropic nastiness we've come to admire! A brilliance we haven't seen since the likes of your early hero, Schopenhauer. And far surpassing, I might add, at least as far as influence may go. But that's what also worries us, and really why I've come.

Nietzsche: 'Us'. You keep saying 'us', as if I should know you. You're not from my damned publishers, are you?

Figure: No, no. 'Damned', perhaps, but I'm not from publishers. We're not in the book business. We've found that such a limited and ineffectual market. Those who read – I mean, *really* read – are half lost to us anyway. No, it's reputation we're more interested in, and when it comes to the reputation of writers, especially for the majority of the 'herd' (as you so love to call them), those who don't read, but who want to appear that they do, spouting all the names in vogue, whether in conformity to pedestrian tastes or as supposed *provocateurs* from amongst the 'knowing' elite, you are our perfect man. Only, we see trouble ahead if things continue as they are.

Nietzsche: If you're not from my publishers, then you must be from lawyers representing my publishers. I am caught in a defamation suit, is that it?

Figure: No, no, your recent presence here in the sanatorium keeps you from any such litigation, I'm afraid. And should keep you from it forever. A shame. A good defamation suit might have really sealed your reputation.

Nietzsche: Then for whom do I take you, if you're not from the class of scoundrels, as your appearance and manner suggest?

Figure: Friedrich, I am disappointed in you. You know all too well who am I, but won't admit it to yourself. Our meeting has been fated for a long time. I can only be but one person, if I am to exist at all. And I think you have to admit that I exist, as sure as I sit before you. What am I called? Various names: Old Scratch. Old Clootie. Black Caspar. Diabolus. Sammael. Woland. Master *Dicis-et-non-facis*. They're all the same to me. Well actually, I prefer the latter, if I had to choose. It makes me out to be such an ironist, an arch-ironist, if you will, which suits me well. Your friend Kierkegaard, whom you've just discovered, I see, should be roused by that title too. Though, watch out, Friedrich, lest in the end you too should become so *earnest*.

Nietzsche: *Dicis-et-non-es* is best. All other names are irrelevant. For I went well beyond you. Well beyond you and your counterpart. You exist far less than even my Zarathustra, who had enough sense to see that Ultimate Good and Ultimate Evil were sheer conveniences, conveniences for the weak.

Figure: There you go with 'sense' again! Keep this up and you'll out-ironize me! Listen, my dear boy, trying to go beyond me is fine. Even Kierkegaard attempted that, and remained the good theologian that everyone now takes him for. But when you claim that you went beyond my counterpart – well, you realize, don't you, that such a move is, and has always been, perceived as the epitome of sinister intent, the apotheosis of diabolical evil. Anyone who claims to supercede my counterpart is, to be sure, party to *der Teufel*. And this is how you yourself are destined to be perceived for the next century or so. So don't go bragging about your nose-in-the-air, better-than-thou, beyond-good-and-evil philosophy quite yet. I'm not here to convince you of my existence. I am here to bargain with you about your own existence.

Nietzsche: My own existence! What could you possibly know of my existence, or, for that matter, anyone else's existence, you who, even if you were to exist, exist only for the negation of existence.

Figure: Not true, my boy. Totally untrue. I happen to care a lot about that old wizened authority they call *esse*, at least in relation to mortal time. For ultimately, mortal time is what we sell. And without the essence of existence, time would be of little use to us. I have time to give, but of course not endless time. I have time with an end, a determined time. But what a time! A time that makes the end inconsequential! I give you my time, and you give me your end. It's that simple.

Nietzsche: You've obviously not read enough of me, if you've read me at all. Eternal recurrence throws you and your 'time' back to the dogs, those creatures who lick themselves because time is so insufferably bound to *ennui*. There never was an end, you fool – except if you hold to some fantasy of 'time' as a way out of your pathetic self-enfeeblement.

Figure: Yes, well, I know all about your theory of eternal recurrence. A clever piece of sophistry. I've even used it myself on occasion. It gives good justification to the glories of the here and now, which have always been a staple of ours. But really now, Friedrich, look at your own here and now. It hardly inspires confidence. This is a hell of a place (if I can use the phrase), hell of a state, for an *Übermensch*. Where's your overcoming now? Where's your willful assertion of power against your own deterioration, your own mental enfeeblement? Where's all this grand yea-saying you once brandished so confidently, so hubristically? Hm? Should I tell you how it stands for you?

Nietzsche [*pause*]: It seems I have no option. 'Pierce on, cruelest thorn.'

Figure: You have one option, which is to hear me out and consider my offer. Now you, dearest Friedrich, have always been of melancholic disposition, accompanied by a little demon bat that flies in the face of the sun, as in *Meister* Dürer's famous woodcut. And there you have sat, in your despondent pose, the sands of time running out above your head, and next to them the hanging bell of death, waiting to knell from the jarring of the pull-cord that disappears out of the frame of your life, as if held by an invisible and sinister hand; and there you still sit, with a writing implement always ready in your grip, your eyes betraying that psychic disturbance from within, which, like the manifold creases of Dürer's garment that furl below your waist, forms convoluted knurls within your brain no instrument of reason or no will to power will smooth or appease. And as you follow the path of that ghoulish bat, while it spreads the word 'melancolia' across what is the only radiance within view – and oh how you have loved your written words, even if they have come on the wings of a devil's hellkite – there in the dark valleys of your thoughts has gestated that disease to which you now succumb so pitiably, that syphilitic result of a promiscuous conjoining between philosophic cerebration and biological perspectivism. You have tried to overcome metaphysics, yes, the queen of sciences, but in doing so you have yielded to the temptations of that prostitute we call intellectual *concern*, a noeticism treated all too sincerely, which Diogenes the Kynic, if you must speak of dogs, was far wiser for having avoided. Why didn't you go live in an urn and leave the concerns of philosophy to those you despise and denigrate? Because, my dear boy, fundamentally, at the heart of it all, you *care*, philosophically, intellectually, philologically, even, dare I say, theologically – call it what you will – you really do care. And in that caring, you have brought about your disease, your incurable, inexorable, metavenereal disease. And now there is no stopping it. You may live for another ten years or so, but you'll live bereft of the thing you truly care about most, your mind. But that's where I come in. Your private picture of melancholy is really a diptych, whose pairing becomes Dürer's other famous engraving, *The Knight, Death and the Devil*, in which your confident, armored, striding self now confronts *moi* – a very unbecoming rendering, I must say, but I'll suffer the portrait for the sake here of our little trope – as I once again hold out the flowing hourglass of time for you to ponder. You see, for all your bold striving, a trait you admired so much in Goethe's Faust, your malady in the brain has caught you out. And really, despite Master Dürer's intention, you will not get by me so easily, not get by me at all, before you trip and stumble over that skull placed at the foot of your path, to which the dogs beneath your horse's belly run with such purpose. But I offer you time. I hold out to you a reprieve of your disease, and a resumption of your mental faculties – a whole other hourglass of devilish sand, of the *genius* time you boasted of so proudly, if ironically, in one of your autobiographical writings. Yes, you can return to your unfinished business with renewed passion and clear-headedness, and others will say of you, just as Pilate said of Christ, and you mimicked of yourself, *Ecce Homo*! – but now, as with Pilate and not with you, they will say this earnestly and with admiration.

Nietzsche: You betray yourself, you hypocrite. You tell me to watch out for Kierkegaardian earnestness, and now you tempt me with the very same thing? Get away, wretch! You feign to show me the source of my illness, but it is this very illness which conjures you up, and without which you would vanish into nothingness. You have exposed yourself as a charlatan: you have proven that it is my perturbed condition that has drawn the semblance and falsity I see before me. And perturbed it must be, to have come up with *you*.

Figure: Feckless logic, dear boy. Sad and feckless. If I am simply the result of your subjective mind, your cherished perspective, maladjusted as it may now be, then why would this perspective so profoundly and so definitively betray itself, and all its self-avowed triumphalism in surpassing good and evil? Why, for that matter, would I betray myself? 'Every kingdom divided against itself is laid waste, and no city or house divided against itself will stand.' That goes for both of us, my friend. If I am a conjuration, you yourself are a conjuration.

Nietzsche: So be it, then. Better a self-made fool than a god's – or devil's – lackey.

Figure: Better a devil-preserved fool than a self-determined lunatic.

Nietzsche: Devil-preserved? And just what would you preserve me for? If I am allowed to finish my *Revaluation of All Values* as I have always intended, you, who are devoid of all value, would become evén more *Dicis-et-non-es* than you are now.

Figure: Oh, don't get me wrong. I would not inhibit you from writing. *Au contraire*. I would insist you keep writing, insist you finish your beloved *magnum opus*. It's just that I would demand you make some small adjustments. Nothing wholesale. Just a little recalibration here and there. Let me tell you something about your own 'art', if I may; let me give you a little *occultus conspectus* into the future reception of your *Werke*. I am a trafficker of time, as I have said – my time, granted, but time nevertheless, and most people are all too happy for any kind of extension or modification, especially with the kind of perks I can offer. As a proven man of the temporal bargain then – just ask the *real* Faust, the historical Faust – I occasionally am privy to what you mortals can only guess at, the future. Admittedly, I don't get to see it all, for omniscience is not my expertise, and I'll confess to you now that it is a most over-rated attribute anyway, since knowledge that encompasses all time, past, present and the whole of future, is of absolutely no consequence to the one who truly wants to live, that is, who lives out of the moment. In this I am in full agreement with you, and, though you may not believe it, living out of the moment is a dictum I actually follow myself. Mostly. But once in a while I get a glimpse into what is to come – a murky glimpse, one predicated on generalities and probabilities, but a glimpse sometimes distinct enough for me to abandon the moment temporarily, while I try to rectify a situation that, once rectified, will make one never want to abandon the moment again. Such a situation I have with you. Now it appears that this coming century will treat you as the naughty boy of philosophy, the rogue, the madman who philosophizes not only with a hammer but with a jester's cap, and not too infrequently with a bit of foam at the sides of the mouth. The religious establishment will revile you, naturally, just as you did them. (One doesn't need to be a seer to know this.) The philosophic establishment, which is where you will be taken up most strictly, will treat you largely as a marginal character, a lone voice in the wilderness, whose ravings have an undeniable intellectual genius, especially your earlier work, but whose destructive message will ultimately be dismissed as a moral critique taken far beyond the boundaries of good judgment, and good taste. Your reputation as a classicist, I'm afraid, seems very limited. I know this last revelation disappoints you deeply. But there is more. Certain political extremists will adopt you, and from what I can see horribly misread you, employing some of your ideas, selected with gross partiality, to justify a system that will become notorious for its atrocities. As these people will come from your own German stock, I should not imagine, given what you have always said about your own people and era, that you will be thrilled with their advocacy and misappropriation of your ideas; but at the same time you should not be all too surprised either, since you have always been misread, and most of all by your own folk. 'A prophet is never welcome in his own town' is a cliché even you can't elude. Well, if it is any consolation, it appears that these political extremists will fail miserably in the end. And yet, as far as I am concerned, there looks to be some delicious fruit born from their temporary regime, and their very failure will in the short term wed your name to the infamy they had perpetrated, and endow you both with a splendidly demonic reputation. Were it to stop there, I would of course designate this all a raging success – for, you remember, it is reputation I am most interested in. But it does not seem to stop there. Something very curious and unexpected appears to take place in the latter part of the century. For reasons I cannot quite make out, but which are somehow connected to all this earlier extremism, you begin to be taken *seriously*. I do not mean taken seriously by some radical group whose very zealotry ensures a thorough misunderstanding of your thought. And I do not mean taken seriously in the sense of a comfortable acclimation to the roundly unironic sincerity of the academic tradition, with all its conservative methodologies. I mean taken seriously as you yourself took your work, with a seriousness about the very playfulness that goes hand in hand with all your creative ambiguity. And what is even more astonishing is that this playful seriousness is then used as an indictment against that earlier reputation, that nefarious legacy of extremism, as if somehow your thought should have warded off, rather than invited, such extremism, and as if now your thought is needed as a necessary corrective or tonic. Well if that was all, we should have a good laugh and let all this attempt at playful seriousness fizzle out in self-mockery, as it must inevitably do. But that is not all. It gets even more preposterous. It seems that, by the end of the century, you are taken up by *theologians*! Yes, hard as it is to believe, it appears that Friedrich Nietzsche becomes a new kind of saint! Irony of ironies! A certain faction of theology adopts the self-styled Antichrist as a new way forward through an expiring secularity. These theologians pick up your cry that 'God is Dead' and preach it themselves! They then pick up your general critique of structures, religious, linguistic and otherwise, in order to put forward the silly idea that theology itself becomes a mechanism for criticism, becomes critical in a playfully ambiguous and self-reflexive sense, and that 'God' dies in order that the God who is not 'God' – oh how I detest that phrase! – might live outside of the philosophical contrivances of ideology and human intention, or some such chicanery. From all I can discern, you become a new kind of *via negativa*, which in turn, through some bloody-minded logic, becomes a *via affirmans*. I know, this is all very incredible, but what should frighten you most is that the theologians who read you this way, though by no means mainstream, are nevertheless largely Jews and Christians! Yes, Christians, the very lot you used to rant against most vituperatively! ... [*deliberate pause*]. So you see our dilemma.

Nietzsche: Very touching. The Devil waxes passionate, and pathetic.

Figure: You are implicated more than I, my boy. And the problem lies in the fact that you were never clear about what you exactly intended. Had you ended with your last three completed books, and particularly that last line of *Ecce Homo* – 'Have I been understood? – *Dionysus versus the Crucified*.' – it would have been patently clear just where you stood, and the chances of Christians, and I suspect even of rabbis, arranging trysts with you that culminate in some bizarre, perverse elopement would be inconceivable. But no, you had to go and qualify that statement in your 'Will to Power' fragments, and say that '*Dionysus versus the Crucified*' is really a problem of the meaning of suffering, the Christian conception versus the tragic conception. Don't you see, dear boy, that such a move is ultimately counterproductive to your critique, because it invites reconciliation? Reading the cross as redemption from life for the sufficiently weak, poor and disinherited is not the only way to read that event. Reading it in the more tragic sense, as an affirmation of the harshest suffering and of a promise of a life eternally reborn from destruction, as you claim, is perfectly viable even within *orthodox* Christian theology. You of all people should know this. Now, I will grant that you wrote all these thoughts hastily, and were not in the fittest of minds; and I will grant that the rest of this 'Will To Power', which is now in the worrying possession of your sister, and which so often suffers from the same imprecision and open-endedness, is the incomplete result of a tired brain and a waning acumen. But that is precisely why I am here: to offer you and your misinterpreted ideas restitution. All this can be fixed. The future which I have just told you about need not be the final outcome. My powers can use that old cause-and-effect formula to our advantage, and sway the course of time from its present destination with a little alteration here and a little persuasion there. It's easy: I give you back your mental facilities for several more years, and you finish the 'Will to Power' in the way that you had intended, with all the potentially misleading passages either expurgated or modified, and with a much more sustained and uncompromising critique against a theology that itself tries to work behind the structures of religion. In your haste, you forgot about the theologians who care about what lies *behind*.

Nietzsche: Behind, in front – this is all still religious language. If you want religious words, I'll quote them back to you: 'Get thee behind me.'

Figure: Don't be so hasty and dismissive. Hastiness has always been your downfall, and I am offering you the chance to redeem yourself. Nor will it take much, as I calculate it. The 'God is Dead' number was a superbly masterminded and well-crafted move, and I'll even continue to allow you to take all the credit for it. But let us not deceive ourselves: it cannot in the end carry the day. Ultimately, it now seems abundantly clear, this 'God' must be kept alive. I do not of course refer to that being they call [sotto voce, *and with a wince*] *mysterium tremendum*, but rather the 'God' of predicable and predicatory religion. For to lose that 'God' completely from the picture seems to invite the search for that other, less definable notion whose reference, thankfully, we've managed to keep to a few marginal authors whom no one reads. You are destined to be a marginal author whom everyone reads, I see – or at least, one whom everyone has heard about being read. And so we need to take measures now to ensure that you don't end up in the wrong hands, and especially not in the hands of these audacious Judeo-Christian pontificators who think they can usurp the 'Antichrist' for their own righteous cause. Better, then, a 'God' of organized religion, who wants to preserve the structures of a timid and safe redemption for the weak, for the poor and for the disinherited, than a bunch of hypercritical theologians who seize your apparatus of critique in order to cloak their piety. They try to peddle such terms as 'apophatic thinking', 'ongoing creation', and 'divine rhetoric' as if they all accord with your notions of tragedy and the creative will. If you want to avoid these mountebanks, you will have to suffer the ready-made 'God' of the cult, even though you have spent your entire *oeuvre* railing against it. Fine, continue to rail, but rail in such a way that you polarize, *you* against *them*, as you did in the finale of *Ecce Homo*. Don't rail so as to extend collegiality with those you rail against! What your final, unfinished work needs, then, is a shift in emphasis. Build up the anti-Christian polemic by *deifying* the individual and its will to power, and tone down the glorification of the creative strength as a gesture of truth. The first is perfectly self-centering; the second is too broad, too vague, and too open for theological interpretation. Forget the hermeneutical nature of your critique – nothing takes you back to theology faster than hermeneutics! – and stick more to the revaluation of *religious* values and morality, as you had done in your earlier main works. Tighten up the argument, so that the interstices of ambiguity cannot be probed and entered by later ironists with sanctimonious agendas. And end on a more venomous note. Do not forget that Dionysus is unforgiving. Finish your work with a more Euripidean Bacchus, one who turns the innocent into serpents and banishes royalty from its kingdom. Greek tragedy is your strength, after all, so play it up. It won't take much. And best of all, you'll be left with plenty of time to enjoy some of your now growing success within certain circles. Who knows, I could even arrange for a little female diversion. How about Wagner's darling, that Cosima you've always itched after? There'd be no better way to humiliate your ex-friend, even if he is already in my immortal company. So what do you say?

Nietzsche [*after considerable silence*]: A fine Devil you make. Temptation succeeds best when delivered with indifference. It succeeds least when the tempter is desperate. You cut a sad figure with all your imploring. And you have the gall to tell me how to write my book, as if now you're an expert on books. When have you written anything of note, I ask? At least your main rival can claim a bestseller. But you, you don't write because you're afraid to lose control to the unknown, the hermeneutical unknown. You have just admitted as much yourself. Fear, cowardice, and desperation define you. And you are stupid as well. You bargain with a madman. You may be able to reason with the indigent, or with the complacent bourgeois, or even the bored aristocracy, but to reason with a delirious man such as myself, who sees you only because he *is* delirious, betrays a stupidity of staggering proportions. And so you let your true colors show, and revert to that old, tired line of defense, that Manichaean maneuver of strict moral partisanship, a black and white dualism that gives you the subtlety of an ox's ass, and makes you into a ridiculous, nugatory, doomed-to-fail villain. I've never had any truck with you, and I certainly won't now, whatever my condition. You're a delusion of a delusion, fit only for one purpose, to return to your *naught*.

Figure: *Ecce homo*, the clever, untimely lover of fate, who thinks he can hide in his subjectivity! You discount my objectivity as if I only exist in the brain. But then this refusal of me is a refusal of self, and if what is objective has nothing of value, then your self, subjectivity's object, dies on the vine as well. '*Ich bin die* Einsamkeit *als Mensch*', you write – but now you would have no more solitude left to be *Mensch*, and no more *Mensch* or humanity to represent in all your solitude. You'd have nothing anymore with which to be delusional, even. All this is truly philistine, and worthy of your overcoming, if there was ever anything worthy. If you behold me, then I am really here for you, and it does not pay to ask about the nature of this 'really', except insofar as you ask it of your subjectivity. You are a diseased genius, and I offer you nothing more than to remain the diseased genius, whose very disease, modified and kept in check by me, will guarantee the future a cure for its own obsessive mediocrity, and whose genius, which owes its very existence to that disease, will continue to frustrate the liberal theologians with their extreme unorthodoxy. The secular will remain the secular, the sacred cult will cower under its hegemony, and neither will pursue the excess, the paradox, the mystical passion that sits buried behind the icy, moribund rhetoric of their own cold war. Together you and I will keep 'religion' and its 'God' alive for the sheer purpose of antagonism, without which all 'hell' will break loose. If you don't want 'hell' anymore than you want 'heaven', this is your only way to ensure the two sides cancel each other out. You see, I can be theological too. Religion is as much my field as anyone's, and surely more than the effete bourgeois'.

Nietzsche: And yet, if you are not a product of the effete bourgeois, you are certainly kept alive by them. You owe them everything. So don't try all this anti-bourgeois palaver on me as your last-ditch effort. I see through you. Your incantations don't work here. If you want to strut this diabolical religious cant, strut it before the 'sane', who will at least join forces or put up a fight. Leave me to my madness. After hearing you plead, I am content with my fate, in both its immediate and future manifestations. And if I lose my mind completely, I'll be happy in the knowledge of at least this much: compared to your anemic performance, I could out-Devil you with little effort. But I choose not to. [*Stands up and takes off his housecoat.*] I choose not to waste my time, however much I may have left. There are much greater beasts to overcome. [*Throws housecoat at the Figure's feet.*] 'What is done out of love always occurs beyond good and evil.'

Figure: 'Love' now! Dear oh dear! I overestimated you, clearly. Or you overestimate yourself. You no more care about love than I care about salvation.

Nietzsche: The problem is you care *too much* about salvation, and about staving it off – eternally.

Figure: And your problem is you *care* too much – about the eternal. Of the recurring same, of the ineffaceable difference, it doesn't really matter. [*Sneering*]

You really *are* theological, when it comes down to it. Perhaps I shall leave you to your newfound Kierkegaard. You seem more congenial bedfellows than I would have guessed. [*Rises to leave. Picks up the housecoat.*] Lost the chill in all your ardent refusal, I see.

Nietzsche: Out of the ice pack into the fire. My fire. You are now naught.

Figure: Well before this naught leaves, let me tell you one last thing: you will never write again. Your solitude will now be silence; your *Mensch* will now be voiceless. A foolish, foolish willfulness you stubbornly possess. [*Tosses Nietzsche back the housecoat.*] But you may yet need this.

[*With housecoat in hand, Nietzsche moves towards a mess of strewn papers that cover the floor. He bends down and brushes them aside, revealing the outline of a large trap door. He finds the latch and raises the lid with some effort. The Figure stands by watching bemused but puzzled. Nietzsche separates the housecoat's belt from its waist. He approaches the figure. In one surprisingly quick and agile motion, which takes the Figure completely off guard, he flings the housecoat over the Figure's head and secures it tightly around his small chest with the belt, pinning the arms to the side. Muffled objections can be heard from underneath the shroud. With a grip on the belt, Nietzsche leads the captive to the edge of the trap door. He quickly returns to the bed and fetches Kierkegaard's booklet on Mozart's* Don Giovanni, *which he subsequently forces between the Figure's chest and the belt that constrains him. After a ceremonious pause, Nietzsche shoves the Figure forward, who immediately disappears into the darkness beneath. He slams the trapdoor shut.*]

Nietzsche: I will always have something to say ...

5 Nietzsche

> Will to truth is a making firm, a making true and durable, an abolition of the false character of things, a reinterpretation of it into beings. 'Truth' is therefore not something there, that might be found or discovered – but something that must be created and that gives a name to a process, or rather to a will to overcome that has in itself no end – introducing truth, as a *processus in infinitum*, an active determining – not a becoming-conscious of something that is in itself firm and determined.
>
> Nietzsche, *The Will to Power*[1]

No one has understood the dramaturgical nature of truth better than Nietzsche. Fictitious more than factual, histrionic more than historical, spectacular more than speculative – this, for Nietzsche, is the character of truth, which, in cothurni and mask, paraded most proudly and most brazenly about the Greek stage. As early as *The Birth of Tragedy* (1872), Nietzsche had asserted that existence of the world and existence within the world could only be justified aesthetically, that art, rather than morality, as he says later in his self-critical preface to this first published work, 'is presented as the truly *metaphysical* activity of man.'[2] And it is on stage where 'metaphysical' activity is best manifested, under the costume and dissimulation of the dramatic act. 'Playing at truth', as he describes it in *Die Morgenröte* (*Daybreak*).[3] For it is on stage where the 'beyond' of the physical, the mask, can *truly* have its say without that kind of hypocrisy which plagues traditional, speculative metaphysics: the claim to a truth existing outside of our material embeddedness in this world, and yet never able to describe our access to that truth except from that embeddedness. In the dramatic mask, however, the material never parades as anything other than what it is, artifice, through which the voice of the actor issues forth. The mask is metaphysical here in the sense of going beyond the actor's own face, to some archetypal emotion or visual topos; and yet in its artificiality and opacity as a covering, it presents the very physicality and materiality which grounds all human action and endeavor. This duplicity, a double expression of the corporeal and the incorporeal, is what links truth most primordially to the stage for Nietzsche. We play at truth, because truth is only ever a doubling, a marriage of artifice and human spirit: Apollo as the mask that is worn, Dionysus as the actor speaking and acting through the mask. Truth is only ever creative.

If for Kant truth functions within the limits of critique (*Kritik*), for Nietzsche truth functions within the creativity of acting – acting as part of a willful make-believe (a making of belief) that demands an unflinching existential commitment to artifice. But what precisely does this artifice look like? And how can we go from the rigors of the Kantian system, in which knowledge tries to be grounded upon a certainty inherent within the system itself, to the craft of artifice which, by its very definition, its reliance on masquerade and metaphor, renders certainty all but irrelevant?

It is not through the whole corpus of Nietzsche's thought that we should piece together this radical dramaturgy, but rather through an early short essay, written in

1 Friedrich Nietzsche, *The Will to Power*, '552 (Spring-Fall 1887)', p. 298.

2 Nietzsche, *The Birth of Tragedy*, p. 22.

3 Nietzsche, *Daybreak*, p. 176.

1873, a year after *The Birth of Tragedy*, entitled 'On Truth and Lying in an Extra-Moral Sense'. This is a famous essay, but famous for essentially one sentence, at the expense of the rest of the essay. So let us begin then not with the sentence itself, which we will come to in due course, but with the beginning of the essay. For here Nietzsche takes to task not simply the inherited moral structures of Western society, as his title would suggest, but the fundamentals of Western metaphysics as they fund our notion of truth in all its commonly adopted senses.

To emphasize the disconnection of traditional metaphysics from the material ground that it takes as its departure, and from the necessary fabrication that must sustain this disconnection, artificial or 'unnatural' as it may be, Nietzsche starts with his own fable. 'In some remote corner of the universe that is poured out in countless flickering solar systems, there once was a star on which clever animals invented knowledge'.[4] In these opening lines, with a gesture of irony and subversion typical to his approach, Nietzsche rewrites the cosmos, and in doing so suggests an epistemogony. 'Epistemogony' is a neologism we use here to underscore a point: we never think of knowledge as coming into being from the hand of a creator or from some process of creation. Knowledge resides by virtue of the fact that things already exist, and we in turn come to *know* them. That we have been obsessed, since Kant, with *how* we come to know the objects given to us at hand does not lead us back to the origin of this *how*, or to the creation of a passage from ourselves to the objects. Kant did not propose a blueprint from which we could then construct and create for ourselves an intellectual apparatus consisting of intuitions and concepts, to be modified and altered according to our specific whims. Intuitions in particular are nothing if they are not our immediate sensibility in relation to an object already given. Kant would never claim he made up a blueprint. He would, however, along with Plato, claim that he discovered the boundaries and outlines of a blueprint already in existence, one that reasonably accounts for our given ontological and epistemological nature. That knowledge arises from his schematism is not yet equivalent to an invention of knowledge as such. Kant assumed knowledge was already in place. His schematism was simply the working out of how that knowledge is appropriated in the thinking and acting subject. But in Nietzsche's fabular view, knowledge is like any other invented device, with its beginnings in whim and accident, except that in the case of knowledge the consequences have led to more harm than good. Of this inventing of 'knowledge' he says, 'That was the most arrogant and the most untruthful moment in "world history" – yet indeed only a moment. After nature had taken a few breaths, the star froze over and the clever animals had to die.'[5]

A star among endless stars, a moment fleeting among countless moments, an arrogance based on a lie, 'pitiless', 'shadowy', 'purposeless', 'arbitrary' – all this describes the human intellect, Nietzsche says, situated as it is among an ever-changing and infinitely possible nature, or φύσις (*phusis*). This nature, in

---

[4] Friedrich Nietzsche, 'On Truth and Lying in an Extra-Moral Sense', in *Friedrich Nietzsche on Rhetoric and Language*, eds. and trans. Sander L. Gilman, *et al.* (Oxford: Oxford University Press, 1989), p. 246.

[5] *Ibid.*

Nietzsche's cosmos, is not subservient to humanity and its intellect, for any such subservience is only another human invention. Nature has its own law, its own concern, and each component of nature, down to the smallest insect or particle, has as much right to call itself the center of the universe as the human mind: 'But if we could communicate with the gnat, we would learn that it too swims through the air with this same pathos and feels within itself the flying center of the world.'[6] Nietzsche's subversion not only of a Christian cosmology but of a deep humanism, sacred or secular, is of course deliberate. He wants to question the very grounds upon which our thinking lies. The intellect is a frail, miniscule faculty with only a shameless, even baseless, arrogance to inflate it above the rest of creation; and in its claims to truth, it first must veil over this embarrassing fact, its delicate and perishable nature, making its first steps to knowledge a 'most untruthful moment'. And philosophers, the acknowledged experts of intellect, have been the worst perpetrators of such veiling.

The young Nietzsche, by the second paragraph, has already altered the boundaries in which the notions of 'truth' and 'lying' operate in the rest of the essay. In the grand scheme of the cosmos, knowledge, the consummation of our intellect's achievement, has no more effect upon us humans and the world than deception, for indeed it requires deception, as self-deception, to come into being in the first place. Nietzsche goes on to say that this is how we survive, how we preserve ourselves as individuals: 'The intellect, as a means of preserving the individual, develops its main powers in dissimulation ... .'[7] And it is from such dissimulation that the worst of humanity arises, for it begins in a consummate arrogance and vanity, and ends in the kind of fraud that, rather than preserving an individual from the hostile forces of the world, pits one against another in cheating, slander, revenge and subterfuge. Amid such delusion and deception, Nietzsche wonders 'how an honest and pure desire for truth could arise among men', and asks 'Given this state of affairs, where in the world does the desire for truth originate?'[8]

Where *in the world* indeed? Nietzsche's suggestion: language. In order to keep from destroying each other, humans band together under some notion of a peace agreement. This idea, indebted to Hobbes, suggests that in order to preserve oneself against the natural state of war that marks both the physical world and human society, one must leave behind multiplicity – multiplicity of selves, multiplicity of desires, multiplicity of territory, multiplicity of law – and unify under some arbitratable system. With such a system in place, 'a uniformly valid and binding terminology for things is invented and the legislation of language also enacts the first laws of truth.'[9] Truth becomes 'fixed': fixed in one place, to be adjudicated in a court of law; but also fixed or rigged by the peace agreement, to be passed off as universally valid for all. Like knowledge in the opening argument, truth arises, once again, out of a duplicity, out of that which, on the one hand, is stationed, even cemented, in the law as a binding universal, and on the other hand is positioned in

---

6 *Ibid.*

7 *Ibid.*, pp. 246–247.

8 *Ibid.*, p. 247.

9 *Ibid.*

the purely conventional, contrived in such a way so as to give law its prima facie validity and to provide it with particular jurisdictions. From this original duplicity (universal vs. conventional), which has the same paradoxical structure as the great invention of the 'third account' in that other famous cosmogony, Plato's *Timaeus*, in which the χώρα (*khora*), the 'receptacle of all becoming' (49a),[10] acts both as a provider of the cosmos and as a part of/place in the cosmos – from this macrocosmic duplicity, there follows individual duplicity, that is, lying. As truth is now essentially the legislated conventions of a particular language, of terms adopted for the purpose of linking the conventional to the universal, lying comes into effect when an individual 'fixes' language for his or her own purposes against the convention. Or, it comes into effect when an individual uses language to make the established conventions stand for a universal condition that does not in fact exist under the system.

We can see this kind of legislation at work in an even earlier cosmogonic narrative, the Hebrew account in Genesis, where in the second creation story of 2.4b and following, the prohibition to eat from the Tree of the Knowledge of Good and Evil is a convention set up by Yahweh, which, once tested and broken, sets truth and lying into their standard orbit. Why did Eve contravene the prohibition? 'The serpent tricked me', she says (Genesis 3:13). That is, she succumbed to the serpent's duplicity. But this duplicity is not yet lying. Throughout his temptation the serpent never in fact *lies* to Eve in the sense just described. He does discount Yahweh's threat that 'in the day that you eat of it you shall die' (Genesis 2:17), and assures Eve that she 'will not die', but presumably he has good reason for this claim, since immortality seems readily available with the second tree, the Tree of Life, which carries with it no prohibition. It is only when the divine convention is broken, and the universal has been established through their punishments, that Adam and Eve must vacate their pre-moral paradise, lest they reach out their hands 'and take also from the tree of life, and eat, and live forever' (Genesis 3:22). Once expelled into this postlapsarian world, with the moral paradigm now established through the transgression, truth and lying come into their own, and we get individual human duplicity now in the direct form of lying when Cain, in Yahweh's presence, disavows knowledge of his brother's whereabouts, the same brother he has just killed (Genesis 4:9). In symbolic terms, the trees of the garden function in the same way Nietzsche says language functions to legislate law. But where does language get its legislative authority? As Nietzsche asks, 'what is the situation with those conventions of language? Are they perhaps products of knowledge, of the sense of truth? Do terms coincide with things? Is language the adequate expression of all realities?'[11]

If, to help answer these questions, and to amplify this argument about convention, we allow Nietzsche to become the serpent in the story of Eden, a role he may indeed have relished, the following dialogue might take place:

---

[10] As it is translated by Donald J. Zeyl, for example, in Plato, *Complete Works*, ed. John M. Cooper (Indianapolis: Hackett, 1997), p. 1251

[11] Nietzsche, 'On Truth and Lying', p. 248.

Nietzsche: Actually, there are two trees of consequence in this garden.

Eve: Two? We were only told of one.

Nietzsche: Of course you were only told of one, for when it comes to setting up the moral structure, only one tree is needed to break the symbolic order of innocence. Let me explain. God labeled two trees with specific designations, one as 'Knowledge' and the other as 'Life'. But as only one tree is needed for an act of violation, God felt compelled, by His own logic, to set the prohibition around 'Knowledge', as what He means by knowledge here is that which arises directly from the sheer act of contravention: the awareness of consequence. But remember, this consequence is pure convention. What did he say the consequence would be?

Eve: That we would surely die.

Nietzsche: Ah, you see? There is nothing inherent in this one tree here that will make you die. The fruit itself will certainly not kill you. Let me assure you – I eat it all the time. The consequence arises simply out of the desire, the *convention*, of God to keep you in your place as humans, a place of 'innocence', or as the word suggests, of no harm. But in this paradise harm only comes from knowing that harm, or evil, is possible, and it is possible only because God has decided to set up the structure in which consequence follows as harm (death). Therefore, the content of this knowledge – 'good and evil' – is in fact completely caught up in its own self-made structures, and is thus no content really at all. What you would 'know' by eating this fruit is simply that consequence here is conventional, is part of a prohibitionary structure whose very purpose is to prohibit the breaking of the prohibition. Do you see the circularity here?

Eve: I do – I think.

Nietzsche: To prohibit knowledge of what makes a prohibition prohibitory (good and evil) involves the same logic, although in a reversed scenario, as reasoning with a fish that, if it would just give you an hour of its time up here in the boat upon your lap, you will explain to it with convincing clarity why yielding to the fisherman's lure and living outside of the waters would be detrimental to its health. The danger that you promise to explain is already made manifest in the act of explaining: in your case, the prohibiting of the knowledge already brings with it the knowledge. The 'knowledge' of good and evil is the potential harm, or loss of innocence, that is brought to you by the knowledge of the potential harm. But you already *know* the potential harm. God told you this earlier, and you just told me it yourself. So ironically, your 'harmless' state of innocence already has built into it the very thing you are being kept from, the threat of harm, and thus acting or not acting against the prohibition seems superfluous, or at least inconsequential. The knowledge that God really is trying to keep you from, and that all who reside in His divine realm already know, is just this: eating or not eating the fruit itself is really inconsequential. It is the mere conventionality of prohibition that makes any particular prohibition effective. Knowing *this* may have its consequences, but let me tell you, the consequences are not all bad.

Eve: I see. So this fruit actually won't kill me? By eating it I will acquire the knowledge of evil, but not necessarily the evil itself, because, as you say, such evil is a sheer contrivance anyway, just as is the knowledge – a knowledge of contrivance. Is that it?

Nietzsche: More or less. The tree and its fruit are only ciphers in the system. God could have chosen any of the other trees for this label of good and evil. Of course, the 'Tree of Life' is another matter, for he couldn't very well attach the prohibition to it, since the consequence of death doesn't accord well with the promise of immortal life. 'Eat of this Tree of Life and you will surely die'– that doesn't work, does it? Even God sticks to a certain degree of logic. That is why there is no prohibition at all attached to the second tree, since the idea of life, and *everlasting* life no less, contravenes what the theologians or the moralists might call the 'prohibitory calculus' of punishment by death which God has constructed. You know, if you are still worried about these supposed consequences of eating this fruit, which, I have to say, is looking more and more delectable as we stand here talking – if *you* aren't going to eat it, I'd gladly take it from you – there is nothing stopping you from going over to the Tree of Life and eating some of its fruit, just to be on the safe side. Nothing, that is, as long as you remain within the confines of this 'prohibitory calculus'. God could always toss you out of it altogether, of course, at which point the option is no longer available. But that would make God rather duplicitous, don't you think? Well, if you want my opinion, leaving this place would be preferable to what you have going here.

Eve: Yes, well I wouldn't know. But I do think I understand a little better now. What you mean is that God could have used anything, not just a tree. He just as easily could have said, 'Do not fish in the Pond of the Knowledge of Good and Evil . . .', is that it?

Nietzsche: You *are* getting the point, yes. What is knowledge? In this case, it is knowing simply the act of knowing, not knowing some object as a thing-in-itself. What is the very thing that would rob you of your innocence? Harm – that is, evil. What harms you? Knowledge of evil, for then you will die. So the knowledge is only a knowledge of itself, not of anything outside itself. And that's the problem with this labeling business. The tree happens to take the brunt of this self-defined and self-enclosed knowledge. But, as you point out, it could have been the pond, or this rock, or this flower, or that bees' nest over there. You are no closer to the 'thing-in-itself' in any of them, if the 'thing' we are talking about is 'good' or 'evil'. 'Evil-in-itself' is just the structure of the prohibition contravened, 'good-in-itself' the structure of the prohibition upheld.

Eve: You've made a compelling case for why I should not worry about eating this fruit. But, conversely, is there any reason, after all you've said, why I *should* eat it?

Nietzsche [*smiling*]: Ah, my dear, if you really think I've made a compelling case for not eating it, then, to all intents and purposes, you've already eaten it. Therein lies the real truth of the matter.

Eve: Hmmm. I see. But then . . . what is truth?

Nietzsche: Well, now, you see what this new knowledge of yours brings you? A critical mind. Bravo – good question. Give me a bite of your fruit, and I'll tell you the answer. Though let's continue to leave Adam out of it – I find him an insufferable bore.

This artificial scenario could go on, of course. But we will leave it to its own devices. Nietzsche in fact supplies his own answers to the questions that set off our scenario, questions about the convention of language, and we find these answers thinly veiled in the next stage of his essay, as it develops an argument against Kant. Nietzsche begins here by questioning the relationship between truth and language: 'Unless he [a human] wants to settle for truth in the form of a tautology, i.e., for empty husks, he will perpetually exchange truths for illusions. What is a word? The portrayal of nerve stimuli in sounds. But to conclude from a nerve stimulus to a cause outside ourselves is already the result of a false and unjustified application of the law of causality.'[12] A word becomes nothing more than a transference of a nerve stimulus to a specific sound, and then to specific written characters. But the connection of the stimulus to the word has no inherent causality. We arbitrarily assign a word to the stimulus:

> We arrange things by genders, we designate the tree [*der Baum*] as masculine, the plant [*die Pflanze*] as feminine: what arbitrary transferences! How far-flung beyond the canon of certitude! We speak of a 'serpent'; the term applies to nothing but its winding, and so it would apply equally to the worm. What arbitrary delimitations, what one-sided preferences for one trait or another of a thing! The various languages, juxtaposed, show that words are never concerned with truth, never with adequate expression; otherwise there would not be so many languages. The 'thing-in-itself' (which would be pure, disinterested truth) is also absolutely incomprehensible to the creator of language and not worth seeking.[13]

The arbitrary transference here is what Nietzsche calls metaphor. The first metaphorical move is from the nerve stimulus to an image in the head or the mind. We transfer a purely physical matter, the stimulus, to a purely noetic abstraction, a mental image which, Nietzsche claims, has no inherent connection to the stimulus. The connection we make is thoroughly arbitrary. Of course, Kant had attempted to ground this connection in synthesis. Modern theories of language and semiotics, or modern philosophies of mind, may too offer their own theories, but no one, not even modern scientists experimenting with the brain and its functioning, can tell us *exactly* what transpires when visual sensation receives a stimulus and an image is subsequently formed in the mind in correspondence to that stimulus. For Nietzsche, this is only ever a correspondence, two things responding to one another, and not a causal connection, one thing necessarily following from another. But even if we grant Kant his synthesis, and modern science or theory the legitimacy to cast serious doubt on this purely 'metaphorical' understanding of correspondence, there

---

12 *Ibid.*
13 *Ibid.*

is yet another metaphorical move far less refutable: 'Then, the image must be reshaped into a sound! The second metaphor.'[14] Here the transference from image to sound is completely arbitrary, with no internal necessity whatsoever, not even the possibility of a physiological necessity as there may be in the first move. Like God in the garden, we simply designate a sound, such as the phonetic sound of the word 'tree', to the image we have of a tree. What precisely links together these two 'objects', sound and image, is nothing other than a willful and yet arbitrary decision on the part of the subject to correlate them, that is, to metaphorize them. This metaphorizing, whether in one or two moves – and we could add more metaphorical moves, as we turn the sound into a written script, the script into gender distinctions, and so on – distances us each time from the essentiality of the 'thing' that we claim to be representing, if not comprehending, in our language. That original essence, the 'thing-in-itself', a term Nietzsche borrows from Kant (*Ding an sich*), is not in any way captured by the legislative structure of the language system that is constructed in this process, just as evil would not be resident in the juice of the forbidden fruit. And here Nietzsche and Kant can be in agreement, for the 'thing-in-itself' becomes unavailable in the process of our claim to knowledge. We only know some representation, or metaphor, of the original thing. But unlike Kant, Nietzsche does not believe the process of representation or metaphorization, however provisional or substitutionary or 'synthetic', is a logical one, grounded in reason. Rather, he concludes the opposite, that 'the origin of language is not a logical process, and the whole material in and with which the man of truth, the scientist, the philosopher, works and builds, stems, if not from a never-never land, in any case not from the essence of things.'[15]

The illogical mechanism of language is treated from a different angle in Paul Ricoeur's monumental work on metaphor. In *The Rule of Metaphor* he points out, using Heidegger, the way in which metaphors become 'used up', or 'worn out', within a kind of 'entropy of language'.[16] What binds two terms together in metaphoricity is what he calls a transposition from 'the proper sense to the figurative sense'.[17] But there are instances when the figurative becomes masked, and masked as the 'proper' (Heidegger's *eigentlich*), as if the figurative shares strictly in its own individuality that is both unborrowed and singular. In such instances the metaphor becomes 'dead', used up, no longer treated as living, taken only as 'proper'. The lineage of the figuration still exists, the transposition is still operative, though now only spectrally, as a hidden *deus ex machina*. Such a metaphor, no longer taken as a metaphor, is what Ricoeur, along with Heidegger, calls the philosophical metaphor, the metaphor effectively killed off by a philosophical masking that wants to legitimate its own figuration within what is assumed as a privileged ontology of the proper (*eigentlich*). This philosophical masking is, of course, the move of metaphysics, which is implicated in its own metaphoricity. Hence Heidegger's famous assertion: 'The metaphorical exists only

---

[14] *Ibid.*

[15] *Ibid.*, p. 249.

[16] Paul Ricoeur, *The Rule of Metaphor*, trans. Robert Czerny (Toronto: Toronto University Press, 1977), p. 284.

[17] *Ibid.*, p. 280.

within the metaphysical'.[18] In fact, we could say, 'metaphysics' becomes just such a dead metaphor, as it tries to mask its figuration strictly in terms of the proper. For Plato, metaphysics is the *proper* starting point, even cosmogonically. Philosophy ever since Plato has traded in dead metaphors, as it trades in metaphysics, since both metaphor and metaphysics mask the transpositional move they rely upon for their existence, that move from a singular entity to its alternative representation or figuration. Metaphysics is worn out metaphor, 'worn out' by the masking, which both *wears away* the explicitness of the transposition, while at the same time *wears forth* the dissimulation of the proper, or, we might say, the dissimulation of the thing-in-itself. Ricoeur's reading of Heidegger and the dead metaphor here is in consonance then with Nietzsche's critique, as Ricoeur himself discloses: 'Heideggerean deconstruction [of metaphor] must now take on Nietzschean geneology [sic], Freudian psychoanalysis, the Marxist critique of ideology, that is, the weapons of the hermeneutics of suspicion. Armed in this way, the critique is capable of unmasking the *unthought* conjunction of *hidden* metaphysics and *worn-out* metaphor.'[19]

Ricoeur follows Nietzsche immediately thereafter in connecting metaphor to the formation of concepts. He writes:

> The efficacy of the dead metaphor takes on its full meaning, however, only when one establishes the connection between the *wearing away* that affects metaphor and the ascending movement that constitutes the formation of the concept. The wearing away of the metaphor is dissimulated in the 'raising' of the concept ... Henceforth, to revive the metaphor is to unmask the concept.[20]

Likewise Nietzsche's next sentence in his essay: 'Let us think in particular of the formation of concepts.'[21] What is the concept here? And what is the link between the metaphoric and the conceptual, or words and concepts? The concept, we know from Kant, is the gathering out of singularity into commonality: 'The former [intuition] relates immediately to the object and is single, the latter [concept] refers to it [the object] mediately by means of a feature which several things have in common.'[22] The concept is not something we find directly or immediately in our interaction with an object or objects. It is rather something we construct out of features we find are shared. But what does it mean to 'share' a feature, in this sense? Do objects in their singularity ever share features? Or is this 'sharing' something we impose? Nietzsche describes it as such:

> Every concept originates by the equation of the dissimilar. Just as no leaf is every exactly the same as any other, certainly the concept 'leaf' is formed by arbitrarily dropping those individual differences, by forgetting the distinguishing factors, and this gives rise to the

18 *Ibid.*, pp. 280, 282.
19 *Ibid.*, p. 285.
20 *Ibid.*, pp. 285–286.
21 Nietzsche, 'On Truth and Lying', p. 249.
22 Kant, *Critique of Pure Reason*, p. 314 (A 320, B 377).

> idea that besides leaves there is in nature such a thing as the leaf, i.e. an original form according to which all leaves are supposedly woven, sketched, circled off, colored, curled, painted, but by awkward hands so that not a single specimen turns out correctly and reliably as a true copy of the original form.[23]

In this critique here of Platonic forms, the origin of the proper for Plato, Nietzsche suggests that what we call the 'shared', or the similar, can only come about by forgetting, by masking the dissimilarities, or indeed by equating them, as if they were not dissimilarities at all. He claims that any such original form can only come about through erasure, an elimination of the distinguishing features of singularity. And he says that we employ words in the same way that we employ forms: 'Every word becomes a concept as soon as it is supposed to serve not merely as a reminder of the unique, absolutely individualized original experience, to which it owes its origin, but at the same time to fit countless, more or less similar cases, which, strictly speaking, are never identical, and hence absolutely dissimilar.'[24] He then extends this to such intangible concepts as 'honesty', the supposed source for an honest act. But to Nietzsche this move is no more sound than saying that the concept 'leaf' is the cause of leaves. Both concepts are formed by omitting dissimilarities, by drawing out from a manifold of features a singular '*qualitas occulta*', and then applying to this forged quality an arbitrary label ('honesty', 'leaf', and so on).

> Overlooking the individual and the real gives us the concept, just as it gives us the form, whereas nature knows no forms and concepts, hence also no species, but only an *x* that is inaccessible and indefinable for us. For even our distinction between individual and species is anthropomorphic and does not stem from the essence of things, although we also do not dare to say that it does *not* correspond to it. For that would be a dogmatic assertion, and as such just as unprovable as its opposite.[25]

We have seen this 'X' before, this variable that here remains ineffable, except in its arbitrary nomenclature which acts as nothing more than a token admission of its ineffability. Here, the 'X' rescues Nietzsche from a thoroughgoing biologism, with which some have charged him.[26] For nature, which knows no forms or concepts, and indeed we who receive that nature through stimuli, are not simply reduced to a biological singularity, or a disparate accumulation of individual physical traits where 'no leaf is ever exactly the same as any other'. There is an inaccessible variable, undefined even by Nietzsche, which enters into the equation, just as it had repeatedly and inexorably for Kant. Only Nietzsche here does not try to 'place' the variable, as had Kant within imagination. He simply allows the 'X' its blind space, its inaccessible presence, which in turn marks our inaccessibility to the essence of the things, the thing-in-itself.

---

[23] Nietzsche, 'On Truth and Lying', p. 249.

[24] *Ibid.*

[25] *Ibid.*, pp. 249–250.

[26] Cf. Heidegger's response to such a charge in Martin Heidegger *Nietzsche, Volume Three: The Will to Power as Knowledge and as Metaphysics*, ed. David Farrell Krell, trans. Joan Stambaugh, David Farrell Krell and Frank A. Capuzzi (New York: HarperCollins, 1991), pp. 39–47, 101ff.

Within the ineffable horizon of the 'X', what then is Nietzsche saying? The concept, like the metaphor, is, if not a false step, then a kind of dissimulation which is no more in relation to the thing-in-itself than any mask is to the one who wears it. Concepts, and their corresponding taxonomies, are 'anthropomorphic', in that they remain determined by the human subject who is creating them, and mediate through that subject, but do not reside as innate qualities of the object itself. The same could be said for metaphors and indeed metaphysics, which always, as Plato found, must resort to 'originals' and 'original forms', to the absolute 'proper' as opposed to the figurative, in order to justify its existence, its transpositional 'meta-' prefix notwithstanding. Such anthropomorphism then does not get anyone closer to the object itself, to an agreement of knowledge with its object, as Kant would want, but keeps one's feet stuck in the human muck and mire of individuality, uniqueness, difference and dissimilarity. If one is going to parade out truth as a concept, it must be done as dissimulation – the dissimulation that asks us to take one thing for something else. Or as Baudrillard defines it, with an emphasis on the negative prefix: that pretends not to have something which it in fact does have – for example, difference.[27] Like language.

And so we come to the well-known passage, Nietzsche's famous question, and his more famous answer:

> What is truth? a mobile army of metaphors, metonyms, anthropomorphisms, in short, a sum of human relations which were poetically and rhetorically heightened, transferred, and adorned, and after long use seem solid, canonical, and binding to a nation. Truths are illusions about which it has been forgotten that they *are* illusions, worn-out metaphors without sensory impact, coins which have lost their image and now can be used only as metal, and no longer as coins.[28]

This definition, equally celebrated and feared – a credal statement for post-structuralists, and indicting evidence for both materialists and idealists – has now had a long day in the sun. Truth is here reduced to human construction, to human relations, and to the manipulations of language. But let us keep in mind that these 'human relations', far from being accidental, casual, or even perfunctory, are for Nietzsche the results of poetry and rhetoric, of an aesthetic heightening and adorning. Granted, the summation of this heightening is illusion, but not illusion in the sense of hallucination; truth is not *not there*, even though we think we see it. Rather, it is there as artistic illusion, in the same sense of an art that deliberately deceives its audience into believing willingly that what they are watching is 'real'. Great art, at its most heightened moments, has always made us forget this very *willingness*, the willingness to suspend disbelief, to be credulous, to let our wills be overcome by dissimulation and make-believe. So truth as illusion is in part about forgetting, forgetting that we have turned the figurative into the proper, forgetting, as Ricoeur says, the entropic nature of language that wears down our metaphors

---

[27] Jean Baudrillard, *Simulacra and Simulation*, trans. Sheila Faria Glaser (Ann Arbor: University of Michigan Press, 1994), p. 3. Baudrillard's definition of 'simulation' is conversely a feigning 'to have what one doesn't have'.

[28] Nietzsche, 'On Truth and Lying', p. 250.

into something fixed and canonical, forgetting that what we want to fix as outside our human capacity is only ever, in that very human want and desire, anthropomorphic at its source. This is a lesson Freud will reiterate not long after Nietzsche, even as Nietzsche here anticipates Freud uncannily: 'Now, of course, man forgets that this is his situation; so he lies in the designated manner unconsciously and according to centuries-old habits – and precisely *by his unconsciousness*, by his forgetting, he arrives at his sense of truth' (Nietzsche's own italics).[29] But as much as this illusory nature within our forgetting can be turned against us, in making truths that are binding upon (and against) our own better nature (Freud), it can be turned in our favor, in the conscious artistry of the imagination (Kant). That is, truth as illusion, even as worn-out metaphor, need not hinder us, or project us towards an all-encompassing nihilism (even of the Nietzschean sort). If the coin has lost its image, there still remains the metal, on which a new image can be engraved. In this economy of truth, our old coinage is never without worth, even if it can no longer trade on the worth of the initial minting. Unlike the paper which replaced it, this coined metal still has value, even if a yet-to-be-determined value. This unrealized value is the 'extra-moral' value of Nietzsche's title to his essay, and it is also part of the economy of art.

No reader of Nietzsche has been more perspicacious in regard to the artistic notions of truth as illusion than Heidegger, just as Heidegger was in his regard to Kant's Transcendental Deductions. In his four volumes of lectures on Nietzsche delivered between 1936 and 1940, which analyze Nietzsche's last writings, especially *The Will to Power*, and not his early writing as we have just been discussing, Heidegger examines the complex relationship for the later Nietzsche of art with truth. In Volume I, 'The Will to Power as Art', Heidegger distills from *The Will to Power* five statements on art:

1. 'Art is the most perspicuous and familiar configuration of will to power.'
2. 'Art must be grasped in terms of the artist.'
3. 'According to the expanded concept of artist, art is the basic occurrence of all beings; to the extent that they are, beings are self-creating, created.'
4. 'Art is the distinctive countermovement to nihilism.'
5. 'Art is worth more than "the truth".'[30]

Each of these statements, and how they were arrived at, are worth detailed analysis. But it is the last statement which begins to qualify the idea of truth as illusion, and begs the question most immediate for us now: what does it mean for art to be worth more than truth? And this question of course begs a further question central to our concerns, the question that Heidegger himself sees as pivotal, and on which he spends much of his subsequent thought extrapolating in his lectures: what is truth? In a later section of the same volume, Heidegger looks at what seemed for Nietzsche a 'raging discordance between truth and art', only to suggest that Nietzsche's notion of truth needs much qualification (hence the inverted commas in

[29] *Ibid.*

[30] Martin Heidegger, *Nietzsche, Volume One: The Will to Power as Art*, ed. and trans. David Farrell Krell (New York: HarperCollins, 1991), pp. 69–76.

the fifth statement above).[31] After an extended analysis of Plato's view of art, and its segregation from 'truth', Heidegger shows that Nietzsche rejects the Platonic understanding of truth as supersensuous, and reinterprets the 'true world' as constituted exclusively by the sensuous world, making its once 'apparent' nature now the most real of the 'true' (in a similar way that Romanticism suggests). Heidegger writes in the final section of the first volume: 'The sensuous is no longer the "apparent", no longer the penumbra; it alone is what is real, hence "true". And what becomes of semblance? Semblance itself is proper to the essence of the real.'[32] The old semblance that Plato had categorically invalidated is now raised to a new valuation. It is first raised by Nietzsche: ' "Semblance" as I understand it is the actual and sole reality of things ... Hence I do not posit "semblance" in opposition to "reality", but on the contrary take semblance to be the reality which resists transformation into an imaginative "world of truth". A particular name for that reality would be "will to power", designated of course intrinsically and not on the basis of its ungraspable, fluid, Protean nature'. Heidegger himself then offers a distinct, unmistakably individual reading of Nietzsche's valuation: 'That [Nietzsche's first sentence on 'semblance' just quoted] should be understood to mean not that reality is something apparent, but that the being-real is in itself perspectival, a bringing forward into appearance, a letting radiate; that it is in itself a shining. Reality is radiance.'[33] If art is worth more than truth, it is worth more than that truth which is posited *contra* semblance. Under Nietzsche's elevated idea of semblance as 'the actual and sole reality of things', anyone who wants to counter semblance in the name of truth must do so with self-deception, that is, must deceive oneself that semblance can be overcome in the appeal to an original, supersensuous 'real'. Art retains greater 'worth' first because art's understanding of truth includes semblance, not opposes it, and secondly because art at least admits that its own imaginative powers are involved, even necessitated, in any such appeal to something 'real' outside of semblance. Art admits to creating, and not discovering, a 'world of truth'.

This strange marriage of truth and semblance becomes confusing, to say the least. If semblance is now the 'actual' reality of things, how does Nietzsche define 'actual' here? Does this term not denote some sense of correspondence with a reality, where reality is some fixable notion, some fixation that we can determine? If the actual corresponds with a fixed entity, how can it in any way be called semblance, a term defined against fixation, by virtue of its dissimulative and apparitional properties? Heidegger gets around this confusion by saying that semblance itself can be 'fixed', that is, can be situated amid a bringing or shining forth (*Schein* – which can also be rendered 'illusion'). This is a brilliantly fanciful interpretation of the matter, which presages Heidegger's own illustrious fixation upon art in his later thought. Rather than understand reality as a fixed ontological entity, a being in the strictly nominal sense of the word, Heidegger revises the notion as a 'fixed' or situated becoming, a being in the more verbal sense of the

---

[31] *Ibid.*, pp. 142–150.
[32] *Ibid.*, p. 213.
[33] *Ibid.*, p. 215.

word. Thus his use of Nietzsche's term 'perspectival', which retains the sense of 'apparition' or the 'apparent' (*Schein*), but adds the sense of situating with the eye, or furnishing the bearings, so that something can come into a field of view. 'Reality is radiance', he says – a letting or emitting of being through perspective.

> Reality, Being, is *Schein* in the sense of perspectival letting-shine. But proper to that reality at the same time is the multiplicity of perspectives, and thus the possibility of illusion and of its being made fast [fixed], which means the possibility of truth as a kind of *Schein* in the sense of 'mere' appearance. If truth is to be taken as semblance, that is, as mere appearance and error, the implication is that truth is the fixed semblance which is necessarily inherent in perspectival shining – it is illusion.[34]

To this illusory truth as fixed semblance, the notion of art is then compared in a culminating passage:

> Life is in itself perspectival. It waxes and flourishes with the height and heightening of the world which is brought forward perspectivally to appearance, with the enhancement of the shining, that is, of what brings a thing to scintillate in such a way that life is transfigured. 'Art is nothing but art!' (WM [*The Will to Power*], 853, section II). Art induces reality, which is in itself a shining, to shine most profoundly and supremely in scintillating transfiguration. If 'metaphysical' means nothing else than the essence of reality, and if it consists in shining, we then understand the statement with which the section on art in *The Will to Power* closes (WM, 853): '... "art as the proper task of life, art as its *metaphysical* activity ... ."' Art is the most genuine and profound will to semblance, namely, to the scintillation of what transfigures, in which the supreme lawfulness of Dasein becomes visible. In contrast, truth is any given fixed apparition that allows life to rest firmly on a particular perspective and to preserve itself. As such fixation, 'truth' is an immobilizing of life, and hence its inhibition and dissolution. 'We have *art* so that we *do not perish from the truth*' (WM, 822). It is '*not possible ... to live with the truth,*' if life is always enhancement of life; the 'will to truth', i.e., to fixed apparition, is 'already a symptom of degeneration' (XIV, 368). Now it becomes clear what the fifth and concluding proposition concerning art avers: *art is worth more than truth*.

Heidegger then adds:

> Both art and truth are modes of perspectival shining. But the value of the real is measured according to how it satisfies the essence of reality, how it accomplishes the shining and enhances reality. *Art, as transfiguration, is more enhancing to life than truth, as fixation of an apparition.*[35]

Heidegger's reading of Nietzsche here attempts to rescue the statement 'truth is illusion' from the wilderness of pure nihilism or pure absurdity, and allow it to

---

[34] *Ibid.*

[35] *Ibid.*, pp. 216–217. The referencing of *Will to Power* here follows both the English version ('WM', followed by the aphorism number, not the page number), and a German version drawn from the multi-volume *Grossoktavausgabe* (Leipzig, 1905ff.) which Heidegger had used (Volume number in Roman numerals followed by the page number – XIV, 368, for example). See 'Editor's Preface' in *Nietzsche, Volume One*, p. xxxii.

contribute to a positive reappropriation of both terms in the equation, 'truth' and 'illusion', so that 'truth' becomes something more than a correspondence theory, and 'illusion' becomes something more than a mocking play of apparitions. If truth fixates an apparition, or fixates the apparent, then art transfigures that apparent fixation, and allows it to appear in or through a becoming radiance, or, looked at another way, in or through a radiance of becoming. This radiance, in opposing a stasis of fixity, 'enhances'; it 'scintillates'; it mobilizes. Art revivifies the dead metaphor, the erased image, the faceless face on the worn coin. It marks the metal, finding a new image, and a new value, within the shining surface of an old symbol for exchange. Art is semblance now in the sense by which image and likeness gain new stature: almost with an iconographic splendor, though without the necessary duality of sensuousness and supersensuousness inherent in the *eikon*, semblance 'images', through transfiguration, the life-giving force of the object, the 'fundamental occurrence of beings'.[36] Hence Heidegger talks about a 'will to semblance', quoting Nietzsche, a will that operates purely on the sensuous level, but a sensuousness that concerns life not in terms of being but of becoming. For this life as becoming, art and truth are both required. 'Art and truth are both necessary for reality.' But, as 'equally necessary they stand in severance.'[37] Art is *worth more than* truth. Even as art necessitates truth, truth as illusion.

Heidegger's own philosophical and ontological enterprise shines forth from these Nietzschean reflections with, some might say, its own blinding effulgence. It rescues from a seemingly useless paradox – the supreme paradox of 'truth as illusion' – an existential program which, in light of Nietzsche's own indeterminate 'will to power', may seem over-determined. But let us keep in mind the perspectival emphasis with which Heidegger reads this later Nietzsche, an emphasis which we will see worked out in Heidegger's later 'Origin of the Work of Art' (with its reworked notion of sensuousness in the *Ursprung*), but which, in revealing the ocular aspect to thinking and thought, remains consonant with Nietzsche's 'biologism'. Here the perspectival position allows us to state at least this much: just as Kant's first Transcendental Deduction gave new authority to imagination (before it retreated to the safety of a rationalism), so too *the perspective with which truth can be grasped is a perspective that gives new authority to semblance*. For in this 'perspectival' resides the two opposing but necessary sides of truth and art that come together in semblance. On the one hand there is truth as 'fixed' perspective, a perspective that is not only fixated but that also 'fixes' (let us keep in mind all the semantic possibilities of the verb 'to fix') something to be something other (an apparition, a dissembling) than what it is in itself, while on the other hand there is art as the 'will to semblance', which sets up perspective on a matter, deliberately and with technical acumen, just as painters set up perspective (whether visual, geometrical, pictorial or emotional perspective) from which to render a scene on their canvas. Semblance as 'perspectival' restores the 'sight' to insight (the sensuousness to the supersensuousness, the stimulus to the concept), just as it brings assembling, dissembling and resembling fully to bear on

---

[36] *Ibid.*, p. 219.
[37] *Ibid.*, p. 217.

sight. Semblance 'sees through', we could say, the assemblage and dissemblage we call metaphor. It remembers or un-forgets what was forgotten. It re-members what was severed – the proper and the figurative, truth and art.

We could compare now a passage from Nietzsche's *The Will to Power*, in which the notion of truth as illusion figures:

> This perspective world, this world for the eye, tongue, and ear, is very false, even if compared for [sic] a very much more subtle sense-apparatus. But its intelligibility, comprehensibility, practicability, and beauty begin to cease if we refine our senses; just as beauty ceases when we think about historical processes; the order of purpose is already an illusion. It suffices that the more superficially and coarsely it is conceived, the more valuable, definite, beautiful, and significant the world appears. The deeper one looks, the more our valuations disappear – meaninglessness approaches! We have *created* the world that possesses values! Knowing this, we know, too, that reverence for truth is already the consequence of an illusion – and that one should value more than truth the force that forms, simplifies, shapes, invents.
>
> 'Everything is false! Everything is permitted!'
>
> Only with a certain obtuseness of vision, a will to simplicity, does the beautiful, the 'valuable' appear: in itself, I know not what.[38]

The 'force that forms, simplifies, shapes, invents' is of course the force of art, and this force is what allows art to be valued more than truth. This force is now something much more primordial, more existential, than simply the art of specific techniques and genres, the art as τέχνη (*techne*) in the Greek sense of a skill. Art, in its own transfiguring capacity, is transformed into a determining force that works its way, by means of semblance, to the very heart of truth, reality, and indeed existence. In Volume III of the Nietzsche lectures, 'The Will to Power as Knowledge and as Metaphysics', Heidegger comments on this very passage, as he returns once more to Nietzsche's valuation of truth as it relates to art. He restates:

> Art alone guarantees and secures life perspectivally in its vitality, that is, in the possibilities of its enhancement, against the power of truth. Hence Nietzsche's statement: 'We have *art* in order *not to perish from the truth*' (WM, 822, 1888). Art is a higher 'value', that is, a more primordial perspectival condition of 'life', than truth. Here art is conceived *metaphysically* as a condition of beings, not merely aesthetically as pleasure, not merely biologically and anthropologically as an expression of life and of humanity, and not merely politically as proof of a position of power. All these interpretations of art that have appeared in the metaphysical history of the West are themselves but essential consequences of the metaphysical definition that Nietzsche utters and that is already prefigured in metaphysical thinking from the very beginning (cf. Aristotle's *Poetics*). Art stands in metaphysical opposition to truth as illusion.[39]

---

38 Nietzsche, *The Will to Power*, '602 (1884)', p. 326.

39 Heidegger, *Nietzsche, Volume Three*, p. 25. Cf. also the previous two paragraphs (pp. 24–25): 'In a note from the year 1884, when the formation of the thought of will to power consciously begins, Nietzsche remarks "that honoring truth is already the *consequence* of an *illusion*" (WM [*The Will to Power*], "602 [1884]"). What does this say? Nothing less than truth itself is an illusion, a mirage; for only if that is true can *honoring* truth be the *consequence* of an "illusion". Yet if a will to truth is vital to our "life", and if life is *enhancement* of life, the ever higher "realization" of life and thus the vitalizing

By 'metaphysical definition' or 'metaphysical opposition' Heidegger does not return us back to a supersensuous understanding of the Platonic kind, though he does link it back to such roots, via Aristotle. The phrase we must highlight here is rather 'a condition of beings', by which Heidegger means something more akin to an existential condition. Art here is not mere aesthetics or cultural/political expression; it is a life-enhancement that operates at the very structure of one's being.

> When Nietzsche speaks *here* of *art*, that is, with a view to thinking beings as a whole metaphysically, he means *not only* art in the narrower sense of familiar genres of art. Art is the name for every form of transfiguring and viable transposition of life to higher possibilities; in this sense, philosophy too is 'art'.[40]

So we see that art has become a 'transposition of life', a fundamental changing of the position or positionality of one's condition into 'higher possibilities'. Art, as Heidegger will phrase it, is about the Becoming of Being, 'a *harmony* with what becomes and its possibilities'.[41] In a critique of Kant's notion of truth, Heidegger through Nietzsche (or Nietzsche through Heidegger) has replaced the understanding of harmony of knowledge with its object with a harmony of being with its becoming. This becomes the 'will to semblance', or the will to art. Heidegger had summed this up earlier by quoting Nietzsche himself:

> But because in Nietzsche's view semblance, as perspectival, also possesses the character of the nonfactual, of illusion, of deception, he must say, 'The will to *semblance*, to illusion, to deception, to Becoming and change is deeper, more 'metaphysical' [that is to say, corresponding more to the essence of Being[42]] than the will to *truth*, to actuality, to Being (XIV, 369). This is expressed even more decisively in *The Will to Power*, no. 853, section I, where semblance is equated with 'lie': '*We need the lie* in order to achieve victory over this reality, this 'truth', which is to say, in order to *live* .... That the lie is necessary for life is itself part and parcel of the frightful and questionable character of existence.'[43]

---

of what is real, and if truth is only "illusion", "imagination", thus something unreal, truth becomes a *de-realization*, a hindrance to and even a destruction of life. Truth is then not a condition of life, not a value, but an unvalue.

But what if all barriers between truth and untruth fall and everything is of equal value, which is to say, of no value? Then nihilism becomes reality. Does Nietzsche want nihilism or does he precisely want to recognize it as such and overcome it? He wants to overcome it. If, accordingly, the will to truth belongs to life, then truth, since its essence is illusion, *cannot* be the *highest* value. There must be a value, a condition of perspectival life-enhancement, that is of a greater value than truth. Indeed Nietzsche does say "that art is *worth more* than truth" (WM, 853, IV; from 1887–88).'

[40] *Ibid.*, p. 123.

[41] *Ibid.*, p. 127.

[42] This is Heidegger's editorial insertion, which, it has to be said, is not particularly helpful, as without great qualification concerning the phrase 'essence of Being', it appears as if he is returning us back precisely to a correspondence theory of truth. We might better qualify: that is to say, the will to semblance out-metaphysicalizes 'metaphysics' in the traditional sense, in bringing us closer to the very condition(s) for existence and becoming of Being.

[43] *Nietzsche, Volume One*, p. 217.

Let us now return to the earlier Nietzsche of our 1873 essay on truth and lying in an extra-moral sense. He has told us that 'Truths are illusions about which it has been forgotten that they *are* illusions', and we now have a better sense of what this illusive quality might entail, even if it is only in seminal form at this early stage of Nietzsche's thinking. He admits here that we 'still do not know where the desire for truth originates', and Heidegger has helped us to see that Nietzsche later finds a desire for truth originating in the necessary 'fixation' that truth must bring, even to the illusory apparitions. But the early Nietzsche shows us that, at the very least, we can discern an 'obligation which society, in order to exist, imposes: to be truthful, i.e., to use the customary metaphors, or in moral terms, the obligation to lie according to an established convention, to lie collectively in a style that is mandatory for everyone.' This kind of lying is described at this early stage in pathological terms, in a passage we have already quoted: 'Now, of course, man forgets that this is his situation; so he lies in the designated manner unconsciously and according to centuries-old habit – and precisely *by this unconsciousness*, by his forgetting, he arrives at his sense of truth.'[44] But we have just seen above that lying will become a necessary weapon against a devitalizing 'truth', a lying that is no longer dictated by a 'designated manner', and a lying that is fully conscious of itself as lying. Let us continue the quote in *The Will to Power*, '853', that Heidegger referred to just above:

> 'Life *ought* to inspire confidence': the task thus imposed is tremendous. To solve it, man must be a liar by nature, he must be above all an *artist*. And he *is* one: metaphysics, religion, morality, science – all of them only products of his will to art, to lie, to flight from 'truth', to *negation* of 'truth'. This ability itself, thanks to which he violates reality by means of lies, this artistic ability of man *par excellence* – he has it in common with everything that is. He himself is after all a piece of reality, truth, nature: how should he not also be a piece of *genius in lying*![45]

This passage, written more than thirteen years after 'On Truth and Lying in an Extra-Moral Sense', is what becomes of Nietzsche's extra-moral lying: it becomes party to semblance, in the best sense (or valuation) of the word – the *genius* of semblance. But we can see this semblance emerging even in the pathological forgetting which characterizes the earlier critique: 'Only by forgetting that primitive metaphor-world ... only by the invincible belief that *this* sun, *this* window, *this* table is a truth-in-itself, in short, only insofar as man forgets himself as a subject, indeed as an *artistically creative* subject, does he live with some calm, security, and consistency.'[46] And of course such calm, security and consistency are only illusions, semblances in the worst sense or valuation of the word – the *self-deception* of semblance.

We must remember that Nietzsche's critique of the metaphorical and conceptual in this essay is not only a critique of Platonism, which is turned on its head, but a critique of Kantianism, which, if not turned on its head, is painfully

[44] Nietzsche, 'On Truth and Lying, p. 250.

[45] Nietzsche, *The Will to Power*, pp. 451–452, probably written around 1886.

[46] Nietzsche, 'On Truth and Lying, p. 252, Nietzsche's own italics.

contorted. Kant's presumption of subject and object, and of the need to bridge the gap that separates the two, even if that bridge becomes a thoroughgoing anthropomorphic reason [*Vernunft*], is not discarded by Nietzsche, but is called back to the original deduction of Kant in which imagination played a central role. Here however, for Nietzsche, the anthropomorphisms do not rely on reason, but on semblance, on *artistic* semblance. The 'adequate expression of an object in a subject' he calls 'a self-contradictory absurdity': 'For between two absolutely different spheres such as subject and object, there can be no expression, but at most an *aesthetic* stance, I mean an allusive transference, a stammering translation into a completely foreign medium. For this, however, in any case a freely fictionalizing and freely inventive middle sphere and middle faculty is necessary.' So he acknowledges both the Kantian move for a middle term, as well as the need for that term. But he refuses Kant's terminology in the very next sentence: 'The word 'appearance' contains many seductions; and so I avoid it as much as possible. For it is not true that the essence of things appears in the empirical world.'[47] Of course, Kant would not say the essence *appears* in the empirical world or in empirical intuition either, if by 'essence' we mean the thing-in-itself.[48] So Kant and Nietzsche are not divided on this point.[49] But Nietzsche does take exception to the idealism which claims that in moving from the empirical to the rational, in drawing out concepts from appearances (a new kind of 'saving the appearances', we might say), a reliable and coherent unity is formed within our judging faculties by which 'reality' becomes known to us. For such a unity is only ever metaphorical in nature, since it must equate objects that are dissimilar, or that, if they *are* similar in and of themselves, we could never possibly *know* as similar. And when such equating solidifies through habit and over time, when one forgets that the metaphor is a metaphor, we call the equation 'necessary', and therefore 'real' in the fixed and constant sense. 'Certainly,' responds Nietzsche, 'every person who is familiar with such meditations has a deep distrust for that sort of idealism, as often as he has very clearly convinced himself of the eternal coherence, omnipresence, and infallibility of the laws of nature.'[50] Even Kant's time and space perceptions do not escape this kind of (self-)illusion. In sum then, what Nietzsche asks us to acknowledge is the sheer contingency of all the self-made structures we call reality, a contingency from which we cannot escape, nor which we can ignore ('because that would amount to ignoring man himself'), but for which we ought to seek 'a new province for its activities and a different riverbed'.[51] It is such a 'new province' that Nietzsche,

---

[47] *Ibid.*

[48] 'As appearances, they cannot exist in themselves, but only in us. What objects may be in themselves, and apart from all this receptivity of our sensibility, remains completely unknown to us.' Kant, *Critique of Pure Reason*, p. 82 (A 42, B 59).

[49] For further elaboration and qualification of this claim, see Nietzsche, *The Will to Power*, Book Three, I, p. 9 – 'Thing-in-Itself and Appearance', pp. 300–307; Heidegger, *Nietzsche, Volume Three*, p. 9 'Tracing the Opposition of the "True and Apparent Worlds" Back to Relations of Value', pp. 57-63; and 19 – 'Truth and the Distinction Between "True and Apparent Worlds" ', pp. 123–130.

[50] Nietzsche, 'On Truth and Lying, p. 253.

[51] *Ibid.*, p. 254.

in all his work, both early, middle, and, as Heidegger's lectures show us, very late, has sought out consistently and radically.

Where is this new province? Nietzsche has pointed the way in the last short section of 'On Truth and Lying in an Extra-Moral Sense'. The new province is 'in *myth* and in *art*', he says, as we would expect him to.[52] And, also expectedly, he points to the ancient Greeks as the one great culture who, excepting Plato, was 'conscious' about the lie – the 'waking day of a mythically excited nation' that is more like a dream:

> When any tree may begin anytime to speak as a nymph, or a god in the guise of a bull can abduct a maiden, when the goddess Athena herself is suddenly seen driving through the marketplaces of Athens on a beautiful team of horse in the company of Pisistratus – as the honest Athenian believed – then at any moment, as in a dream, anything is possible, and all nature crowds around man as if it were only the masquerade of the gods, who only make a joke of deceiving man in all forms.[53]

Here is life as illusion, truth as illusion, humans allowing themselves to be deceived consciously and wittingly. The goal is to be deceived 'without harm', innocently, yet knowingly, like the Maenads of the Bacchic cult. What is the harm? The harm, the prohibition, is here also against knowing good and evil, but now 'good and evil', 'truth and lying', as constructs within the conceptual framework of a strict and binding morality, an 'enormous structure of beams and boards of the concepts, to which the poor man clings for dear life'. When the 'liberated intellect' turns from this kind of harm, as did the ancient Greeks in their art and mythology (and the two were never separated), the structure and framework become 'just a scaffolding and a plaything for his boldest artifices. And when he smashes it apart, scattering it, and then ironically puts it together again, joining the most remote and separating what is closest, he reveals that he does not need the emergency aid of poverty, and that he is now guided not by concepts but by intuitions.'[54] Kant is turned topsy-turvy. Intuitions guide us, not reason. And these intuitions guide us not towards abstractions but toward creativity, towards the rebuilding and reconfiguring of smashed illusions.

They guide us, ultimately, towards the stage, towards the place of acting with masks. Acting is fundamentally intuitive, but its intuition is characterized by dissimulation. Intuition is dissimulated – the sensible is paraded as something other than what it is – as the actor simulates. This is the role of the mask, as it covers up the emoting, intuitive self. Dionysus and Apollo come together, as in *The Birth of Tragedy*, and as late as *The Will to Power*:

> *Apollo's* deception: the *eternity* of beautiful form; the aristocratic legislation, *'thus shall it be for ever!'*

[52] *Ibid.*

[53] *Ibid.*, p. 255.

[54] *Ibid.*

Dionysus: sensuality and cruelty. Transitoriness could be interpreted as enjoyment of productive and destructive force, as *continual creation*.[55]

For what is this mobile army of metaphors if not truth parading about, now unconsciously, now self-consciously, in costumes and masks, with the mask as Apollo's eternal form (beauty, legislation, understanding, concept, reason) through which the productive and destructive force of Dionysus (sensuality, cruelty, transitoriness, intuition) issues forth (*scheinen*)? This is the truth of theater, and the theater of truth. Truth here must be theatrical, as it is the will to semblance and the will to art.

[55] Nietzsche, *The Will to Power*, '1049 (1885-1886)', p. 539. See also the following sections, '1050–1052', which culminate in the famous reworked phrase from *Ecce Homo* which opens '1052 (March-June 1888)': '*The two types: Dionysus and the Crucified*'.

6 Kundera

1

The Czech novelist Milan Kundera writes: 'By his refusal of systems, Nietzsche brought deep changes to the way philosophy is done: as Hannah Arendt defined it, Nietzsche's thought is *experimental thought*. His first impulse is to break up whatever is rigid, to undermine commonly accepted systems, to open rifts for venturing into the unknown; the philosopher of the future will be an *experimenter*, Nietzsche said; free to go off in various directions that could, conceivably, come into conflict.'[1]

2

Kundera again: 'Nietzsche's refusal of systematic thought has another consequence: an immense *broadening of theme*; the barriers between various philosophical disciplines, which have kept the real world from being seen in its full range, are fallen, and from then on everything human can become the object of a philosopher's thought. That too brings philosophy nearer to the novel: for the first time philosophy is pondering not epistemology, not aesthetics or ethics, the phenomenology of mind or the critique of reason, etc., but *everything human*.'[2]

3

In his own work Kundera is clearly, self-admittedly, influenced by Nietzsche's approach. His writing style is neither rigid nor imposed upon by a system; his novels experiment, are broad in theme, go in various directions. And yet they philosophize. Amid the unfolding stories of his narrative, the author stops to ponder, to ruminate, to investigate large themes, themes with wide variety, ranging from kitsch to immortality. Such philosophical commentary never disguises itself as speculation within a particular character's consciousness. It does not slip in between action or dialogue or description. It is often its own chapter, written as a singular task. And it announces itself for what it is, a step back from the story, an authorial intrusion, a philosophical interlude that breaks completely, or at least ostensibly, from the action, from the 'plot', to consider the wider implications of a particular notion, a social construct, an ideology, or even a religious concept. It is a deliberate disruption of the novelistic convention, a contravention of the tacit agreement with the reader that narrative will simply 'tell the story'. The author turns around, faces his reader, and says, 'Now consider this complex phenomenon, consider this philosophical point, but consider it my way for a moment.' And we are struck by this audacity.

---

[1] Milan Kundera, 'Works and Spiders', in *Testaments Betrayed*, trans. Linda Asher (New York: HarperCollins, 1995), p. 174.

[2] *Ibid.*, p. 175.

4

The reason Kundera's philosophical point of view excites our interest is because, despite the intrusion, Kundera's philosophizing is never outside the *context* of his story. It always arises from the details of the narrative he is creating. It is always one with his characters' lives, with their world, with the words they speak and the thoughts they think, even if it is he, Kundera, who does the philosophizing, and not his characters. It is a philosophizing that is always *existential*, but in the most uncategorical sense of the term, that is, in a manner which does not hold to some philosophical program or abstruse intellectual edifice, but which understands philosophy as *doing*. This is an author who puts philosophical concepts into his titles – *Being*, *Identity*, *Immortality* – in order to show philosophy as bound to narrative, as part of a storied history. Thus when, for example, he talks about immortality, it is never as an abstraction, never as pure theory, but in relation to particular lives: in this case, the lives of his own invention, his characters in *Immortality*, but also the historical and artistic life of a particular artist, Goethe, who, by all accounts, thought long and hard about immortality. 'Immortality. Goethe was not afraid of the word.'[3]

5

In an essay about his compatriot Franz Kafka, Kundera writes about the term 'Kafkan': 'This term, drawn from an artist's work, determined solely by a novelist's images, stands as the only common denominator in situations (literary or real) that no other word allows us to grasp and to which neither political nor social nor psychological theory gives us any key.'[4] The more English cognate 'Kafkaesque' is now an entry in English dictionaries. And even those unfamiliar with Kafka's novels and stories have a sense of what this term refers to: the nightmarish quality of a world where dream and reality are indistinguishable, and where the invisible hand of an oppressive Force chokes off the air that one has been accustomed (even taught) to draw upon for individual identity and rational self-estimation. Kundera admires in particular the wholly unique nature of Kafka's philosophical and literary sensibility, as it captures more powerfully than any other medium or any other experience the modern predicament and paradox of living in an Enlightenment age benighted by its own ultraviolet glare. The term 'Kafkan' also brings the 'literary' and the 'real' together, as this 'real' found in our actual experience of Enlightenment (and post-Enlightenment) can be described now *only* by a 'literary' reference. It is premature to suggest that a similar term or neologism might be used in regard to Kundera – 'Kunderan' or 'Kunderaesque'. Kundera's sensibility and world have not yet reached, nor may never reach, the radically visionary power of the earlier Czech writer to whom he owes such a great deal:

---

[3] Milan Kundera, *Immortality*, trans. Peter Kussi (London: Faber and Faber, 1991), p. 54.

[4] Milan Kundera, 'Somewhere Behind', in *The Art of the Novel*, trans. Linda Asher (New York: HarperCollins, 1988), p. 100.

Kafka's ability to have articulated a 'reality' before it actually arrived. But Kundera is one of the first writers to give voice to a new kind of literary language, one that is still literary in the traditional understanding of 'literature', but one that transgresses the traditional boundaries of what a novel is supposed to offer, and that is unafraid to 'philosophize' as a matter of course. This is not to suggest that Kundera is the first to philosophize through the novel, nor even through literature in general. We know that, in the West, Parmenides began this tradition. And Plato, arguably, perfected it – if to his own chagrin. Dante, Voltaire, Hölderlin, Borges, the French Existentialists – there are plenty of examples to be had, and plenty within the subcategory of the 'philosophical novel' alone, including such recent and more popular novelists as Robert Pirsig and Jostein Gaarder. The marriage of literature with the grand ideas of philosophical speculation is not what distinguishes Kundera's work as unique. It is rather his vision of what literature and what philosophy must *do* that places Kundera in a separate field. Both literature and philosophy must concern existence, the problem of existence. This existence must be understood within a contextualized form, and Kundera invokes both Husserl (*die Lebenswelt*) and Husserl's pupil Heidegger (*in-der-Welt-sein*) to situate this form philosophically,[5] while his novels themselves situate this form aesthetically. But existence for Kundera is never about aesthetics or about philosophy *per se*; existence is about life, which assuredly contains both aesthetics and philosophy within its sphere, but which itself, fundamentally, is situated elsewhere. *Life is Elsewhere*. Where is this *elsewhere*? It is where Kundera continually brings us in his writing, a place where the novel becomes something other than simply a reduction of experience. For Kundera, novels ought not to reduce; novels ought to expand, open us up to somewhere *else*.

6

Of *Life is Elsewhere*: 'I wanted to solve an esthetic problem: how to write a novel which would be a 'critique of poetry' and yet at the same time would itself be poetry'.[6] A philosophical problem as well.

7

Life is Elsewhere is a portrait of a poet as a young, lyrical man. The coming to life of a poet. The coming to death of a poet. The poet rethinking poetry. About poetry no longer in the service of some aesthetically disinterested 'beauty', but in the service of the people, of the revolutionary people, striving towards utopian ideals. Poetry and slogan conjoined: '*Power to the Imagination*', '*Dream is Reality*', '*Poetry is in the street*'. Poetry in the street – life and work once again fused. Such is the lyric, the life that becomes the work, the passion of life as the passion of work. The

[5] Kundera, *The Art of the Novel*, pp. 3–4, 35.

[6] Milan Kundera, 'Preface', in *Life is Elsewhere*, trans. Peter Kussi (London: Penguin, 1986), p. vii.

Communist creed, but the Romantic creed also. Yet *life is elsewhere*. 'Life is elsewhere' is the Surrealists' creed, or André Breton's appropriation of Rimbaud for the final statement of Breton's *Manifeste du surréalisme* (1924).[7] Rimbaud had fled poetry for life elsewhere – Africa, for instance, and gun-running with the natives. But for the Surrealists, life is yet elsewhere still, below the real, behind the real: dream is reality. Life is not the dream of an ideal, not that which we expect or hope for; life lies at the level of the sub-rational. The Surrealists felt that what they shared in common with Rimbaud was a critique of a cultured, bourgeois understanding of 'life', and the championing of another, disruptive, perhaps even violent way to reconceive the 'real' of life (and perhaps even the Lacanian 'Real' behind life). Kundera appropriates the statement 'life is elsewhere' for the title of his novel. It was not his first choice, he tells us. 'The Lyric Age' was his working title, until his publishers put up resistance.[8] He subsequently changed it to *Life is Elsewhere*, and with this change, the statement becomes perpetuated yet again, but now in a completely different register. The 'elsewhere' is not in a disruptive, dialectical opposition, even though Jaromil, the young poet of the novel, follows such a disruptive and violent course, and succumbs to the pathos of his own lyrical narcissism. The 'elsewhere', for Kundera, lies in a *mode*. It is not in a 'more real' or a 'sub-real' location, which are two elusive realms, but in a mode between realms: the mode of possibility (Aristotle) or experiment (Nietzsche) that gives exigency to the real as *existence* (Heidegger). 'A novel examines not reality but existence. And existence is not what has occurred, existence is the realm of human possibilities, everything that man can become, everything he's capable of. Novelists draw up *the map of human existence* by discovering this or that human possibility. But again, to exist means: "being-in-the-world"'.[9] This Heideggerean *being* furnishes the mode, a mode which is 'elsewhere' to some pre-given reality or prescribed locality. But, consistent with Heidegger, this mode also does not lie outside the realm of the novel as a work of art. 'The novel's sole *raison d'être* is to say what only the novel can say.'[10] Life is within the novel as (that is *qua*) elsewhere. 'The origin of the work of art is art.'[11]

8

The critique of the work of art is art. Oscar Wilde and Milan Kundera are at tea. Kundera says: 'No, friend, not the critic as artist, but the artist as critique. There is a great difference.'

---

[7] '*L'existence est ailleurs*' – André Breton, *Oeuvres complètes, I*, eds Marguerite Bonnet *et al.* (Dijon: Gallimard, 1988), p. 346. Rimbaud had actually written: '*La vraie vie est absente. Nous ne sommes pas au monde.* [The true life is absent. We are not in the world.]' – Arthur Rimbaud, *Complete Works, Selected Letters*, (Chicago: University of Chicago Press, 1966), '*Une Saison en Enfer, Délires I*', pp. 186–188.

[8] Kundera, *Life is Elsewhere*, p. v.

[9] Kundera, 'Dialogue on the Art of the Novel', in *The Art of the Novel*, p. 42.

[10] *Ibid.*, p. 36.

[11] Martin Heidegger, 'The Origin of the Work of Art', in *Poetry, Language, Thought*, trans. Albert Hofstadter (New York: Harper & Row, 1971), p. 39.

9

Immortality is a way of living elsewhere. The Greeks have always taught us this, much more than Christian theology. What Christian theology has taught is that immortality is a way of dying.

10

In *Immortality* we see Kundera's way of philosophizing-in-the-world:

> I was always fond of the American President Jimmy Carter, but I felt something approaching real love when I saw him on the television screen, jogging with a group of fellow workers, trainers and bodyguards; his forehead suddenly began to sweat, his face became distorted with pain, fellow joggers rushed to his side clutching and supporting him: it was a minor heart attack. Jogging was supposed to be an occasion for showing the nation the President's eternal youth. That's why cameramen had been invited, and it was not their fault that instead of an athlete bursting with health they had to show an ageing man with bad luck.
>
> A man longs to be immortal ...[12]

11

If lyricality is the passion of youth, and immortality the afflatus of the old, then the two come together supremely in Mann's *Lotte in Weimar* – the aged Goethe reconfronting his youthful passion, as immortalized by the modern novel.

12

The temptations of the Garden serpent: also the passion of youth and immortality. Mephisto uses these same temptations as well, except that for Faust immortality becomes a matter of allegiance.

13

In Mann's *Dr. Faustus*, immortality has only one allegiance: the work of art. The novel as a 'critique of immortality' and yet at the same time itself immortal.

[12] Kundera, *Immortality*, p. 56.

14

'And what about Werther?', asks Kundera. 'Is he sensitive and noble? Or an aggressive sentimentalist, infatuated with himself?' (We might ask the same questions of Jaromil the poet in *Life is Elsewhere*.) 'The more attentively we read a novel, the more impossible the answer, because the novel is, by definition, the ironic art: its 'truth' is concealed, undeclared, undeclarable.'[13] Yes *and* no. Truth, now, is elsewhere as well.

15

Kundera's *Immortality* and Mann's *Lotte in Weimar* share much in common – deliberately, one should think. In Mann's novel, Goethe's dalliance with a young married woman becomes the point of departure not only for the earlier writing of *Werther* but now for a later tale of the two old lovers, a recapitulation of *Werther* in modern mythical dress, where the realism (or pseudo-history) of the elderly exchange is mythologized by Mann in and through the irrepressible legacy of what happened before – not the original dalliance, of course, but its literary transposition, *Werther*. In Kundera's novel, Goethe returns again, likewise to confront an earlier passion of youth. But this time, the passion comes not as a passion of advanced years, Lotte at sixty, but as youth itself, a twenty-six year old 'child', daughter of a certain Maximiliana La Roche with whom Goethe had had yet another dalliance when he himself was twenty-three years old. The similarities between the two anecdotes, Mann's and Kundera's, are telling, but in Kundera's case the disparity of age – the 'child', La Roche's daughter, was in her mid-twenties, while Goethe was now in his sixties, with no longer 'a single tooth in his head' – makes the theme of Kundera's novel that much more salient. In Part Two of *Immortality*, subtitled itself 'Immortality', which stands in juxtaposition to a fictional narrative set up in Part One (much like Bulgakov's *The Master and Margarita*), Kundera tells us of an actual historical encounter. La Roche's daughter, Bettina Brentano, was the sister of the famous Romantic writer Clemens Brentano. She had recently married the poet Achim von Arnim. (Arnim, according to André Breton, was an important precursor to and influence upon the Surrealist movement, with its 'Life is elsewhere' decree.) Bettina visited Goethe in Weimar on several occasions between 1807 and 1811, only a few years before the widowed Charlotte Kestner. For Bettina, daughter of a woman who had once excited, however briefly, the romantic imagination of the now famous German poet, there was a natural attraction to Goethe from the outset, and in time she too desired the romantic privilege her mother once claimed. As Bettina and her husband rose within the artistic circles of nineteenth-century Germany (Bettina is famed for exchanges with Schleiermacher, Beethoven, and some say even Marx) she sought out the attention of Goethe himself. She began by visiting Goethe's mother, who lived in Bettina's own city, Frankfurt. After many successful meetings, in which Goethe's mother was all too

[13] Kundera, 'Sixty-three Words', in *The Art of the Novel*, p. 134.

willing to speak of her son and his childhood, Bettina went to Weimar and introduced herself to Goethe. Their encounters were at first paternal, as one might expect with such a gap in age. But Bettina's childish flirtation was calculating, and Goethe's old habit of womanizing was by no means beyond recrudescence, and in 1810 their dallying culminated in a moment of intimacy, when the old Goethe placed his hand on the exposed breast of this young and enterprising woman. Kundera writes: 'After their parting, the traces of that magic moment stayed with them for a long time. In the letters that followed their meeting, Goethe called her *Allerliebstes*, dearest of all. Yet this did not make him forget what was at stake, and in the very next letter he informed her that he was beginning to write his memoirs, *Poetry and Truth*, and that he needed her help: his mother was no longer among the living, and nobody else was capable of summoning up his youth. Bettina had spent much time in her presence: let her write up what the old lady had told her and send it to him!'[14] Summoning up his youth! – a fine phrase that recalls Goethe's own self-description in *Dichtung und Wahrheit*, 'to summon up his dim mental powers [*verdüsterten Seelenkräfte*]' by 'his guiding genius', that it might prompt him, 'in his capable youth, to capture and describe the recent past.' And now, in the place of his own genius, he solicits a young admirer! We might justly accuse the old romancer of seduction here. Of course Bettina obliged, but she had ulterior motives for doing so. Not love, suggests Kundera, not even seduction, but immortality. Immortality? Whose? Her own, or Goethe's? Both, perhaps. The Romantic *Zeitgeist* of the time was fulsome not only with thoughts of death (we need only think of the representative Werther) but also with seeking an aesthetics of immortality. Bettina, like those great Romantic souls around her, was seeking immortality in her own way. Or perhaps we should say, in Goethe's way. For Bettina was collecting the correspondence which she herself had maintained with Goethe in those short years: her letters expressing her boundless, loving admiration for the poet, and Goethe's letters offering a judicious but accepting reply. So as she wrote down and delivered to Goethe her conversations with his mother, to be a source for the more famous *Dichtung und Wahrheit* (Goethe actually called them his 'Confessions' to Bettina), Bettina was at the same time amassing her own memoirs, for her own (auto)biography of the great German figure. Despite subsequent estrangement, resulting from the hostile intervention of Goethe's wife Christiane, these memoirs, prolific even by Romantic standards, were published after Goethe's death (1832) as *Goethes Briefwechsel mit einem Kinde*, or *Goethe's Correspondence with a Child* (1837). They reveal to us all the foregoing exchange and involvement – Bettina's amorous fellowship with Goethe and her literary intrigue – with the passion of a confessional, in which innermost thoughts and motivations are disclosed. The popularity of these revelations soon contributed significantly to the already considerable Goethean lore. And yet, as Kundera tells us, this publication, based on verifiable (and later rediscovered) correspondence between Bettina and Goethe, had been highly doctored and romanticized by Bettina after she received posthumously, upon request, all the letters she had sent to Goethe. 'When she read them she was disappointed: her whole story with Goethe

[14] Kundera, *Immortality*, p. 72.

seemed a mere sketch, perhaps a sketch for a masterpiece but a sketch all the same, and a very imperfect one at that. It was necessary to set to work. For three years she kept correcting, rewriting, adding. Dissatisfied as she was with her own letters, those from Goethe pleased her even less. When now she reread them she was offended by their brevity, their reserve, and even, at times, their impertinence. At times he wrote to her as if he took her child-like mask literally, as if he were bestowing mildly indulgent lessons on a schoolgirl. That is why now she had to change their tone: where he called her "my dear friend" she put "my dear heart", she toned down reprimands with flattering postscripts and added sentences that acknowledged Bettina's power over the fascinated poet as his inspiring Muse.' So here we have a life being tampered with imaginatively yet again, poetry passing as history, though without the expected markers to delineate the boundary between fact and fiction. A shameless coloration, we might charge, which did not stop with Goethe's side of the conversation: 'Of course, she rewrote her own letters even more radically. No, she didn't alter the tone, the tone was just right. But she altered, for example, their dates (to erase the long pauses in their correspondence, which might deny the constancy of their passion), she discarded many unsuitable passages (for example the one in which she begged Goethe not to show her letters to anyone), she added other passages, dramatized various situations, expanded to a greater depth her views on politics, art and especially on music and Beethoven.' It was a brilliant and successful ruse, for as Kundera informs us, 'Nobody questioned the authenticity of the correspondence until 1920, when the original letters were discovered and published.'[15]

16

Amid the recognized tendency of humans to rewrite their history, we can think of the Christian Gospels, those biographies of Jesus where the personal perspectives and distinctive theologies of each Gospel writer alter an original story so as not to deny 'the constancy of their passion'. In the Christian case, however, the original versions are never available. Bulgakov, in a long tradition of regospelization (a tradition which Albert Schweitzer's scholarly *The Quest of the Historical Jesus* (1906) helps illuminate, under the drive for some historical veracity, which nevertheless yields works of pseudo-history), emphasizes for us this lack of an original record when Yeshua (Jesus) says of Matthew, his sole chronicler: 'But once I caught a glimpse of that parchment and I was horrified. I had said not a word of what was written there.'

17

What is Kundera saying in his book *Immortality*? Why is he so interested in a piece of fabricated biography concerning a young woman whom Goethe only knew

[15] *Ibid.*, pp. 82–83.

passingly late in his life? Kundera is interested in immortality, to be sure, and the way in which we try to extend our life and our reputation by corralling the vagaries of our experience within the manipulated structures of language, of memory, and of print. But there is more. Kundera returns to 'history' to show once again, as Goethe himself showed, the fusion of life and work, or of poetry and truth. But unlike Mann, there is no attempt to remythologize the encounter. Kundera does not tell us the story of Bettina von Arnim to bind us, through a reconfiguration of the past, both historical and literary, to some notion of an absolute art. He rather demythologizes the encounter. That is to say, he shows the myth of Bettina's love affair with Goethe as a myth, which is neither absolute nor binding. The life may still be in the work, the novel may still say only what a novel can say, but the story is caught up in its own mechanism as story and presented to us as such. This is precisely why Kundera chooses a figure in Goethe's life who took it upon herself to rewrite and fictionalize her own involvement with the poet, instead of choosing someone who, like Charlotte Kestner, remains always at the mercy of another artist (Goethe or Mann, for example). We might see here a clear transition from a strict modernism to a strict postmodernism in the move from Mann to Kundera, where Mann's modernism prefigures Kundera's postmodernism, or where Kundera's postmodernism reworks Mann's modernism by pushing it to its logical conclusion. For in Kundera's novel, Bettina, who never inspired a *Werther* from the great poet, writes a *Werther* herself, though she passes it off as fact. Kundera's postmodernism then both depends upon and supersedes its modernist predecessor. But a strict literary criticism cannot capture the full extent of what Kundera is doing here. For Kundera involves his own self as narrator in the equation. He relates Bettina's motivations as philosophically driven – by thoughts of immortality – yet relates them as someone consciously philosophizing not simply about immortality but about writing as immortality, not simply about the act of writing but about the relation of that act to life, not simply about the life of the character but about the life of the author, not simply about authorial reality but about authorial fiction. What complicates all these textual strata further is that he does not reserve his own authorial commentary merely for the historical/philosophical passages about Goethe, or about Beethoven, or about Rubens (Rilke, Rolland, Eluard, Hemingway), but incorporates himself into the very fabric of the fictional narrative that runs along side, and eventually interweaves with, these speculations on such great figures of the past. The entire novel begins: 'The woman might have been sixty or sixty-five. I was watching her from a deck-chair ...', and we soon learn that this 'I' is not simply an 'invented' first-person narrator. It is Kundera the novelist. Near the end of the novel the narrator is introduced to one of the characters by another character: 'He joined us at the table and Avenarius made a broad gesture in my direction: "You don't know his novels? *Life is Elsewhere*! You've got to read it! My wife claims it's outstanding!" '[16] This is the very 'novelist' who had been making personal intrusions, declarations and asseverations all along, whether within his history of Goethe or within his story concerning the fictional characters of Agnes, Paul, Professor Avenarius, and others. That his history should be about storytelling then is not surprising – Kundera the

[16] *Ibid.*, p. 374.

storyteller is de-euhemerizing the stories of Bettina the storyteller who is immortalizing Goethe the storyteller. This meta-narrativizing epitomizes Kundera's fundamental difference with Mann. It also emphasizes a different way to conceive of the interconnection between life and art. Art is less about the mythical or the real or the mythically real than it is about the *possible*, about the artist rendering for us what *might* have happened, or better what is possible to happen, between the 'facts'. So too, life is less in the mythical or in the real than it is in the space of the *possible*. But then where precisely is this space of the *possible* located? It is, as it has always been, *elsewhere*. And this *elsewhere*, as *elsewhere*, lies, as it always has, in the imagination – the imagination as elsewhere.

18

Aristotle in his *Poetics* states 'that the function of the poet is not to say what *has* happened, but to say the kind of thing that *would* happen, i.e. what is possible in accordance with probability or necessity' (1451^a).[17] Aristotle later states: 'Probable impossibilities are preferable to implausible possibilities' (1460^a).[18] The first statement shows that Aristotelian μίμησις (*mimêsis*) has little to do with strict imitation: there is always something *additive* to imitation. The second statement would suggest that imagination gets the better of the day over imitation. Indeed, as Aristotle summarizes: 'it is impossible for people to be as Zeuxis painted them, but that is an idealization of the truth; one should surpass the model' (1461^b).[19] The suggested term 'idealization' here[20] functions in a world of metaphysical certainty or possibility; the term 'imagination' functions in a world of metaphysical uncertainty or impossibility. Imagination has no choice but to surpass the model.

19

Where does one go to surpass the model when there is no universal ideal? Elsewhere. Let us call this elsewhere 'X'.

[17] Aristotle, *Poetics*, trans. Malcolm Heath (London: Penguin, 1996), p. 16.

[18] *Ibid.*, p. 41.

[19] *Ibid.*, p. 45.

[20] The original Greek meaning of the first part of Aristotle's sentence, with the opening clause 'it is impossible' (καὶ εἰ ἀδύνατον) as a later interpolation, is less than obvious: (καὶ εἰ ἀδύνατον) τοιούτους εἶναι οἷον Ζεῦξις ἔγραφεν ἀλλὰ βέλτιον· How the 'better' (βέλτιον) actually functions grammatically and syntactically here is uncertain. But the second half of the idea, that 'one should surpass the model', is unambiguous: τὸ γὰρ παράδειγμα δεῖ ὑπερέχειν. – *Aristotelis: De Arte Poetica Liber*, ed. Rudolf Kassel (Oxford: Oxford University Press, 1965), 46. The philology required for this passage, in moving from the ambiguous 'original' in the first half to the unambiguous 'rising above' (ὑπερέχειν) the 'model' or paradigm (παράδειγμα) in the second half, seems an appropriate metaphor for what we are trying to say regarding the process of imitation, with its additive nature that 'betters'.

20

In *Immortality*, Kundera refers to Aristotle's *Poetics* and its discussion about episodes. A story, however much it presents 'probable impossibilities', must be reduced to its universal form, says Aristotle; episodes are then added as mere elaboration and detail. They are not integral. But Kundera points out that universals are only ever made up of episodes – this is precisely Nietzsche's point in 'On Truth and Lying in an Extra-Moral Sense'. Kundera: 'Life is as stuffed with episodes as a mattress is with horsehair, but a poet (according to Aristotle) is not an upholsterer and must remove all stuffing from his story, even though real life consists of nothing but precisely such stuffing.' (Cf. Nietzsche's reference to leaves, to their fundamental dissimilarity with one another, and to the concept of 'leaf', which is formed by forgetting about all the dissimilarities. The mattress shell for Kundera here equals the concept.) 'For Goethe, meeting Bettina was an insignificant episode; from a quantitative viewpoint, she took up only a tiny interval of his lifetime, and moreover Goethe tried as hard as he could to prevent her from ever playing a role in his life, assiduously keeping her outside his biography. But it is precisely here that we realize the relativity of the concept of the episode, a relativity Aristotle did not think through: for nobody can guarantee that some totally episodic event may not contain within itself a power that some day could unexpectedly turn it into a cause of further events. When I say some day, it can even be after death; this was precisely Bettina's triumph, for she became part of Goethe's life story when he was no longer alive.'[21] An important phrase, 'assiduously keeping her outside his biography'. Life indeed is elsewhere.

21

Bettina von Arnim requested her letters from Goethe's executor Chancellor von Müller. The Chancellor yielded easily to the request, but with one request of his own: that he might have one or two pages of this correspondence for his own as a keepsake. In the Preface to *Goethe's Correspondence with a Child*, the English version translated by Bettina von Arnim herself, she records the Chancellor's desire: 'I shall always possess in it [the correspondence] a doubly dear memorial, as if it were a drop of your heart's blood, which had flowed as a tribute to the greatest and best of men.'[22] As Faust signed over his life with his lifeblood, so too, the Chancellor implies, Bettina has signed over her life in blood to the one whom she so admires. And like Goethe's Faust, Bettina gains in the transaction: she gains a life and a reputation she would have never enjoyed otherwise. But she does so by adding to the biography of both herself and Goethe, by surpassing the model. Her life and Goethe's life become a work of art, as Goethe had taught her. Kundera: 'A character is not a simulation of a living being. It is an imaginary being. An experimental self.'[23]

---

[21] Kundera, *Immortality*, pp. 338–339.

[22] Bettina von Arnim, *Goethe's Correspondence with a Child* (Boston: Houghton Mifflin; Cambridge: Riverside Press, 1868 [?]), p. viii.

[23] Kundera, 'Dialogue on the Art of the Novel', in *The Art of the Novel*, p. 34.

22

The Romantic interest in turning a passionate death into something larger than life began with Goethe's *Werther*. We might say it finds its apotheosis in Goethe's *Faust*, because the stakes are eternal, and Faust's eternal death is in the end transmuted into an eternal life. The transmutation of death into life is a central religious concern. Since the Romantics, the transmutation of life (the lyrical, the biographical, the sanguinary) into art is a central aesthetic concern, with religious import. Let us reiterate that this Romantic transmutation (in which death is always drawn along) does not involve imitation. It is ampliative, like Aristotle's *mimêsis*, or even, more to the point, like Kant's synthesis.

23

It is not unreasonable to say – and we have already intimated – that the striving, ambitious Bettina von Arnim endeavored to be another Lotte, before whom Goethe might throw down his now elderly life, and generate another work, another *Werther*. In Kundera's view, this ambition was driven by the complex of immortal longing, manifested in an immortal work of art. When Bettina realized no immortal work involving herself would be forthcoming from Goethe, she took matters into her own hands.[24] But her quest for immortality was not restricted to her involvement with Goethe. For she realized later that she had found her own Werther in Karoline von Günderode, a young poet and canoness with whom she developed a close relationship in the years leading up to the canoness' death in 1806, just before her friendship with Goethe. This relationship is described with distinctly lesbian ardor in a letter to Goethe's mother that makes up the first section of *Goethe's Correspondence with a Child*. Günderode's subsequent involvement with a philologist named Friedrich Creuzer seemed to have caused a breach in the friendship with Bettina, and the resulting relational turmoil eventually led to a drastic Ophelian response: Günderode plunged a knife into her bosom and died on the banks of the Rhein while still only in her twenties. This event gave way to a later work by Bettina, *Die Günderode*, or *Correspondence of Fraulein Gunderode and Bettine von Arnim* (1840), a publication similar to *Goethe's Correspondence*,

---

[24] But was no work forthcoming in fact? In 1810, the same year Bettina bared herself to Goethe, literally and not literarily, Goethe wrote a poem in the first-person called '*Das Tagbuch*' ('The Diary') about a married man who, stranded while traveling, falls prey to the beauty of an inn maiden. The man is on the verge of taking full advantage of the situation when the maiden, pure yet all-giving, succumbs to slumber at the midnight hour. With internal debate, the man remembers his diary, in which he writes nightly to his loving wife at home, and instead of giving in to the vulnerable maiden, he gives in to his diary, and writes a veiled confession to his wife, affirming his unbroken love. The act of writing here preserves fidelity. So Goethe may have understood his predicament with Bettina. But for her part, Bettina would have seen the situation in quite the reverse. The act of writing for her preserves her 'seduction'. And if Goethe believes his Bettina is actually asleep, safely removed from his own thoughts, so he may take control of the dilemma in his own power and on his own terms, Bettina will wake with a vengeance: her own 'diary', *Goethe's Correspondence with a Child.*

where letters of exchange become highly reworked and romanticized, with questionable fidelity to the original. Bettina had not only found her Werther, but in her letter to Goethe's mother she claimed to have prophesied her friend's suicide. In describing her time together with the canoness poet, she made a point of telling Goethe's mother: 'We read Werther together, and conversed much upon suicide'.[25] And later, upon certain clues from Günderode herself, her premonition was voiced directly: 'I described how she would kill herself; in a red gown, with loosened bodice, and close beneath her breast, the wound. This was called wanton wildness in me, but it was unconscious excitement, in which I described the truth, with perfect accuracy.'[26] The 'truth' here remains deeply suspicious, knowing as we do that these letters were written well after the fact, and with such embellishment that any claim of 'accuracy' with the original event loses much of its meaning. But accuracy and the 'real' is not Bettina's chief concern. This is why, as Kundera tries to tell us, she was never interested in Goethe as an object of personal love, but only as an amplification of the real, a larger than life, immortal figure. She betrays herself even in this letter describing her interactions with Günderode, when she speaks of the relation between Nature and inner beauty: 'The great and piercing eye of the spirit was arrested by an internal ray of light, (it must perforce drink it in), without being able to free itself by self-willed reflection; my friend knows well what enchantment is caused by this spell-bound gaze on a ray of light, (the spirit of color), and he knows, also, that the semblance is no semblance, but *truth itself*.'[27] Or as she speaks rapturously of visions and dreams: 'Did I open my eyes? all was gone! all was still! and I perceived no interruption, only I could no longer distinguish this so-called real world (in which other men maintain that they exist) from this world of dream or fancy ...'.[28] Kundera does not mention Günderode, and Bettina's flights of Romantic fancy concerning her. But he might well have, as the conflation of life and work here too is in the service of an immortality. The immortality of death, of self-imposed death, of a death imposed by premonition – or as the Greeks might have said, by oracle.

24

Did Pilate have any premonition that by imposing death upon his eccentric prisoner he would invoke an immortality of death? Did Judas?

25

Dream is reality. A poetic injunction that runs through Bettina von Arnim, her husband, André Breton, Kafka, Bulgakov, Mann, and Kundera. We should also

---

[25] von Arnim, *Goethe's Correspondence with a Child*, p. 51.
[26] *Ibid.*, p. 65.
[27] *Ibid.*, p. 54. (von Arnim's own italics.)
[28] *Ibid.*, pp. 54–55.

add, each in their own way, Ricoeur's 'three masters of suspicion': Marx, Nietzsche and Freud.

26

Freud would have had a model analysand in Bettina von Arnim. Of her relationship with her father, an Italian merchant, Freud would have written volumes, his insights based solely on her relationship, at once paternal and quasi-erotic, with Goethe. Dream-fulfillment played out in reality, or in the text. And yet desire plays itself out on more levels than the paternal and the erotic, as Kundera shows us, and as *Die Günderode* confirms. Desire for death – for the immortality of death. The dream for reality beyond the real. The realization of this dream within the real through death. Here Bettina, and Kundera's portrayal of her, is more Lacanian than Freudian. Let us recall some of Lacan's famously abstruse words: 'Being of non-being, that is how *I* as subject comes on the scene, conjugated with the double aporia of a true survival that is abolished by knowledge of itself, and by a discourse in which it is death that sustains existence.'[29] Or again: 'If I have said that the unconscious is the discourse of the Other (with a capital O), it is in order to indicate the beyond in which the recognition of desire is bound up with the desire for recognition.' But this is not merely Bettina's desire for Goethe's recognition, or for recognition from the public who read Goethe. It is a desire for the beyond, the elsewhere. Lacan immediately adds: 'In other words this other is the Other that even my lie invokes as a guarantor of the truth in which it subsists.' The Other as poetry invoked as truth. And immediately qualified with a point in concert with – rather, directly owing to – Nietzsche and Heidegger: 'By which we can also see that it is with the appearance of language the dimension of truth emerges.'[30] Bettina *writes* her way into the Other ... Goethe, Günderode, herself, death.

27

Freud's own Lacanian fulfillment: during the writing of *The Interpretation of Dreams*, his son Ernst reported that his father would emerge from his writing for mealtime 'as if he were sleepwalking'.[31]

28

Kundera cites the lesser known novelist Hermann Broch, with his trilogy *The Sleepwalkers* (1931), as one of his greatest influences. He sees in the trilogy a

[29] Jacques Lacan, 'Subversion of the subject and the dialectic of desire', in *Écrits: A Selection*, trans. Alan Sheridan (New York: W.W. Norton, 1977), p. 300.

[30] Lacan, 'Agency of the letter in the unconscious or reason since Freud', *Écrits*, p. 172.

[31] Steven Marcus, *Freud and the Culture of Psychoanalysis* (New York: W.W. Norton, 1984), p. 16.

prefigurement of the 'future possibilities of the novel'. It is not just the way Broch brings the past and present together ('polyhistoricism'), but the way dream and reality are brought together, fiction and fact. 'In Broch's light', he tells us, 'I read Thomas Mann's *Doctor Faustus*, a novel that examines not only the life of a composer named Adrian Leverkühn but several centuries of German music along with him. Adrian is not only a composer, he is the composer who brings the history of music to an end (his greatest work is called *The Apocalypse*). And he is not just the last composer (the author of *The Apocalypse*), he is also Faust. His gaze fixed on his country's diabolism (he wrote the novel toward the end of the Second World War), Thomas Mann ponders the contract that the mythical doctor – the incarnation of the German spirit – made with the devil. The whole history of his country suddenly looms up as the single adventure of a single character: a single Faust.'[32]

29

On the publication of *The Interpretation of Dreams*, Freud wrote of the book: 'The big problems are still unsettled. It is an intellectual hell, layer upon layer of it, with everything fitfully gleaming and pulsating; and the outline of Lucifer-Amor coming into sight at the darkest centre.'[33] Freud: in the Faustian lineage.

30

Broch's *The Sleepwalkers* is Kundera's great inspiration, but for Kundera it only hints; it does not achieve. What it hints at is what Kundera wishes to achieve: a new kind of art. He states this wish in programmatic terms: '(1) a new art of *radical divestment* (which can encompass the complexity of existence in the modern world without losing architectonic clarity); (2) a new art of *novelistic counterpoint* (which can blend philosophy, narrative, and dream into one music); (3) a new art of the *specifically novelistic essay* (which does not claim to bear an apodictic message but remains hypothetical, playful or ironic).'[34]

31

In an interview entitled 'Dialogue on the Art of Composition', which is not a transcript but an edited dialogue, and edited by Kundera himself, the interviewer says of Kundera's approach: 'You've spoken of novelistic counterpoint as uniting philosophy, narrative and dream. Let's consider dream. Oneiric narrative takes up all of Part Two of *Life is Elsewhere* . . .'. Kundera responds: 'Oneiric narrative; let's say, rather: Imagination, freed from the control of reason and from concern for

[32] Kundera, 'Notes Inspired by "The Sleepwalkers" ', in *The Art of the Novel*, p. 55.

[33] Marcus, *Freud and the Culture of Psychoanalysis*, p. 17.

[34] Kundera, 'Notes Inspired by "The Sleepwalkers" ', in *The Art of the Novel*, p. 65.

verisimilitude, ventures into landscapes inaccessible to rational thought. The dream is only the model for the sort of imagination that I consider the greatest discovery of modern art. But how can *uncontrolled* imagination be integrated into the novel, which by definition is supposed to be a *lucid* examination of existence? How can such disparate elements be united? That calls for real alchemy!'[35] The alchemy of a Faustian nature, in which Mephisto must now be seen through the imaginations of Blake and Bulgakov. And of course of Nietzsche.

32

An allegory of critique: Kundera's Goethe, now deceased and speaking with Ernest Hemingway from the 'other side', tells of a dream. 'It was my last dream, after that I had no more or else they were confused and I could no longer distinguish them from reality. Imagine a small puppet theatre. I am behind the scenes, I control the puppets and recite the text. It is a performance of *Faust*. My *Faust*. Did you know that *Faust* is at its most beautiful when performed as a puppet play? That's why I was so happy that no actors were present and I alone recited the lines, which on that day sounded more beautiful than ever before. And then I suddenly glanced at the seats and saw that the theatre was empty. That puzzled me. Where was the audience? Was my *Faust* so boring that everyone had gone home? Was I not even worth booing? Bewildered, I turned around and I was aghast: I expected them out front, and instead they were at the back of the stage, gazing at me with wide-open, inquisitive eyes. As soon as my glance met theirs, they began to applaud. And I realized that my *Faust* didn't interest them at all and that the show they wished to see was not the puppets I was leading around the stage, but me myself! Not *Faust*, but Goethe!'[36] In the allegory, critique is not the audience behind the stage. (But the audience's desire to see Goethe and not *Faust* allegorizes a perfect amalgamation of life and work.) Nor is it the puppet strings. Nor is it Goethe's realization of the situation. It is the dream itself. A critique of the critique would be Kundera's imagining of this dream.

33

Kundera on the specific word 'imagination': ' "What did you mean by the story about Tamina on the children's island?" people ask me. That tale began as a dream that fascinated me; I dreamed it later in a half-walking state [sleepwalking?], and I broadened and deepened it as I wrote it. Its meaning? If you like: an oneiric image of an infantocratic future ... However, the meaning did not precede the dream; the dream preceded the meaning. So the way to read the tale is to let the imagination carry one along. Not, above all, as a rebus to be decoded. By insisting on decoding him, the Kafkologists killed

[35] Kundera, 'Dialogue on the Art of Composition', in *The Art of the Novel*, pp. 80–81.

[36] Kundera, *Immortality*, p. 93.

Kafka.'[37] We might say the same for critique: it is not, above all, a matter of decoding. By insisting on critique as a technique (Fichtean, Marxian, literary critical, demythological, deconstructive, and so on), critical theorists have put the meaning before the dream, and killed off critique's potency.

34

Goethe: 'You never go further than when you no longer know where you are going.' As echoed by Rimbaud: 'He reaches the unknown, and when, bewildered, he ends by losing the intelligence of his visions, he has seen them.' As echoed by Freud: 'we cannot do without men with the courage to think new things before they can prove them.' As echoed by Kundera: 'And it matters little whether the preconceived truth is called revolution or dissidence, Christian faith or atheism, whether it is more justified or less justified; a poet who serves any truth other than the truth *to be discovered* (which is *dazzlement*) is a false poet.'[38]

35

In *Immortality*, Kundera imagines a conversation between Goethe and Hemingway as they are 'strolling down a road in the other world'.[39] In yet another world, somewhere else, Kundera and Oscar Wilde are reposing in relaxed conversation. 'My dear Milan,' says Wilde, 'all this palaver about Bettina – I'm afraid I beat you to it. Don't you remember? My Cecily in *The Importance of Being Earnest.* The young, impressionable object of Algernon's untiring affections. Do you remember her box of letters? In her incorrigible romanticizing, she had written to the Algernon she had yet to meet and supplied all of his written responses herself. She had them engaged, broken up, and reunited again – well before she was ever to lay eyes on the man. Cecily outdid Bettina, I'd say. She never waited till death, but began when her fanciful little heart moved her!'

Kundera was nodding. 'Yes,' he said, 'but your Cecily is a mere trifle compared to Bettina. Bettina at least went on to contribute something significant to German Romanticism, especially as a woman.'

Wilde laughed. 'Of course Cecily's a mere trifle, my dear. Remember the play's subtitle: 'A Trivial Play for Serious People'. That is, *for* serious people, not *about* serious people. I should have thought that this was well in line with your sensibility. You are always going on about laughing, about the playful, about the ironic. You even named one of your novels "The Joke", for goodness sake.'

---

[37] Kundera, 'Sixty-three Words', in *The Art of the Novel*, p. 132.

[38] Goethe, *Maxims and Reflections*, p. 118; Rimbaud, letter to Paul Demeny, May 15, 1871, in *Complete Works, Selected Letters*, trans. Wallace Fowlie, p. 307; Freud, letter to Wilhelm Fliess, December 1895, in Marcus, p. 15; Kundera, 'Somewhere Behind', in *The Art of the Novel*, p. 117. Is Kundera's 'dazzlement' here the same as Heidegger's *Schein*, we must wonder?

[39] Kundera, *Immortality*, pp. 238–241.

'Yes, but strangely, I am actually quite earnest about it all.'

'Earnest about humor! How delicious. How charming. But a little passé, I should think. All this recent postmodern levity, with its vogue academic theory, surely that's had its time in the spotlight now. I say this with regret, of course. Only what is out of fashion is ever worth celebrating.'

Kundera smiled, but continued: 'Not passé. At least, not yet. I don't think our typical academicians have ever understood what being earnest about humor really means. To them, irony is a device to be studied, to be rationalized by a theory. I suppose I don't fault them for this approach, since they are constrained by the presuppositions of their profession, which even they admit are unyielding. But then again, they could have all followed Kierkegaard, had they the courage. As for you, I suspect a little dissembling on your part – you were more earnest about your mannered levity than you were ever willing to let on, I would hazard to bet.'

'Perhaps I was', said Wilde. 'But I was never serious-minded. There is a difference. In matters of truth, an earnest soul knows the value of a smirk, while the serious mind speaks only through gritted teeth. A clenched jaw is always a betrayal of self-doubt. I am certain that that is why Hemingway always had his jaw clenched. To be perfectly honest, I don't know what you see in that man. He doubted himself at the very core. He doubted even his Christian name. His death has very little heroism, and even less Romanticism, as I can see it.'

'In my portrayal of him with Goethe, I added to his character, you'll remember: I bring him levity, and make him laugh easily.'

'But an insufferable man, altogether. One should always choose bravura over bravado. Far better the bravery of pretense than the pretense of bravery. A writer who shows off *in deed* but not *in language* is, after all, a writer afraid of himself. I should have thought that if you focused on any Ernest, you'd have chosen the later one named Becker (if one is to speak of going out of fashion). Is it not he who brought Kierkegaard, Freud, heroism and the denial of death all together? Irony and dream therapy entwined? And did he not say "The urge to immortality is not a simple reflex of the death-anxiety but a reaching out by one's whole being toward life"? Does this not capture the essence of your book *Immortality* better than an obsession with bullfighting?'

Kundera was again nodding his head. 'Yes, that seems to capture it, especially the phrase "one's whole being toward life". It's Heidegger. And the *raison d'être* of the novel. But I suggest to you that that's what Hemingway had his eye on too.'

'Well maybe he did,' said Wilde dismissively, 'but his style was as grey as a park pigeon. And style is three-quarters of life. The rest is rhetoric.'

'We can't all be peacock feathers', said Kundera, as a jesting smile stole across his face. 'And you never were, at least not all the time.' The smile changed expression. 'You turned to Catholicism on your deathbed, I recall.'

Wilde's own face became earnest. But it soon regained a smirk: 'Yes, well, I could not resist its pageantry.'

'So you see', said Kundera, 'you always had "earnest" within you. You and I are closer than you probably care to admit. And you and old Papa are closer than *I know* you care to admit. Your last stanza of the *Reading Gaol* suggests you understood him all too well.'

Wilde had grown pensive. 'Gaol is a self-revealing place. Your own novels' characters know that. But the truth it reveals is a private place.'

'I shall never forget,' responded Kundera, respecting the new tone his conversant had assumed, 'reading the description of your first trial. One of your questioners, an old schoolmate, had quoted your own words to you, as an attempt at self-indictment. The line went something like "A truth ceases to be true when more than one person believes in it." Your rejoinder has never left my mind: "Perfectly", you said. "That would be my metaphysical definition of truth; something so personal that the same truth could never be appreciated by two minds." I have thought about this often, and always admired your integrity and self-honesty even amidst such a soul-destroying interrogation. I don't think I fully agree with your definition, but it seems to me wonderfully Nietzschean and a perfect sentiment for our modern dilemma. And if I don't fully accept the idea as an intellectual or philosophical tenet, I nevertheless believe that I write my novels in the shadow of its claim. When, for example, I write about immortality across the ages and concerning various personages – my own included – I am not writing under some universalist claim or some liberal humanist understanding, but as if the idea needs to be explored and appreciated from a myriad of angles, refracted endlessly through the prism of history and textuality and individuality and, ultimately, possibility.'

Wilde had been listening intently, having moved his elbows forward onto his knees. 'And the mask. You forgot the mask.'

Kundera spread his fingers as a prompt for a further explanation. Wilde leaned forward even more.

'I quote myself, and in doing so I admit, at least to some ironic degree, of being earnest: "Man is least in himself when he talks in his own person. Give him a mask, and he will tell you the truth." '[40]

[40] The quote from Ernest Becker comes from *The Denial of Death* (New York: The Free Press, 1973), pp. 152–153; the reference to Wilde's trial from Marcus, pp. 207–208; the final quote from Oscar Wilde from 'The Critic as Artist', in *Oscar Wilde: Plays, Prose Writings and Poems* (London: J.M. Dent and Sons, 1975), p. 45.

7 Gadamer

Modus: a measure, a manner, a way, a way forward. Mode. *Modus operandi*. Modality. Modern. Modernity. Interconnection of method with time. Being with time.

Modern: the now, the new, the newly measured, the new way forward. Succession of the new upon the new. Aggrandizement of the new. Means of the new. New meaning.

Postmodern: going beyond the measure by means of the measured. The new as the old, as the new. The measuring of the means. A new means of measuring the old means. The measure as already measured. The measure of meaning.

Modern consciousness: a new measure of knowing. Of coming to know. Of knowing one's ability and capacity to know. Mode of self-knowing. Self-consciousness. Consciousness aware of itself as consciousness. Knowledge of self as consciousness. Grounding knowledge in self-reflexivity. Self-knowledge as self-certainty. Means of self-meaning. Measure of being.

Postmodern consciousness: mode of knowing the mode. Meta-reflexivity. Coming to know the coming to know. Consciousness all too aware of itself as consciousness. Self-conscious consciousness. Knowledge of self as mere means with no end. Self-knowledge as self-division. Self-meaning beyond measure. Measureless being.

In the foregoing question of a new approach to interdisciplinarity, we have been suggesting a new mode, a new way of carrying out the task of critique, a new art of 'critical counterpoint', as Kundera might call it. But we now must realize that this new mode, as a way of thinking, as a way of operating, consciously, through language, through discourse, through text, must lead to a new kind of consciousness. For a new consciousness has been implied in each of the thinkers we have explored so far, if by consciousness we mean a measure of being that allows the question of our knowledge (or our self-knowledge) to remain a question of our coming to knowledge, and therefore of our coming to being. And in this *modus* of consciousness we are led in turn to a new understanding of truth and a new valuation of truth. Not that this truth is an endpoint, a pot of gold at the end of an operational arc, but that this arc, in all its variegated, polychromatic splendor, is itself truth, which nevertheless lies elsewhere to our immediate grasp in self-consciousness.

What do we mean by this, that truth as an operational mode does not lie in our immediate grasp in self-consciousness? What is this mode of consciousness if it is not rooted, by its very participation in the project of modernity since Descartes, in self-consciousness? Does not Hegel the great dialectician lead consciousness to an acme of absolute self-consciousness, by which the interfusion of the universal with the individual reaches its utmost fulfillment, and renders to us the truth of self-certainty?[1] We cannot deny a certain indebtedness to dialectic, even of the Hegelian kind with its *Aufhebung*, since new consciousness, in breaking with the

[1] Hegel, *Phenomenology of Spirit*, B, IV.

old form of thought and establishing the new, must always remain fundamentally and constitutively under the horizon of the polarity it has created. Does not a rainbow reveal itself only upon the coexistence of two opposing conditions? If, as we have been suggesting all along, a new consciousness lies in the form and in (we should always acknowledge) the *legacy* of critique, then, as Habermas has shown us, it has Hegelian roots. But Habermas has also reminded us of the ground-breaking work of Horkheimer and Adorno, how the Hegelian dialectic can be turned on itself, how critique, through a 'left' orientation, inverts Hegelian absolutism to pragmatic materiality, and becomes deeply critical of subject-centered rationality and its adjoining self-certainty.[2] In this analysis, 'self-consciousness' becomes only a consciousness that, in being aware of itself as consciousness through radical reflexivity, divides rather than unifies, and loses the primacy of the self as a place of grounding certainty. Horkheimer and Adorno's analysis of Odysseus before the Sirens has shown us most trenchantly this divisive and disruptive nature of Enlightenment dialectic: just when the self is most in possession of itself, it is at the point of losing it. It can only remain itself when it binds itself to a mast and thwarts its very desires. 'The strain of holding the I together adheres to the I in all its stages; and the temptation to lose it has always been there with the blind determination to maintain it.'[3] Is this not what Bettina von Arnim discovers as she tries to immortalize death?

Why then, if modern self-consciousness threatens the ground of its own authority and stability, should we make the mode of consciousness and its operational force so critical? We must understand that consciousness has always been, from its very inception within our philosophical vocabulary, a modal term with an inbuilt capacity for shift and play. Even Husserl, in analyzing the Cartesian foundation of modern consciousness, in order to forge 'a radical new beginning for philosophy', understands that the essential property of every consciousness is the ability '*to change into continually new modes of consciousness of the same object*'.[4] The history of modern philosophy has been the history of this shift or change, even as it has tried to remain fixed upon truth as its object. There is always an elsewhere to consciousness, even as it shifts on itself. Did not Odysseus know this best, he who, before the advent of modern consciousness, found his self's survival dependent upon a giving up of that self, upon a denial of that self, in order to find a way to something new, if never fully captured?

In its shifting, we might say then that the mode of modern consciousness also moves beyond the given methods it has inherited. With Descartes and the *cogito*, the modern self was born as a method, a way of transposing doubt to certainty. Through this self subsequent methodologies were formed, which in turn have developed, through Enlightenment's determined utilization of the self's rational framework, into various disciplines. But as the self has given way to the play within its own consciousness, so too its methodologies have given way to the shifting

[2] See, in general, Jürgen Habermas, *The Philosophical Discourse of Modernity*, trans. Frederick Lawrence (Cambridge: Polity Press, 1987), and specifically Lectures I–III.

[3] Max Horkheimer and Theodor Adorno, *Dialectic of Enlightenment*, trans. John Cumming (New York: Continuum, 1999), p. 33.

[4] Edmund Husserl, *Cartesian Meditations*, trans. Dorion Cairns (London: Kluwer Academic), p. 45.

ground upon which these methodologies have been placed. If the philosophy of Cartesian self-consciousness was the Enlightenment's greatest single inheritance, then we could say that the modern mode of consciousness now surpasses philosophy proper, so that a critical consciousness takes shape by going beyond the methodologies of philosophy, of criticism, of art, of theology, or of any other relevant discipline *sui generis*. A new mode of critique would not be bound by methodology, in whatever disciplinary form, even if it would have to yield to a new method for its 'truth'. But of course this unbound freedom raises once again the difficult question of the nature of the relationship between truth and method.

In the Introduction to his *Wahrheit und Methode* (*Truth and Method*) Hans-Georg Gadamer pronounces that a 'new critical consciousness must now accompany all responsible philosophizing which takes the habits of thoughts and language built up in the individual in his communication with his environment and places them before the forum of the historical tradition to which we belong.'[5] Like Descartes, like Kant, like Nietzsche, like Husserl, like Heidegger – all *modern* philosophers par excellence – Gadamer calls for a new approach, but under the horizon of historical tradition. *Wahrheit und Methode* presents the now famous concept of *wirkungsgeschichtliches Bewusstsein*, most often rendered as 'historically effected consciousness', a consciousness that is not isolated or 'differentiated' from the whole of our life experience, but one that is integrated with our past influences, our present prejudices, and our future possibilities – that is, following Heidegger, and now Kundera, with the authentic experience that confronts us in the form of being-in-the-world itself. For Gadamer, the methodologies we have constructed for our historical thinking, our philosophical thinking, our aesthetic thinking, and even our theological thinking, those 'sciences' that ask us to differentiate ourselves from the object under scrutiny, and form judgments from a consciousness fundamentally distanced from what is being judged, are put in a qualified opposition to 'truth', to the truth of being as it functions directly in the world. What Gadamer strives for is a different consciousness altogether, a different way to measure ourselves against truth, or within truth.

Gadamer, we could say, works for a consciousness that remains embedded in the world. Like Kundera's picture of a President clutching his side before the television cameras, as his mortality cuts through the abstraction of his title and the symbolism of his office (both of which demand that we address the one elected forever after as 'Mr. President' and not as, say, Jimmy Carter), so Gadamer's historically effected consciousness wishes to cut through the symbolisms and abstractions of our Enlightenment history, inasmuch as these have abstracted the 'self', while at the same time to remain true to history as it informs and shapes our understanding of being, and aging, in the world. In this consciousness, the self remains integrated within and not set against the world. The 'truth' that it would thus encounter, the 'truth' Gadamer wants to cut through to, at the expense of methodological distancing, is the truth that brings about history in its first blush, that brings about

[5] Hans-Georg Gadamer, *Truth and Method*, 2nd, revised edition, trans. Joel Weinsheimer and Donald G. Marshall (New York: Continuum, 1997), p. xxv.

(or 'effects') the very details and vicissitudes of life as we encounter them before we can historicize them, so that in our later historicizing, which is inevitable, we do not lose sight of the existentiality that sets any history first into motion.

To get to this more existential notion of truth, Gadamer must think beyond the 'methods' which have created and maintained the distance of the self from the world, in contradistinction to its integration of being-in-the-world. These 'methods' are the methods of the sciences. Like all modern philosophers, and indeed modern theologians (Gadamer, we should not forget, maintained close associations with Rudolf Bultmann, and Gadamer's own work is infused with theological concern), Gadamer feels compelled to pose the question of consciousness and its validation under the rubric of modern science ('science' as found within consciousness both epistemologically and etymologically). And this seems reasonable enough, for the broad context of science would appear to supply the most essential and exclusive parameters for the question of historical, hermeneutical or even aesthetic consciousness as it pertains most specifically to methodology, just as it had done for the Descartes of the *Meditations*, or more directly for the Kant of the *Prolegomena*. But Gadamer's enquiry assumes the overall context of the *human* sciences (in German, *Geisteswissenschaften*), not the natural sciences in their general form. And more specifically, it returns to the humanist tradition, and begins not with the question of truth as fact, in the sense that natural science understands verifiable 'fact', but with 'the question of truth as it emerges in the experience of art' (section title to Part One of *Truth and Method*). With Gadamer art has a priority: the human sciences must be subsumed under the precinct of art, and not the other way around, as is so often the case in strictly historical enquiries. Gadamer explains his approach in his Foreword to the Second Edition: 'My starting point is that the historical human sciences, as they emerged from German romanticism and were imbued with the spirit of modern science, maintained a humanistic heritage that distinguishes them from all other kinds of modern research and brings them closer to other, quite different, extrascientific experiences, especially those peculiar to art.'[6] These 'extrascientific experiences' transcend the methods and methodologies of any disciplinary field of enquiry, and are best manifest in the field and practice of art, beginning particularly with the Romantics, who were the first to understand that the 'methods' of art must first be sourced in something far more primordial than the mechanical logic and classicism of eighteenth-century aesthetics.

The heritage of German Romanticism, which Gadamer will later trace out in connection to hermeneutical theory leading up to and culminating in Schleiermacher, we have already seen in our own analysis of Goethe, whose writings nevertheless included much in the way of natural science (even if they were still imbued with an aesthetic classicism). Goethe's merging of his own life with his work becomes the first great modern gesture, beyond the classical tradition, of another kind of consciousness as truth, where the truth of the modern scientific rationality (conceptual knowledge), which claims to be the measure of all things, of life as we observe it, is transposed to the truth of an aesthetic understanding of life

---

6 *Ibid.*, p. xxviii–xxix.

(or 'art') as we *experience* it. (Gadamer will make much of this term 'experience' as it is rendered in the German '*Erlebnis*', especially in connection to Goethe.[7]) And that this consciousness, as we have seen in the Werther/Goethe dyad of Goethean tradition, becomes *self*-consciousness – this is no accident, since poetry and truth here gain their unity and (paradoxically) their universality under the mantle of the self (*Aus meinem Leben* [*From My Life*] – the first half of Goethe's autobiographical title). This move to the self through aesthetic consciousness, or to the aesthetic through the self, is the very heritage by which the human sciences will come closer and closer to 'extrascientific experiences', as the truth of the self in self-consciousness, the basis of all science if not just the 'moral sciences' of *Geisteswissenschaften*, becomes necessarily aestheticized in the methods of imaginative understanding (the work). Thus the question of truth, even now within any scientific context, becomes a question of art, and a question of method.

On the contribution of poetry in the search for truth, Gadamer writes: 'When Goethe gave this title to his autobiography, he was clearly referring to the positive role that poetic recollection plays in truth itself, and not just to the poetic freedom he allowed himself in telling his life story.'[8] And we have explored the way this recollection, or memory, figures in the aestheticization of Goethe's life first by Goethe himself, and then by Bettina von Arnim, only to be surpassed later by Thomas Mann, whose *Lotte in Weimar* makes of memory a memorial itself, and turns art into a self-contained world of self-memory. Gadamer is uncomfortable with this extreme kind of aestheticization and memorialization, which in Mann especially, at the height modernism, becomes an aesthetic anamnesis, a strangely inverted Platonism, whereby the pure Form is always art. This approach to aesthetics results directly in the kind of distancing of the self that Gadamer, along with earlier critical theorists, feels is the central problem of modernity. He calls the consciousness that has developed from such a Goethean understanding *aesthetic consciousness*: an abstraction through aestheticization, by which consciousness universalizes a work of art beyond its immediacy in the world, beyond even its content, and places it in a pure aesthetic sphere, where it exists autonomously, differentiated from anything outside this sphere, and yet total in its universal aspect. As traced by Gadamer through German Romanticism, beginning with Kant,[9] this aesthetic consciousness leads to an alienation of the self, since the aesthetic experience must remove any of the features that contextualize both the work and the creator/viewer of the work, in order to bring it to the purity of its self-contained truth. Hence the term 'disinterested', as taken from Kant, although Gadamer prefers the term 'differentiated': 'Thus through "aesthetic differentiation" the work loses its place and the world to which it belongs insofar as it belongs instead to the aesthetic consciousness. Correlatively, the artist too loses his place in the world.'[10]

---

[7] *Ibid.*, pp. 60–81.

[8] Hans-Georg Gadamer, 'On the contribution of poetry to the search for truth', in *The Relevance of the Beautiful and Other Essays*, ed. Robert Bernasconi, trans. Nicholas Walker (Cambridge: Cambridge University Press, 1986), p. 105. This essay was first published in *Zeitewende Die neue Furche* XLII (1971) under the title 'Wahrheit und Dichtung'.

[9] Gadamer, *Truth and Method*, pp. 81ff.

[10] *Ibid.*, p. 87.

Gadamer criticizes such consciousness as disembodied from the world of being (or from 'a "hermeneutic phenomenology" of Dasein', he says in explicit reference to Heidegger[11]). Inasmuch as recollection or memory is tied to such a disembodied consciousness, either through a Platonic metaphysics or through Kantian transcendentalism, that consciousness may be said to link poetry with truth (however romantically aestheticized that truth then becomes) through a removal of being from the scene. It is this very removal that Gadamer wants to avoid, and that Kundera insists *needs* to be avoided if art is going to survive beyond modernity.

What Gadamer is leading us towards, and what Kundera has pointed us to with a practitioner's clarity, is not an aesthetic consciousness as such, but something we could rather call a *poetic consciousness*. Poetic consciousness would be different in many respects from aesthetic consciousness. Poetic consciousness would function as a mode of being itself, not as an aesthetic experience (*Erlebnis*) that transports us to a pure aesthetic sphere. It would understand mode as fundamentally *poesis*, a making, a return to the measuring, the tailoring, the fabrication of the means. It would not disembody through differentiation, but embody, through the very lineaments of the work, the corpus of one's being, one's life. It would involve the fabrication of text and the concurrent entextualization of being. Poetic consciousness would bring poetry and truth together not as a positive role of one in the other (the present case for any of the disciplines functioning within the standard view of interdisciplinarity now), but as inseparable features of a modality, by which the self becomes 'made' and the work becomes open to all of life's possible makings. The 'world' of the 'being-in-the-world' would then be brought back into the picture because the world would itself become 'made' in the modality. This may seem a Kantianism indeed, except that the transcendental consciousness of Kant would now give way to the poetic capacity of imagination as a primordial and existential *poesis*, from which, as we saw, Kant shrunk back.

Gadamer takes us back to Kant as one of the main sources for the philosophical development of aesthetic consciousness. We know that by the time of the Third Critique, Kant had made a crucial distinction, as the development of his critical philosophy galvanized around two basic poles: understanding that legislates theoretical knowledge, and reason that legislates practical knowledge, or practical precepts. These poles had become the first two Critiques, pure and practical reason respectively. They in turn accord with Nature and Freedom respectively, the two divisions to which all of philosophy, according to Kant, can be reduced. In the Kantian scheme these divisions undergo further subdivision: the realms of the sensible and supersensible, even though the latter realm, the supersensible, is ultimately inaccessible to us as a matter of theoretical cognition, and must be consigned to a practical reality only. Nature, through sensible intuition, allows us to arrive at cognitive knowledge at least of an object's representation (never of course the *Ding an sich*, the thing-in-itself), whereas Freedom allows us to act according to an internal moral law which is not intuited or intuitable, but which nevertheless,

[11] *Ibid.*, p. 96.

being *a priori*, binds us to the same pure logical structures as that of understanding, and imposes upon us universal validity. But these concepts of Freedom and the supersensible carry with them inherent problems, for if the supersensible is not open to theoretical cognition in any formal way, how can it legislate for us universal validity in the same way as natural phenomena and their laws? Is not Freedom fundamentally at odds with law? The answer here for Kant lies in the will (or will as desire), which, while purely autonomous, expresses the principles of an imperative to act according to a universal law, which the will elects to embrace and enact, making free will and a will under moral law identical, even if now on the basis of the Subject (the one who wills) and not the Object (the predicate of a knowing subject).[12] This is basic Kantian ethics. But then a further question arises: how do we pass from the one realm to the other, from our theoretical employment of reason upon an Object (our cognitive faculty), to our practical employment of the will that in freedom expresses through autonomy the moral law within the Subject, based on the supersensible? Kant tells us that the two realms, being grounded upon *a priori* concepts of reason, must not reside exclusive of each other: 'the concept of freedom is meant to actualize in the sensible world the end proposed by its laws; and nature must consequently also be capable of being regarded in such a way that in the conformity to law of its form it at least harmonizes with the possibility of the ends to be effectuated in it according to the laws of freedom.' Kant concludes:

> There must, therefore, be a ground of *unity* of the supersensible that lies at the basis of nature, with what the concept of freedom contains in a practical way, and although the concept of this ground neither theoretically nor practically attains to a knowledge of it, and so has no peculiar realm of its own, still it renders possible the transition from the mode of thought according to the principles of the one to that according to the principles of the other.[13]

This ground of unity of the supersensible across both Nature and Freedom Kant finds anew in the faculty of judgment, to which the *Critique of Judgment* will be devoted. In this Third Critique, judgment becomes the 'middle term between understanding and reason.'[14] Once again we find Kant seeking a middle term, but not now within judgment as it is laid out in the First Critique, that is, between sensibility and understanding, the place of *das Unbekannte* = *X* as we saw earlier, but between that very understanding once it is attained and the autonomous will whose appeal is to something other than intuited sensibility, that is, to the supersensible. Once again Kant requires a bridge, and once again imagination comes into play, only not now as a mode unto itself (unknown and 'blind' in its functioning) but rather as part of an aesthetic consciousness through which we come to judge something as beautiful (or sublime). Unlike logical judgments, judgments of beauty contain no universal validity that is conceptually binding: how

---

[12] Cassirer, *Kant's Life and Thought*, 250.

[13] Kant, *Critique of Judgement*, Introduction, II, 176 (p. 14).

[14] *Ibid.*, III (p. 15).

a work of art (or of nature) is judged is purely an individual matter, whose determining ground is strictly subjective. Our aesthetic contemplation of beauty is what Kant calls the judgment of taste, or 'reflective judgment' (as opposed to 'determinant judgment' of the First Critique), and the question that pertains most pressingly to this judgment is how we can still talk about a universal beauty or a universal pleasure through a faculty that is outside the jurisdiction of the validating structures of logic which grant *a priori* universality. There are no laws of beauty, and yet there seems possible an agreement about beauty that transcends pure subjectivity. On what foundation does such an agreement sit? The answer to this question lies in this expanded notion of the faculty of judgment as 'reflective judgment', and is worked out, in Books One and Two of the Third Critique (the Analytics of the Beautiful and the Sublime), as the judgment of taste. How we know something to be beautiful and yet universal in its applicability to truth in a work of art will involve the very same faculty which allows passage from Nature to Freedom. Such a judging faculty, through art and the sphere of aesthetics, will unify philosophy into its cohesive whole.

Now, Gadamer finds Kant's explication of the judgment of taste problematic, for the aesthetic consciousness that is required and developed in this judgment, and which helps to furnish the ground of unity across Nature and Freedom in the supersensible, is grounded, as we have seen, upon a radical subjectivization. Taste, says Gadamer, should not be simply a personal preference or predilection. 'The concept of taste undoubtedly implies a *mode of knowing*. The mark of good taste is being able to stand back from ourselves and our private preferences. Thus taste, in its essential nature, is not private but a social phenomenon of the first order.'[15] Kant's major contribution in these matters of taste (his revolution, some say) is in discovering a validity for taste that goes beyond the private sphere – and more, in discovering a universality for taste which is *a priori*. Gadamer explains:

> In taste nothing is known of the objects judged to be beautiful, but it is stated only that there is a feeling of pleasure connected with them *a priori* in the subjective consciousness. As we know, Kant sees this feeling as based on the fact that the representation of the object is suited (zweckmäßig) to our faculty of knowledge. It is a free play of imagination and understanding, a subjective relationship that is altogether appropriate to knowledge and that exhibits the reason for the pleasure in the object. This suitedness to the subject is in principle the same for all – i.e., it is universally communicable and thus grounds the claim that the judgment of taste possesses universal validity.

Herein lies the Kantian principle of taste as an '*a priori* effect of the beautiful located halfway between a mere sensory, empirical agreement in matters of taste and the rationalist universality of a rule.'[16] But the underlying problem for Gadamer is that this principle is based on a purely 'subjective relationship', one for which knowledge proper has no significance. Aesthetic consciousness may be universally communicable, but not in terms of theoretical knowledge. It is only

---

[15] Gadamer, *Truth and Method*, p. 36. (Gadamer's italics.)

[16] *Ibid.*, p. 43.

suited (*zweckmäßig*) to our knowledge, not constitutive of it. It may constitute a new cosmos, as Cassirer calls it, but this cosmos is 'the whole of subjectivity'.[17] In Gadamer's words, 'there is no other principle of judgment, no criterion of concept and knowledge than that of its suitability to promote the feeling of freedom in the play of our cognitive faculties.'[18] This suitability may be *a priori*, and have an appeal to universality within the transcendental critique that looks upon it as a mode (towards, ultimately, a finality, to which the second half of the Third Critique is devoted), but it is still entirely within subjectivity. As Kant himself says, 'the judgment of taste is not determinable by means of concepts. Hence it can only have its ground in the subjective formal condition of a judgment in general. The subjective condition of all judgments is the subjective judging faculty itself, or judgment.' The mode as faculty is only ever subjective. Or, we might say, the supersensible is only a matter of the Subject, and not the Object, even as it brings its operational freedom into accord with the faculty of understanding and its laws. 'Taste, then, as a subjective power of judgment, contains the principle of subsumption, not of intuitions under *concepts*, but of the faculty of intuitions or presentations, i.e. of the imagination, under the *faculty* of concepts, i.e. the understanding, so far as the former *in its freedom* accords with the latter *in its conformity to law*.'[19] (We can see here both Kant's stress on judgment as *mode* or modality, and his understanding of imagination carried over from his reappraisal in his second edition of *The Critique of Pure Reason*, since imagination remains subsumed under the faculty of concepts, or understanding.)

This Kantian move to place aesthetic consciousness or aesthetic judgment outside the realm of knowledge, beyond the mediation of concepts, and towards an estimated communicability of subjective feelings, is where Gadamer finds the early roots of that shift in the human sciences towards 'extrascientific experiences'. And it is against its subjectivity or subjectivization, particularly as it is later developed by thinkers who pick up the Kantian mantle, from Fichte and Schiller onwards, including Goethe himself, that Gadamer reserves his main criticism and concern. For such a move must necessarily involve an abstraction, an abstraction of the Subject beyond the very ontological embeddedness in the world by which its subjectivity first gains its openness to life experience. And when this abstraction is turned from a *mode* of knowing, as it remains in Kant, to the very *content* of aesthetic experience, as it becomes with Kant's successors, then an 'indissoluble contradiction with the true experience of art', or with the true experience of openness to life, arises.[20] For the very reason of this openness to life experience, Gadamer shares with Kant a deep commitment to upholding the universal nature within art and beauty, to finding that shared understanding of an artistic work that allows us to talk of its 'truth' beyond the hermetic interiority of private preference and opinion, or beyond the impenetrable walls of solipsism. But he finds Kant's solution in aesthetic judgment a dangerous trajectory, if 'experience' is to find its

---

[17] Cassirer, *Kant's Life and Thought*, p. 319.

[18] Gadamer, *Truth and Method*, p. 55.

[19] Kant, *Critique of Judgement*, ' Analytic of the Sublime', §35, p. 143.

[20] Gadamer, *Truth and Method*, p. 97.

post-Heideggerean fullness within an openness that precludes the 'destructive consequences of subjectivism' and the 'self-annihilation of aesthetic immediacy'.[21] By 'self-' here Gadamer means both the identity of the artist and the identity of the viewer of the artist's work, both of which are lost or annihilated by abstracting the aesthetic experience outside of the 'interest' (ontological and otherwise) one brings to and maintains with the work. The 'method' involved in such abstraction (such 'disinterestedness', or 'differentiation') is what Gadamer tries to work against, as he seeks to retrieve the 'truth' of art lost in the subjectivizing nature of aesthetic consciousness that has evolved from the Kantian scheme.

But Kant is important for Gadamer as more than just the source of a root problem. Gadamer's retrieval of the question of artistic truth stands in relation to truth in the human sciences and, ultimately, to truth in language in the same way as reflective judgment stands in relation to freedom in ethical action for Kant. If both can solve the problem of how to account for artistic truth and aesthetic validation, if both can determine the role of art in the larger pursuits of truth in general (historical, ethical, existential, and so on), then both can justify going beyond rational science to 'extrascientific experience' in our understanding of the world – to freedom of the will and of the imagination on the one hand, and to hermeneutical ontology as a critical horizon of language on the other. So Kant remains indispensable, even if his critical emphasis must be reoriented. And surely we see this indispensability most clearly in Gadamer in his retention of the aesthetic experience as a *mode*:

> If we want to know what truth is in the field of the human sciences, we will have to ask the philosophical question of the whole procedure of the human sciences in the same way that Heidegger asked it of metaphysics and we have asked it of aesthetic consciousness. But we shall not be able simply to accept the human sciences' own understanding of themselves, but must ask what their mode of understanding in truth is. The question of the truth of art in particular can serve to prepare the way for this more wide-ranging question, because the experience of the work of art includes understanding, and thus itself represents a hermeneutical phenomenon but not at all in the sense of a scientific method. Rather understanding belongs to the encounter with the work of art itself, and so this belonging can be illuminated only on the basis of the *mode of being of the work of art itself*.[22]

Gadamer, in section two of *Truth and Method's* first part, will offer his idea of what this *mode of being* or this means of consciousness might look like, of where it might take its starting point, and of how it will counter the subjectivism of the Kantian aesthetic legacy.

But before we disclose this understanding, we need to ask of Gadamer a question that by now has become insistent. It is a fundamental question of truth, made all the more pressing by Oscar Wilde's definition. Why does Gadamer seem to adhere to a notion of truth which is inveterately tied to an Enlightenment understanding, and which Kant himself brought to its pinnacle, the notion of truth

[21] *Ibid.*, p. 95.

[22] *Ibid.*, p. 100. (Gadamer's italics.)

as basic *agreement* that carries universal applicability? Why must truth, whether in art, in history, or in language, bear a universality, necessarily and without reserve? We recall that for Kant, truth in the most nominal sense was the agreement of knowledge with its object. Presupposed in this idea of 'agreement' is at least the possibility, if perhaps never the consummation, of universal validity. Gadamer seems to subscribe to this paradigm at the very core of his thought. He does so not merely in the first part of *Truth and Method*, where the question of artistic truth is posed with a view to a shared understanding, one that transcends not just subjectivism but any immediate experience which bars transparent understanding between one being and another. But this paradigm also determines the book's culminating theory of hermeneutics: 'By seeing that language is the universal medium of this mediation [between the past and present], we were able to expand our inquiry from its starting point, the critiques of aesthetic and historical consciousness and the hermeneutics that would replace them, to universal dimensions ... Thus hermeneutics is, as we have seen, a *universal aspect of philosophy*, and not just the methodological basis of the so-called human sciences'.[23] And it carries even beyond *Truth and Method* to Gadamer's following work – for example in the 1971 essay '*Wahrheit und Dichtung*', later republished under the title '*Über den Beitrag den Dichtkunst bei der Suche nach der Wahrheit*' ('On the contribution of poetry to the search for truth'), in which Gadamer reiterates Heidegger's reading of the Greek ἀ-λήθεια (*aletheia*) as unconcealedness or openness, and yet uses a very Kantian description to define the nature of this (poetic) truth: 'It can also be put in this way: when we say a "true friend" we mean that here the word accords with its concept. This man actually corresponds with the concept of a friend.'[24] So why this subscription to truth? Why not another less bound to Enlightenment presuppositions? Why not, for instance, Nietzsche's understanding of truth in an extra-moral sense, truth as an illusive metaphor, truth as *extra*, somewhere else? Gadamer was willing to pursue the 'extrascientific', but why not the 'extra-universal'? Or more to the point, why not the truth of his greatest influence, Heidegger, to whom he has shown in other respects a full allegiance: the agreement (if one must insist on agreement) with the 'unsaid'?

Let us ask the question another way. What would the consequences have been had Gadamer begun not with the aesthetic consciousness of *The Critique of Judgment* but with the imagination of *The Critique of Pure Reason*? Or pushing the matter to its furthest extreme, what if he began with the unrevised notion of imagination in the Transcendental Deduction A? Of course he could never have begun here under the presupposition of truth as an agreement or correspondence that leads to universal claims. But let us suppose for a moment that he relinquished this presupposition. How would his truth and method have emerged under the rubric of an imagination that leads not to universals but to an unknown and unsaid? To an ineffable 'X'? Let us repeat the question we posed with Kundera: Where does one go to surpass the model when there is no universal ideal? We may find Gadamer would end up at the very place he in fact does end up in the second

23 *Ibid.*, pp. 475–476. (Gadamer's italics.)

24 Gadamer, 'On the contribution of poetry to the search for truth', p. 108.

section of Book One, that is, at the concept of *play*. But this concept would now become something very different than what it actually became in *Truth and Method*, and what it continued to be in Gadamer's subsequent writings.

Play: game, sport. The action of gaming. Sporting conduct. Abiding by the rules of the game. Suspending all realities for a playful contrivance. Recreation. Re-creation. Beginning anew with each game. Losing oneself in the game. Primacy of the play over the consciousness of those involved. Willingness to be played. Being game.

Player: active participant. Actor. One who acts according to the script. One who assumes a role. One who is serious about not being serious. One who competes. Contestant. Playing for. Performer. Playing *to*. Self-identification through audience.

Playing: mode of play. Means of the game. Role-taking. Mediation. Imitation. Representing. Recreating. Make-believe. Making believe. Willing suspension of disbelief. Going along. Caught up. Being there.

Play on words: Multiple meaning. Ironic meaning. Odysseus as μῆτις (*metis* – wisdom, craft, cunning, and yet, before Polyphemus the Cyclops, μή τις (*me tis*), Nobody). The famous riddle solved by Oedipus – the human being as most feeble on four feet, that is, when crawling as a baby. Oedipus' own name, 'swollen foot', as given to him in infancy, and its proximity to *oida*, 'I know'. Mephisto's autograph in *Faust*: '*Eritis sicus Deus, scientes bonum et malum*'. Nietzsche's *Ecce Homo*. *The Importance of Being Earnest.* Kundera's *The Joke*.

In the interstice between two dissimilar sides lies an originary power to produce, and in its producing to conjugate either side, and in its conjugating to give an impression of unity, of wholeness, even of commensurability. But only an impression – an illusion, we could say, albeit a very important and vital illusion. Between subject and object, between subject and predicate, between the interior and the exterior, between question and answer, between sensibility and understanding, between sense and apperception, between the sensible and the supersensible, between intuition and concept, between *Dichtung* and *Wahrheit*, between the work and the life, between the fictional and the real, between *mythos* and *logos*, between the *as if* and the *is*, between the model and the original, between the figurative and the literal, between the ironic and the straightforward, between method and truth, between past and present, between present and future, between already and not yet, between mortality and immortality, between seriousness and playfulness – but all these are only convenient markers – there lies an unknown place which acts as the structural 'ground' for both sides. This 'ground' is of course only ground in a hypothetical sense; it is not 'real' estate, as the phrase goes. An inexpressible 'X' marks its spot, a location ultimately indeterminable, though nevertheless acknowledged as existing, somewhere, but elsewhere to the two sides that it unfolds. It therefore has abyssal qualities, where vision and speech lie in blind and mute latency. But it is also the wellspring of potentiality and power behind this latency, the primal, inceptive source of the new *qua* new, that which allows being to exist as productive being, as creative being, as visionary and as enunciatory being, the propelling energy behind the verbal force, that deep and mysterious chasm that stands at the center of (or prior to) the infinitive 'to be', allowing all of its conjugations, giving essence to this most reductive, most rudimentary, most nascent copula, a copulative energy that brings to life, that bears life, that determines the life of the two sides (and perhaps more besides) between which it resides and issues forth. Its situation then is less a locus, a fixed locality, as it is a mode, a modality, which provides the possibility for and the means of any manner of consciousness. The Romantics called this imagination, 'the highest and most original faculty in man' (Schleiermacher),[25] as they took a cue from Kant (despite his retreat from the 'surprising' and inchoate nature of his initial finding in the Transcendental Deduction A), and then invested it with divine characteristics, or at least divine origins. But as an originary mode we must maintain (still in Kant's wake) its critical stature, its *how* over its *what*, even though its ultimate limits, and its own self-consciousness, remains (*contra* Hegel) unknown to us.

By maintaining a critique of this unknown 'X', we move towards a new kind of consciousness, a poetic consciousness, in which the mode of *poesis* becomes determining as mode. In this move we also shift by necessity towards a new understanding of truth. Truth amid such consciousness can no longer be reduced to a correspondence theory, a theory of basic agreement with universal parameters and universal jurisdiction, since the *what* is not the primary focus of the critical orientation. The *how* predominates, and in its predominance truth now must neither accord, conform, align itself, agree to nor agree with some pre-established or metaphysical ideal that has traditionally constituted the realm of the *what*. Truth would now go even beyond Heidegger and his agreement with the unsaid of the *what*. Truth, in the *how*, would have no recourse to the measure that enables the commensurability assumed within the *what*, no distinct point of reference with which to measure itself either against or as a preeminent standard, for it would become subsumed by measuring itself, by pure modality. What then would truth become within pure modality, within the modality of a constituting *poesis*? Truth, unleashed from the necessity of fixed measurement, would become *play*. For play is what we have when internal components no longer measure up with each other. We need only think of Hamlet and Claudius the King.

With play we return to Gadamer, and to his Section Two of *Truth and Method*'s Part One. But with the help (yet again) of Kant. In *The Critique of Judgment*, as we have briefly seen above, Kant introduces the idea of 'free play'. In the contemplation of the beautiful, the representation upon which our contemplation is based is not, as we saw, bound by concepts: 'the judgment of taste is not determinable by means of concepts.'[26] Our contemplation is thus, by its very

[25] Friedrich Schleiermacher, *On Religion: Speeches to its Cultured Despisers*, trans. John Oman (New York: Harper and Row, 1958, rpt. 1986), p. 98.

[26] See n. 19 above.

nature, free to roam spontaneously outside the dictates of law that characterize our cognitive faculty.

> The cognitive powers brought into play by this representation are here engaged in a free play, since no definite concept restricts them to a particular rule of cognition. Hence the mental state in this representation must be one of a feeling of the free play of the powers of representation in a given representation for a cognition in general. Now a representation, whereby an object is given, involves, in order that it may become a source of cognition for all, *imagination* for bringing together the manifold of intuition, and *understanding* for the unity of concept uniting the representations. This state of *free play* of the cognitive faculties attending a representation by which an object is given must admit universal communication: because cognition, as a definition of the Object with which given representations (in any Subject whatever) are to accord, is the one and only representation which is valid for every one.'[27]

We see here that free play is still wedded to the requirement of universality, since cognition by definition must be universally valid for all. But despite such requirement, this free play remains fundamentally subjective in nature, since it does not appertain to concepts in any definitive way. The 'subjective universal communicability' arises, we recall, from the *suitability* of the subjective experience to a cognition in general, and we repeat Gadamer's words: 'there is no other principle of judgment, no criterion of concept and knowledge than that of its suitability to promote the feeling of freedom in the play of our cognitive faculties.'[28] This freedom then works across both imagination and understanding, as it places itself, while still bound in subjective relationship, into conformity with the law. This clever solution of a notorious sticking point for philosophy over the ages (and especially for modern philosophy) – the reconciliation of the two antithetical sides of freedom and law – is a masterful philosophical stroke, with what seems to be play as the great arbiter. But even though this play functions across the two heterogeneous faculties of imagination and understanding with the purpose of bringing them into what Lyotard has called a 'dynamical synthesis', we have seen above that, even in its play, this synthesis does not appear to be equally weighted: the subjective power of judgment contains a 'principle of subsumption' by which the imagination is ultimately subsumed under the faculty of understanding and reason.[29] This is certainly in accord with the Transcendental Deduction B of the First Critique. And yet even if, on account of ambiguity that persists on this matter in the Third Critique, we must suspend a final reckoning of whether or not one side actually gives in to the other, we can nevertheless say that the free play, which is a play of the *powers* of each respective faculty (and not their content), never assumes an autonomy. It is always in the service of an overall synthesis of reason. As Jaspers says: 'The transition is not "to another thing, but to another way of using reason." ' Jaspers's summary of this point is helpful: 'This

[27] Kant, *Critique of Judgement,* ' Analytic of the Beautiful', §9, p. 58.

[28] See n. 18 above.

[29] See n. 19 above; and Jean-François Lyotard, *Lessons on the Analytic of the Sublime*, trans. Elizabeth Rottenberg (Stanford: Stanford University Press, 1994), pp. 23-25; 123ff.

going beyond the understanding does not mean that there are two worlds between which we might shuttle back and forth, losing the one when we are in the other. Rather, there is only one reason, which goes astray unless, in one simultaneous operation, it holds together what it cuts apart. The universe in which we live is one. In Kant truth is only in the totality.'[30]

Gadamer does not seem interested in the power play between imagination and understanding as such; rather, he argues that the main deficiency in Kant's solution of free play is that it still binds us to a thorough subjectivization. The play only plays within a subjective relationship that stands outside of knowledge as concepts. The play still leads to 'differentiation' of the self with the world. Gadamer wants to disabuse us of this subjective differentiation. He wants to let play break truly free, free even from the self, in order that it might lead us towards a purer existentiality. Gadamer wants play to refer to 'the mode of being of the work of art itself'.[31]

Gadamer's reorientation of play from the freedom of subjectivity to the mode of the work of art itself is an important development in our understanding of artistic truth, a development that of course owes much to Heidegger. If play is fundamentally a mode, a question more of *how* than of *what*, then what it mediates and acts as a mode *for* becomes now a necessary consideration, or reconsideration. In Gadamer, we find that play (*Spiel*) is part of the essential presentation of a work of art: 'the presentation or performance of a work of literature or music is something essential, and not incidental to it, for it merely completes what the works of art already are – the being there of what is presented in them.'[32] The Heideggerean ontology at work here is that of the work itself, which is properly evinced through what Gadamer calls a transformation into structure. In this transformation, the work becomes a structure commensurable only with itself: 'it is, so to speak, its own measure and measures itself by nothing outside it' (a point echoed by Kundera in regard to the novel). Upon this self-realization, beyond direct control from the artist or the audience, and beyond certainly their Kantian subjectivities, the work is transformed 'into the true': 'It is not enchantment in the sense of a bewitchment that waits for the redeeming word that will transform things back to what they were; rather, it is itself redemption and transformation back into true being.'[33] Such a 'true being' is the ontological destination Gadamer has been striving for from the start. And in the passage from aesthetic being and historical being to, ultimately, hermeneutical being, and from the respective consciousnesses they leave behind to the 'historically effected consciousness' (*wirkungsgeschichtliches Bewusstsein*) they

[30] Jaspers, *Kant*, p. 83. Cassirer *Kant's Life and Thought*, on the same matter: 'But now it can be seen yet more clearly that this course, which is rooted in the essence of Kantian methodology, does not abort the wealth of intuitive actuality and water it down into a system of flimsy abstractions, but that, on the contrary, Kant's original concept of knowledge has undergone an extension and deepening that only now makes it feasible to survey the *whole* of natural and spiritual life and to conceive it as intrinsically a single organism of "reason" ' (p. 360).

[31] Gadamer, *Truth and Method*, p. 101.

[32] *Ibid*., p. 134.

[33] *Ibid*., p. 112.

eventually culminate in, play gives Gadamer the early modality he needs for the presentation of 'true being'. And through this modality, the audience's own being becomes united with the work in a communion of play, as 'the being of the spectator is determined by his "being there present" (*Dabeisein*)'. Especially in drama, in the festival play, Gadamer claims that to 'be present means to participate'.[34] This is already a kind of hermeneutics, though one that does not privilege one or the other side of the interpretive divide.

This modality of play, as it ushers in the being of both work *and* life, is then an essential contribution to the redefinition of truth and its method of revelation *in general*, and not simply to the redefinition of artistic truth and artistic revelation in the narrow sense. But here we must again question the nature of this more general truth as Gadamer conceives it. For if his notion of 'true being' in its basic ontological structure continues to operate within the paradigm of truth as agreement, we must admit that any such play will have its limitations. If we look at Gadamerian hermeneutics as a whole, we might say it is predicated upon universalist conceptions, since the hermeneutical task becomes a basic task of agreement, as it seeks through language to establish a universal connection between one interpretive being and another: '*Being that can be understood is language*. The hermeneutical phenomenon here projects its own universality back onto the ontological constitution of what is understood, determining it in a universal sense as *language* and determining its own relation to beings as interpretation.'[35] This point is reiterated in the title of Gadamer's 1966 essay 'Universality of the Hermeneutical Problem', and explained in the essay itself: 'What I am describing is the mode of the whole human experience of the world. I call this experience hermeneutical, for the process we are describing is repeated continually throughout our familiar experience. ... Only the support of the familiar and common understanding makes possible the venture into the alien, the lifting up of something out of the alien, and thus the broadening and enrichment of our own experience of the world.'[36] So the familiar and the common, however explicit they are made, structure the very possibility for the unfamiliar – that is, truth begins in the known. Most commentators read Gadamer in this way. David Klemm, for example, paraphrases Gadamer's central hermeneutical point: 'What is true about linguistic understanding must be true about being as such. When our words bespeak the linguistic conditions under which we experience a meaningful world at all, they disclose truth.'[37] That is to say, truth is a result of shared meaning with universal backing. But David Couzens Hoy chooses to read Gadamer's hermeneutics differently. Hoy admits that there are strong universalist tendencies in many of Gadamer's passages, but he insists that, hermeneutically, Gadamer keeps open the relative nature of our understanding of language and history as whole concepts, showing that Gadamer

---

[34] *Ibid.*, p. 124. See also pp. 129–134, 151; and the essay 'The festive character of theater', in *The Relevance of the Beautiful and Other Essays*, pp. 57–65.

[35] Gadamer, *Truth and Method*, pp. 474–475.

[36] Hans-Georg Gadamer, 'Universality of the Hermeneutical Problem', in *Hermeneutical Inquiry, Vol. 1: The Interpretation of Texts*, ed. David Klemm (Atlanta: Scholars Press, 1986), p. 188.

[37] David Klemm, 'Introduction to "Universality of the Hermeneutical Problem" ', in *Hermeneutical Inquiry, Vol. 1*, p. 177.

never presumes an objective reality outside of our understanding, but that our understanding of the whole 'is always tied to the interpreter's own standpoint'. He adds: 'Gadamer's position, as I read it, is not a metaphysical position but a *critical* one. It addresses itself to the conditions of understanding and interpretation, and is not an ontology of what really exists independently of our interpretations.'[38] Rather than subscribing to a metaphysical-realist position, then, or to a 'metaphysical monism', Hoy suggests that, if Gadamer's universalist tendencies cannot be completely dispelled, his hermeneutics could be seen as working within a 'critical monism', while still allowing for disruptive or deconstructionist readings even of the 'monism' that it purports.[39] Hoy's emphasis here on the *critical* may help to rescue Gadamer's general understanding of language from a thoroughgoing universalism. Yet for the question of truth, Hoy's concession to a 'monism', however critical, may still belie the general tendency we have just seen in Gadamer's work, even outside of *Truth and Method*, towards a universal *known*. And if so, Gadamer's insistence upon universal criteria for truth in the common and the familiar, which is in basic agreement with Kant, would therefore restrict the capacity of play in its role as mode or mediation, since the structurality of play would then always be such that it leads to understanding, to what is *known*. In this light, it is no surprise that the notion of play in *Truth and Method* drops out of the discussion after Part One. Play, in its excess and freedom, in its newness and spontaneity, cannot in the end act as a constitutive ground for universality. Play can only be a 'clue' to ontological explanation and ontological truth. Its modality can lead us to truth. But it cannot *be* truth.

Yet we suggest truth *can* be play. And play can be truth. If our consciousness as mode does not have to adhere to a pregiven, corresponding measurement, and conform either to itself as self-consciousness, or to some other extraneous coordinates, whether aesthetic, historical, linguistic, or metaphysical, because it is itself the mode which allows measurement in the first place, through a *poesis* that drives the mode as modality, and keeps (critically) the *how* at the basis of every *what*, then play enters a new realm, where the open-endedness of re-creation maintains its primacy over the closure of agreement. This we call *poetic consciousness*, which remains locked neither in Kantian subjectivity nor in Gadamerian universality (nor 'monism'). Poetic consciousness is free to play out its constituting *poesis* at any level, and across any lines, since it is that which first provides the means for the lines to be drawn. As Gadamer sought a new ground for the human sciences, under Enlightenment's predominant horizon of the natural sciences, and invited the aesthetic to help inform the ontological 'explanation' that counters those explanations given through the methodologies of our various 'scientific' disciplines (aesthetics included), so we can now say that, in poetic consciousness, the lines of our disciplines must necessarily yield to a place which supersedes them all, and thereby renders every one not merely integrated but 'poetically' bound one to another. Let us be clear: the lines do not converge upon

---

[38] Hoy and McCarthy, *Critical Theory*, p. 199. See Hoy's entire section 'Gadamer's Hermeneutical Pluralism', pp. 188–200.

[39] *Ibid.*, p. 200.

this place as if it is a nodal source; the lines yield to its 'ground', and in yielding, disappear, subsumed into the soil of its creative, fertile power. This is the real point at which interdisciplinarity is seeded and emerges forth. Not in some prescribed cross-fertilization of method, nor in some prescribed unity of truth. *Interdisciplinarity arises when truth becomes play in poetic consciousness.* Here, truth becomes method, the modality of play, while method becomes truth, the play of modality. True interdisciplinarity means the absolute loss of distinction between truth and method *in play as play*. And this consciousness remains critical insofar as this play remains the *modus operandi*, even if, in its operation, it is directed from, and even towards, an unknown.

Dare we imagine such a truth? Dare we put ourselves at the service of such a variable as play, an unknown 'X', a gap in the measurement? But we have been imagining such a truth all along. In the textual collisions of philosophy with art, of theology with poetry, of history with present, of account with revaluation, of explication with revision, of the theoretical with the imaginative, we have been moving towards a new understanding, a new critique, a new hermeneutics. Consciously, but in the dark, we have probed the interstices of textuality itself, and found not one Text, not one Canon, not one Method, not one Truth, but the play of texts across each other as truth. In order to read this play and this truth, we must assume a consciousness by nature *excessive*, that goes beyond the known, that is taken up, caught up in the play. We must go beyond ourselves. We must play into the hands of a new kind of immortality, yet to be revealed.

8 Sophocles

Art tells the only truth that ultimately matters. It is the light by which human things can be mended. After art there is, let me assure you all, nothing.

Iris Murdoch[1]

If there was ever a beginning point to truth, no one has made any claim on it. No one has written, 'In the beginning there was truth.' They have written this of God the Creator, of the Word, and, in *Faust*, of Mind, of Force and of Act. But not of truth. For truth cannot be discovered in a pre-existing realm. Truth is encountered in the searching for it. *One comes to truth.*

Hélène Cixous has written 'In the beginning, I adored' and 'In the beginning I desired.'[2] These words are a deliberate attempt by the author to place herself as an acting subject at the center of her religious, that is to say, her scriptural, experience. Cixous being-in-the-world as woman. What she first adored was not a fixed idea, a static object. What she first adored was not the object of truth, or the object as truth. What she first adored and desired, she tells us in her autobiographical essay '*La venue à l'écriture*' ('Coming to Writing'), was the human act of writing. Scripturality. Writing of God. Writing as God. *Writing* as God. She writes, as a Jewish woman, of *coming to writing*, of coming to God. In the same way, out of our faith, we write of coming to truth, we write *coming to truth.*

Why this adoration? Why this love affair with truth? Nietzsche asks, 'Where in the world does the desire for truth originate?' His question is not about the origin of truth, but about the origin of its desire. Why this need to know the truth, to know of truth? This is a question of coming to truth. A question of *how*, not *what*. A critical question of how we come to truth.

Sophocles, the ancient Greek tragedian, knew the necessity and the centrality of this critical question. He did not ask 'What is truth?'. Rather, he examined with probing insight how one comes to truth. In the Theban plays, his Oedipus becomes the great – some may argue, the greatest – seeker of truth. *Oedipus the King* becomes a relentless quest of the self, a self questing for the truth concerning the exceptional nature of its fated existence. But unlike Cixous there can be no adoration in this search, no adoring what Oedipus found. Sophocles fashioned Oedipus the King upon the anvil of Aeschylus, who had forged the famous maxim that one suffers into truth. Oedipus comes to truth through suffering. All the more pressing then Nietzsche's question: from where does the desire for truth come?

To suffer is to recognize, as Aristotle suggested in the *Poetics*.[3] To suffer is to recognize one's self as the bearer of being-in-this-world, and all that this being

---

[1] Iris Murdoch, *The Black Prince* (London: Penguin, 1973), p. 416.

[2] Hélène Cixous, *Coming to Writing*, ed. Deborah Jenson (Cambridge, Mass.: Harvard University Press, 1991), pp. 1, 8. '*Au commencement j'ai adoré*', '*Au commencement j'ai desiré*' – '*La venue à l'écriture*', in *La venue à l'écriture* (Paris: Union Générale d'Editions, 1977), pp. 9, 16.

[3] For Aristotle, the notion of ἀναγνώρισις (*anagnorisis*, 'recognition') is a central component of tragedy's structure, and he refers to Sophocles' *Oedipus the King* as a supreme example: '*Recognition* (ἀναγνώρισις), as in fact the term indicates, is a change from ignorance to knowledge, disclosing either a close relationship or enmity, on the part of people marked out for good or bad fortune. Recognition is best when it occurs simultaneously with a reversal, like the one in the *Oedipus*.' *Poetics*, trans. Malcolm Heath (London: Penguin, 1996), pp. 18-19, or 1452^{a}–1452^{b}. See also 1454^{b}–1455^{a}.

entails. It is to recognize the fragility of being, as much as the fragility of goodness. One cannot recognize one's self as readily in goodness, for goodness assumes a harmony of relations, beginning with the relation to one's very own self, and, as Kierkegaard saw, the self is not constituted by happy self-relation. The self understands itself as self in the horizon of its own mortality, its inevitable non-existence in death, which casts over it an abiding despair. And suffering brings this mortality, and hence this despair, to the surface of our physical and conscious being most emphatically. 'But to arrive at the truth one has to pass through every negativity'.[4] In suffering we know ourselves again as divided beings in a world of pain, divided by the death that is in life. We re-cognize our fragility in the immediacy of this pain. We re-cognize our self in each encounter with suffering.

But these encounters are not without their desire. Before Freud, Kierkegaard's conception of the self left us with a radical despair that could be overcome by the Christian understanding of redemption. For Kierkegaard, this redemption was a matter principally of recognition and not of desire. One recognizes their fundamental state of despair, and responds accordingly; one does not desire it. After Freud, Horkheimer and Adorno show us the centrality of desire in the very constitution of the self. Once again their reading of Odysseus before the Sirens becomes a beacon for us. Odysseus, the hero who 'has reached maturity through suffering',[5] chooses to expose himself to the irresistible charms of the Sirens' song. He plugs the ears of his seafaring companions with wax, while he binds himself to the mast in full susceptibility to the destructive lure of the Sirens' music. He chooses to confront Nature in all its primeval force. He need not: he too can plug his ears. But under Circe's suggestion and council, he elects to delight in the sweet enticement of the distant chant. This is pure desire, desire not just as a libidinal drive (though it is certainly this), but desire as will, the will of the self to confront its own potential demise in desire. Desire works to the abandonment of the self both in pleasure and in annihilation. 'The dread of losing the self and of abrogating together with the self the barrier between oneself and another life, the fear of death and destruction, is intimately associated with a promise of happiness which threatened civilization in every moment.'[6] The self becomes a self when it distinguishes itself from Nature – to become the civilized human being. The self that is left undistinguished is not a self; it is a human bound to an enchanted but uncivilized world, whose enchantment continually threatens to subsume our very humanity. In order for Odysseus to distinguish himself against the Sirens, as someone distinct from enchantment, as a self-abiding self, he must bind himself to his own mast, lest he fall prey to the intoxicating sounds, and be subsumed by the destructive forces of Nature. His men, with their plugged ears, know no better, and thus they know no selfhood. But Odysseus desires selfhood. And so he sets himself against Nature by ensuring a distance through his self-imposed bonds. But the moment he gains his self by maintaining this distance, fastened to his own pole in

---

[4] Søren Kierkegaard, *The Sickness Unto Death*, trans. Alastair Hannay (London: Penguin, 1989), p. 74.

[5] Horkheimer and Adorno, *Dialectic of Enlightenment*, p. 32.

[6] *Ibid.*, p. 33.

the symbolism of a phallocentric gesture, he also loses his self: his desires give in to the sounds, and he demands instant release to join them. This is the dialectic of the Enlightenment self. The moment this self comes into existence it desires its self-destruction. It only survives this destruction by its previous rationalizations, but those rationalizations are necessitated by the initial desire to know and experience what can destroy it.

Odysseus is a man who needs to know. He chooses to hear the Sirens' song so he can recognize himself. Having suffered the ordeal, he can later, in retrospect, re-cognize his self in desire, as he retells his story to his hosts the Phaeacians, who desire to know who Odysseus is. And while Horkheimer and Adorno politicize this self-aware Odysseus as a prototype of the bourgeois man, controlling Nature by the enforced labor of his workers (it is Odysseus' crew who row him to safety beyond earshot of the songs), the authors nevertheless see the old paradox at work in their allegorical reading: that in order to save one's self, one must lose it. This is the divided self. Desire leads to the suffering of self-division, which leads to self-recognition. To know oneself again, to revisit oneself as a distinct self, is to split oneself from the immediacy of one's own experience. It is to make of the self a safe artifice: 'Artifice is the means by which the adventuring self loses itself in order to preserve itself.'[7] So Odysseus, in Book XII of Homer's epic, relates this episode with the Sirens as a story, one that he retells to the Phaeacians. He loses himself in the plot of his tale, only to find himself. This loss is prefigured earlier in Book VIII when the blind Demodocus sings movingly of the Trojan War, and Odysseus, having not yet revealed his identity to his hosts, but now reduced to tears by the song, twice pulls his cloak over his head. Loss of self-composure requires concealment. To recompose oneself, one must recompose one's story, and thus Odysseus soon after tells the elaborate tale of his own self-adventure. He 'unconceals' himself in composition, just as, within that very composition, while in the land of the Cyclops, he first conceals himself as 'Nobody', only to announce boastfully, upon his escape, his true identity as Odysseus, son of Laertes. But of course, this move of self-revelation becomes a curse, for the blinded Polyphemus, son of Poseidon, prays to his father for vengeance, and Odysseus must struggle homeward against the self-stripping forces of Nature. As later with the Sirens, self-assertion becomes self-effacement.

To lose oneself in the plot – this is also Oedipus the King, the allegory of self and desire recharged by Sophocles. For what is Oedipus if not a man whose insatiable desire to know himself (the Delphic dictum, whose oracles, ironically, Oedipus has been resisting all his life) brings him to incalculable suffering? There is a dialectic at work here too, but now a dialectic of, we might say, post-Enlightenment. Like Odysseus, Oedipus encounters the terrifying juxtaposition of raw Nature and human distinction. For Oedipus this juxtaposition is embodied in the Sphinx. As Hegel suggests, the Sphinx creature, with a lion's body and a virgin's head, combines the brute strength of Nature with the abstract principle of the Spiritual.[8] This combination is what Odysseus himself enacted before the

[7] *Ibid.*, pp. 48–49.

[8] Georg Wilhelm Friedrich Hegel, *The Philosophy of History*, trans. J. Sibree (New York: Dover Publications, 1956), p. 213.

Sirens, where the abstract principle becomes his own self. But here with Oedipus an advance has already taken place, for Oedipus encounters the Sphinx as a self already distinct. He solicits no help from Nature and no help from the gods: '*I* stopped the Sphinx! With no help from the birds,/the flight of my own intelligence hit the mark.'[9] There is no Circe to guide him, no crew to bind him from impending disaster. Oedipus faces the Nature/Human riddle on his own accord and with his own private cunning. And it is no accident that the riddle – what walks on four, two and three feet, but most feebly on four? – involves not brute Nature but humanity, humanity in every stage of its pedestrian life. To solve the riddle vanquishes the dualism of the Sphinx in favor now of the human face, and the Sphinx, the symbol of the Human not yet fully emerged from Nature, must cast itself over the rocks to its death. (Sophocles, rightly, does not include this episode with the Sphinx as part of his play's plot. Oedipus enters the stage already emerged from Nature – though of course not from Fate.) Oedipus, whose own identity is marked by his feet made swollen in infancy,[10] is thus well equipped to solve the mystery. He explains that the human walks through the stages of life on four, two and then three feet (the third foot being a cane used by the elderly), and with his explanation he gains victory over the Sphinx, gains in human stature, and marches on to his glory in Thebes. He overcomes Nature as did Odysseus, who averted his many perils and sailed on to his home in Ithaca. But Oedipus goes to Thebes a different man than Odysseus goes to Ithaca. Though more of an emergent self, Oedipus has not yet recognized this self. His real suffering has yet to begin.

The desire to know makes Oedipus the King the quintessential tragic figure. In his relentless search – 'I must know it all/must see the truth at last'[11] – he comes to self-recognition. In his fervid desire to find the cause of his city's plague, that is, the identity of the murderer of Laius, his real father, he sets in motion the fated mechanisms that will reveal his own self to himself. But in his recognition, precisely what will he recognize? Is it the *truth* of himself? By the end of *Oedipus the King*, Oedipus, through suffering, has no doubt come to recognize who he actually is. This recognition is consummated, ironically, in the gouging out of his eyes, those instruments with which he drew the distinction between himself and others in the world around him. These eyes are no longer needed, for sight becomes a matter of pure interiority, whose inwardness is already instigated in the self-imposed act of blinding: 'But the hands that struck my eyes was mine,/mine alone – no one else –/I did it all myself!/What good were eyes to me?'[12] Had Sophocles ended his Theban plays here, with this double act of self-assertion and self-effacement, we could claim that the truth of Oedipus' self had been comprehensively revealed, and that Oedipus had poignantly, catastrophically, self-destructively *come to truth* in the manner of Sophocles' great rival and predecessor Aeschylus.

---

[9] Sophocles, 'Oedipus the King', in *The Three Theban Plays*, trans. Robert Fagles (New York: Penguin, 1982, 1984), lns. 452–453, (p. 182).

[10] Abandoned on the slopes of Cithaeron by his parents, who have heard the oracles, his infant feet are pinned with shackles.

[11] Sophocles, 'Oedipus the King', lns. 1168–1169 (p. 222).

[12] *Ibid.*, lns. 1470–1473 (p. 241).

But Sophocles does not, in the end, present truth in so final and so afflicting a manner. One more play before the end of his career and his life, one last visit to the Oedipus character, would distinguish both Sophocles and his Oedipus anew. In this ultimate play, the less famous *Oedipus at Colonus*, which was produced posthumously in 401 BCE, four or five years after Sophocles' death, the question of truth emerges on a completely different level. But this level is one that we have been exploring since we first began, and one that now, through the textual performance of this final play in the Theban cycle, we are ready, like the aged Oedipus, to face squarely.

The plot of *Oedipus at Colonus* is not complicated. It does not have the complex turns of *Oedipus the King*, for example. Nor is it set in Thebes, but rather, as the title indicates, in Colonus – or more accurately, at the sacred grove of the Furies just outside Colonus. Into this grove wanders Oedipus and his daughter Antigone, in exile from Thebes. This is the grove of the chthonic Furies, the Eumenides, and therefore it is a place of ritual. Here, in a space not to be trespassed, not to be desecrated, where all the proper rites are due, the blind, impoverished, enfeebled Oedipus will have his vindication. In a reversal of what Aristotle's *Poetics* states, that the action of the play should govern all other components, this sacred site takes over control, and governs all the play's action. For it is this place *as a place* where ultimately truth emerges – both the truth of Oedipus, and the truth of the gods. Oedipus, wandering the land in shame, a vagabond in exile, enters the sacred grove and realizes that here is the place where he must reckon with the truth. Here he must confront his final hour. Here the brunt of his mortality, brought on by the events of his life with such severity and with such cruelty, he will now face with new recognition.

At the beginning of the play, we can already anticipate that the space of the grove will be a conflictual space, even before Oedipus' conflict with the local citizens, with Creon of Thebes, and with Oedipus' son Polynices. For the grove is a place where divine realms meet: Apollo, the Olympian sky god, whose oracle had named this very spot as Oedipus' final resting place, and the Furies, the Terrible Goddesses of the earth, whose wrath overtakes those guilty of familial murder. Two divinities, two realms, whose conflict had been dramatized in Aeschylus' earlier *Eumenides*, which ends only as the chthonic goddesses of the earth, the Daughters of Darkness and of blood vengeance, are placated, and submit to their new task as guardians of the Athenian city under their new name of the Kindly Ones. But here in Sophocles' play the Furies have not thoroughly transformed into the civilized gods of the city they were persuaded to become. Their grove remains outside the city limits, where they are to be feared as much as to be praised. They remain both the Terrible Goddesses and the Kindly Ones, a double role that Oedipus himself will assume, as he confronts the differing intentions of Athens and Thebes. The grove is a place that brings opposing sides into confrontation.

But the site is also called the 'Brazen Threshold', for it leads to the underworld. It is then a liminal place, an in-between place, which concedes to neither side in the confrontation. It stands between the goddesses of the earth and the gods of the sky. It stands between uncultivated nature and the developed city. It stands between blood vengeance and civil law. Like Bulgakov's balcony, it is neither purely inside nor purely detached. It accepts both resident and alien. And so Oedipus arrives as one made both resident by the oracle of the sky god Apollo and alien by his Theban history and deeds. In this double role, Oedipus will encounter conflict; but he will also encounter the culmination of his fate, the end prepared for him by the gods as the future hope of Athens. Thus conflict merges with resolution, and the grove becomes a place that keeps both sides open, both sides of a fundamental opposition, while at the same time it provides the possibility for vindication.

The vindication of Oedipus is a complex matter. In the course of his encounter with the local citizens of Colonus, the arch-sufferer is forced to revisit his sufferings. But this painful journey back to his past now ends with claims of innocence: 'I am innocent! Pure in the eyes of the law,/blind, unknowing, I, I came to this!'[13] The question of blame and culpability, a question which presses heavily upon the action of *Oedipus the King*, now gives over to the assertion of 'innocent as ignorant'. Oedipus, whose name suggests knowing (*oida*), did not know. As king he did not know his true identity, and as an individual he did not know his true self. He could not recognize, in his determined search for murderer and perpetrator, that he himself was the guilty party. He could not comprehend the Fate so insistent upon his life. Outside of knowledge, then, how can blame be properly apportioned? The self-infliction of the earlier play now gives way to a self-absolution. The man caught up in Fate's cruel necessity yields no longer to the moral injunctions directed against his life by the probing Chorus of the final play. At the in-between threshold in the grove of *Oedipus at Colonus*, where neither law nor vengeance has reign, where only his impending death has certainty, Oedipus finds self-vindication beyond the customary jurisdictions of good and evil. His sufferings were certainly deserved – even Oedipus will concede to this – but the actions that brought them on, his own actions, were done without the willfulness that warrants moral guilt. As they were fated by the gods, so the gods hold responsibility. Oedipus is caught in between individual will and the will of higher powers, and at this place, at this aporia, he realizes that traditional morality has no footing.

This individual exculpation finds reinforcement through the divine oracle of Oedipus' death. Apollo has willed that his precise location of death will bring blessing to the hosts he has lived among, and disaster to those who have refused him sanctuary. Aware of this oracle, both Creon and Polynices petition Oedipus to rejoin their side. But with Tiresian blindness Oedipus sees through their selfish desires, sees through their false offers of haven. He turns prophet, and prophesies against them. The gods may have cast his life in misfortune, but they have endowed his death with the powers that determine misery and fortune for others. This is a vindication from on high, which now allows Oedipus, the new prophet and seer, to claim victory for Athens, his now benign hosts at Colonus, and defeat for Thebes, the troubled city he long left behind. In his death he will 'harvest all the rest' of his life's misfortunes, and make of them something positive and useful.[14] His departing words as he leaves the stage thus speak to Theseus the king of Athens about matters concerning renewal and regeneration:

---

[13] Sophocles, 'Oedipus at Colonus', in *The Three Theban Plays*, lns. 615–616 (p. 317).

[14] *Ibid.*, ln. 658 (p. 319).

'and in your great day remember me, the dead,/the root of all your greatness, everlasting, ever-new.'[15] Oedipus in the end comes to purpose.

But is this purpose yet truth? Is vindication, the righting of justice, equivalent to truth? Or we could approach the question another way: is vindication all the truth Oedipus seeks? Is vindication all the truth Sophocles offers? In the sacred grove, Oedipus may become his 'own master',[16] at least in terms of his earthly existence and his earthly renown, but is this the kind of truth we ought to expect here? A truth only of personal and political restoration and justification? A truth that validates a life of suffering without excusing the suffering? A truth that, in the final reckoning, confers upon the unfortunate a mark of integrity, whether it be a personal integrity, or, in the case of Sophocles' late fifth-century Athens on the verge of defeat to Sparta, a civic integrity? But truth here cannot amount simply to comeuppance, nor acquittal. We are in the space between vengeance and law. Nor can it amount solely to absolution, a removing of all the stain. For *Oedipus at Colonus* still ends with tragedy, as the final notes struck by the daughters carry us forward to the tragic action of *Antigone*, the first play written in the Theban cycle. The bloodline of Oedipus will continue to suffer. The famous question of the Chorus in *Oedipus the King* still resounds here in the final play: 'If all such violence goes with honor now,/why join the sacred dance?'[17] If Oedipus comes to truth, it is not through the gods' renunciation of violence, not through their reversal of fortune, not through their divine favor which now makes all his suffering inconsequential, or which now gives everything meaning. Oedipus has no more 'reason' for his fate than when he first understood its consequences. Oedipus, here in this last play, no longer suffers into truth. Oedipus comes differently to truth. He comes to truth through immortality.

Immortality. A question of death. A question of not-death. How does one come to death? How does one come to not-death? Oedipus, conscious in the end of his own self to a degree few others will experience, faces what his self has always carried with it, his not-self. Not-self: a site/sight through blindness. A place of blindness. A seeing of the darkness within. Had Oedipus plunged a dagger into his heart rather than into his eyes at the end of *Oedipus the King*, he would never have fully possessed himself. But now here at the end of *Oedipus at Colonus*, when, blinded, he is most in possession of himself, when he most recognizes himself, he does something paradoxical – he gives himself up. He loses his life, and by so doing saves it. But unlike Odysseus before the Sirens, Oedipus gives himself up consciously, knowingly, in full self-possession. How? How does he dispossess himself in self-possession? How exactly does he join the sacred dance?

Oedipus embraces the gap of the unknown.

---

[15] *Ibid.*, lns. 1764–1765 (p. 376). Fagles' worthy translation of the following: εὐδαίμονες γένοισθε, κἀπ᾽ εὐπραξίᾳ / μέμνησθέ μου θανόντος εὐτυχεῖς ἀεί (as in Sophocles, *Fabulae*, ed. A.C. Pearson (Oxford: Oxford University Press, lns. 1554–1555)).

[16] σαυτοῦ κρατῆς, Sophocles, 'Oedipus at Colonus', ln. 449 (p. 307), Sophocles, *Fabulae*, ln. 405.

[17] Sophocles, 'Oedipus the King', lns. 983–984 (p. 210).

The exact site of Oedipus' death in the sacred space is a site unknown. Where Oedipus took his departure to the underworld is unmarked, invisible, known only to his escort, Theseus, king of Athens. No one else has access to the event: 'we couldn't see the man – he was gone – nowhere!'[18] With a small entourage of daughters and attendants, Oedipus climbs to the place of final reckoning and vanishes before all sight, leaving no trace of physical death, no mortal moment, no burial plot, no grave marking. The site remains hidden, unspoken. 'But these are great mysteries …/words must never rouse them from their depths.'[19] Yet the mysterious site remains a gravesite nevertheless, insofar as Oedipus, a mortal, took his leave there at the preordained place. But where is 'there'? The messenger, who relates this event, cannot say. In the liminal grove of the chthonic goddesses, there remains only a story of the unknown, a retelling of the marvels and the mysteries that happened at a hidden site offstage.

The profound nature of this unknown comes to us in a play. In the Homeric epic, Odysseus' story of the Sirens is retold as a narrative, one which Odysseus himself relates to the Phaeacians. In Sophocles' play, Oedipus' story is staged, is enacted. But the climax of the action, the great moment of departure, cannot be enacted. It must be retold as a narrativized event that happened *elsewhere*. Oedipus is gone, offstage, no longer present to tell of his death. But the death of the self can never be self-described. Blanchot writes of 'the instant of my death henceforth always in abeyance.'[20] This is the moment of immortality: the telling of a death that is not-death. The non-presence of death becomes a presence only through retelling, through the artifice of the one who is still in the world, but who is unable to point exactly to the site of the event. The best we can do is point out the boundaries and the limits of the sacred space, and recreate the story from within. So Cixous writes: 'I have nothing to say about my death. It has been too big for me up to now. In a sense, all my texts are "born" of it. Have fled from it. Are its issue.'[21]

Sophocles the playwright, the meta-messenger who retells the story, who marks out the space within the precinct of his own hometown (Sophocles was born at Colonus), can also claim that his *Oedipus at Colonus*, which was produced posthumously, issues from his death. For here, in inscribing the hidden place of Oedipus' death, Sophocles marks out the unknown that is in all death, his own death included. But the markers around this unknown are the stuff of the play, of the tragedy. Like all great playwrights, Sophocles reduces his world to the stage. Yet in this final work, the focus becomes even more confined, even more focused and intense. The sacred grove is his stage, the place marked out as a threshold between country and city, between earth and sky, between, ultimately, human and divine. And in this grove, at this threshold, is a play – the playing out with masks

[18] Sophocles, 'Oedipus at Colonus', ln. 1871 (p. 381).

[19] *Ibid*, lns. 1727–1728 (p. 375).

[20] Maurice Blanchot, *The Instant of My Death*, trans. Elizabeth Rottenberg (Stanford: Stanford University Press, 2000), p. 11.

[21] Cixous, *Coming to Writing*, p. 36. 'Je n'ai rien à dire sur ma mort. Elle a été trop grande pour moi jusqu'ici. D'une certaine manière tous mes textes en sont "nés". L'ont fuie. En sont issus.', *La venue à l'écriture*, p. 42.

and speeches, with songs and dances, of a coming to truth. It is a play that plays itself into truth, as it leads to a great moment of truth. But that moment, upon which the entire play converges, is absent from the stage. It stands as a great gap into which all other action peers unknowingly. The final culmination of all that is Oedipus is an unknown site. And yet, as with Sophocles, we play around that site.

Is it appropriate, is it just, to use 'play' at so crucial, so weighty a moment? Can one rightfully play with suffering, play with one who has suffered so extremely and so deeply? But play can be very serious, we are reminded, very earnest. And suffering is precisely the play, the play of tragedy. Play is effected when two internal components no longer measure up with each other, which in this most extreme of cases are the self and the not-self. Here is play at its most significant, its most powerful, play that leads inevitably to despair and suffering. But such play also leads, as we see with *Oedipus at Colonus*, to re-creation and rebirth. Play, even in its most tragic and devastating, always assumes creation and re-creation. The play, as art, is created and performed each time anew. Like a rite. A performance enacted through the mask, through liturgy. Play and religion – and for the ancient Greeks theater *was* religion, a religious festival. The Dionysian moment: being torn asunder and reborn. The unity of play and religion, which binds together pain and release, suffering and rebirth. And so Sophocles ends his career in a sacred grove, a religious space, with his character facing the contrasting passions of death and renewal, of suffering and apotheosis, of mortality and immortality. A threshold experience that plunges one into the abyss of the in-between by retelling of the abyss that is hidden offstage. A playing, and playing out, of the mode of play as it opens out into the unknown.

In theater, on the stage, the text and the performance are inseparable. The play is the text, but the play is also the performance of that text, the life that is breathed into the text on the stage. The synonymous expression of text and performance. Work and life in creative amalgamation. A sacred dance. Oedipus, no longer as king, but in exile at Colonus, becomes the play itself, the manifestation of work and life, text and performance coming to truth at the unknown site. The play, as suffering, finds its apotheosis at the moment when the gap of the brazen threshold opens up, and the question of truth is laid bare in all its purity. The play then plays itself into a performance that ultimately it cannot enact, but can point to as a site that is elsewhere, offstage, critical to the action in its absence – governing the action. As performance, as *poesis*, the play acts out the *how* of its own truth, and leaves the *what* and the *where* of that truth's location unrevealed. Oedipus, the one who journeys to that location, becomes then the mode of the being of the work of art, as he carries the play to the unknown site, elsewhere. And this mode, this enacting of the *how* as pure enactment, as it leads to the abyss between self and not-self, is immortality: not in the desire to live forever, not in the desire to avoid death, but in the surpassing of death by death, in play, in the naked space between measurement and limit. Oedipus 'prevented from dying by death itself' is sustained through the abyss. 'Dead – immortal.'[22] Measureless being.

---

[22] Blanchot, *The Instant of My Death*, pp. 3, 5.

This allegory of a new dialectic between self and not-self, in which a confrontation with the gap in the threshold both cancels and preserves either side, leads not to Hegelian synthesis (whether of its 'Left' or 'Right' manifestations), but to re-creation out of the unknown that marks the culmination of the play – 'in your great day remember me, the dead,/the root of all your greatness, everlasting, ever-new.'[23] This promise of prosperity and renewal is spoken to Theseus, king of Athens, who is the only one to see the divine burial site foretold by Apollo. He is a privileged witness. But what mortal can ever become such a witness? What mortal can be granted such privilege? Who is this king, who accompanies Oedipus to his place of immortality? Who embraces the mode as a future possibility? It is we the audience, we who watch the play, and in watching participate in the life and death that is being acted out. It is we who grant the performance credibility. It is we who, in our very watching, provide the bearings that demarcate the space of the stage. It is we who accompany the action to its place of truth. Yet how can we embody the king of Athens, the sole witness to Oedipus' great moment, when we in fact never witness that moment, when we hear it only secondhand, from the messenger who retells what he saw elsewhere, offstage? Herein lies the profound nature of Sophocles' art. In witnessing the play, we witness all that surrounds the moment of the gap, the place that marks out the question of truth as the future. We do not see that place in performance, but we hear of it through the artifice of re-creation. And in hearing, we are invited to that place as our own future performance, to be made out, as Gadamer suggests, of what we have witnessed before, of what we have already participated in, and the possibilities of its re-creation elsewhere. This is Theseus, who will prosper only from the secret center of that place, the promise of a future that both is revealed to him now and, to ensure its coming to pass, is hidden in the unknown. Death and life conjoined. And thus this coming prosperity is of the same nature as the instant of anyone's death. How does one relate one's own death, at the precise moment it takes place? One does not. One only relates it as a future event. Or as artifice. This is Sophocles, who assimilates the future into the artifice, and makes of death something immortal, forever future.

And the instance of truth? How does one relate truth, now and in the future? Only as a coming, through artifice. The instance of play.

In this instance we must not be afraid to recreate ourselves. We must draw again on that courage the Greeks so proudly exhibited on their stages, as they tried on new roles and new masks in playing out the instance of their death. In this courage we must abandon ourselves to the rapture of such an instance, as we give over the grounding space that our self once held. 'Rapture as a state of feeling explodes the very subjectivity of the subject.'[24] This is the rapture of the performance, the transportation of the self to the unknown. Like the mask that brings new identity, like the mask that crosses genders, so we must also not be afraid to move beyond the dominance of an Apollonian masculinity within our Enlightenment heritage.

[23] n. 15 above.

[24] Heidegger, *Nietzsche, Volume One*, p. 123.

The Nietzschean cry to embrace the Dionysian we have already heard, but with Sophocles, we also hear the cry of the chthonic goddesses, whose new earthly fecundity must also stand alongside the principles of civic virtue and rationality, as Sophocles' play suggests. 'We must move on, move on!', these goddesses urge,[25] and we must be willing to follow them beyond the logic of only one kind of self, of only one kind of truth that is figured in rational abstraction and predetermined certainty. Like Cixous, we must be willing to rewrite ourselves into a new if dangerous space. This call is more than the vague concluding lines to Goethe's *Faust*, famous though they have become – '*Das Ewig-Weibliche / Zieht uns hinan*' ('The eternal feminine / draws us on'), lines which Kundera suggests are little more than a 'clumsy male imitation of a beautiful female gesture'[26]. Rather it is the call to risk the severing of oneself in the gap that opens up in the grove of the Terrible yet Kindly Goddesses of blood and earth, a call for the masculine to be thrown into the feminine, and for both to be reconfigured, like two lovers who, in embracing the other, abandon themselves to the unknown of what will be. It is a call Cixous has made personal in her text, as if rewriting *Oedipus at Colonus* in her own terms:

> I have been all the couples between whom abysses opened up, or rather I have been this two-bodied flesh that the jealously of the world seeks to dismember, against which are pitted the dirty alliances of kings, laws, surly egos, families, accomplices, go-betweens, representatives of the Empire of Appropriation, of the worst kind of proprietorship, the mouthpiece of the 'you are (what is) Mine,' not Adam and Eve who lose only the paradise of the blind, who are banished only from the point of view of the divine, who are born at last, who emerge, who become: I was the couple hacked apart, severed, condemned in its flesh for having found out the secret of pleasure, because in its body Eros marries masculine and feminine . . .[27]

In her exile she comes to writing, and in her writing she comes to love, which transforms her into a new space, 'the space and the desire for endlessness',[28] just as Oedipus comes to immortality in the secret space of the grove. It is a place Iris Murdoch, as both philosopher and artist, has likewise inscribed: 'All artists dream of a silence which they must enter, as some creatures return to the sea to spawn. The creator of form must suffer formlessness. Even risk dying of it.'[29] In coming to this place, we come to the space where the Olympian and the chthonic merge, the sky and the earth, Apollo and the Eumenides, the prescriptions of the past and the openness of the future, and our identity is re-inscribed in the play that remains between them. This becomes our coming to truth.

Heidegger developed his coming to truth, his ἀλήθεια (*aletheia*), with its un-concealing or un-forgetting, most fully through the writings of Parmenides, where truth is also a goddess, ἀλήθεια as θεά.[30] In Heidegger's specialized reading, this

---

25 Sophocles, 'Oedipus at Colonus', ln. 1845 (p. 380).

26 Kundera, *Immortality*, p. 384.

27 Cixous, *Coming to Writing*, pp. 24–25.

28 *Ibid.*, p. 44.

29 Murdoch, *The Black Prince*, p. 414.

30 Heidegger, *Parmenides*, pp. 1–16 and esp. pp. 161–163.

goddess moves us from concealment to disclosure, a revelation of Being as Being-in-the-world. But the elderly Sophocles modifies this truth with goddesses who reveal a concealed site, an unknown 'X'. Their truth involves a coming to that site. It involves not what is revealed, or the locality of its revelation, but approaching that space through the play of two opposing sides – allegorically, Athens and Thebes (and all the other opposing sides we have previously set up). Here Sophocles would remind us that Heidegger's goddess, Truth, reveals her thought to Parmenides through story (*mythos*). Parmenides philosophical account of truth is a poem. A 'didactic poem', perhaps, but a poetic construct (in Homeric hexameters) nevertheless, in which any revelation, any un-concealment, is already part of an artifice of truth personified in the goddess who bears the name. What is brought to light in truth is brought about through the 'Persuasion' of narrative ('for she attends upon Truth', as the goddess tells Parmenides) and less through the discursive philosophy the later Greeks would develop.[31] As much as the earlier Heidegger may try to 'hypostatize' this goddess as a universal concept,[32] he will later come to understand the importance of the mode of art she represents, and the mode of being present in all artifice and text. Cixous understands this mode as she writes herself into being, but she also understands the chthonic abyss into which that being must plunge. Where even the later Heidegger conceives of the mode of being of the work of art as disclosing a definite and certain site, Cixous understands the Sophoclean unknown that keeps truth as a coming to truth and not as a triumphant arrival, achieved once and for all. The Greek goddesses of both Parmenides and Sophocles keep truth open.

The question 'What is truth?' then is an open question, open to the creative interpretation of play in the artifice and rhetoric of *poesis*. A poetic consciousness takes us there, even in our most rigid disciplines, as it works out of the 'ground' of our being-in-the-world that is the unknown site of imagination, a 'ground' that is a gap. From this space arise Bulgakov's Master and the Master's Pilate; from this space arise Goethe and his Werther, Goethe and his Faust; from this space arise also Bettina von Arnim's Goethe, Mann's Goethe, Kundera's Goethe, and of course Goethe's Goethe. These texts converge, merging one into the other, because they are all texts hyper-conscious of the poetics constitutive of both work and life.

And yet this poetics is not merely the self-involved reflections of a self-contained world, though the self is always involved, at times to its peril. In this poetics we confront, unavoidably, the other, the sacred other. Pilate posed his question of truth to the one person who understood his dilemma between self and not-self, to the personification of truth who stood before him awaiting his very verdict, and in doing so, in both posing the question and casting his judgment, Pilate urged on the coming to truth, urged on truth to the site of divine departure and immortality. This path is the passion of suffering, of death and of rapture – Oedipal in its intensely human experience, and in its moment of unknown when

[31] Parmenides, in *The Presocratic Philosophers*, eds. G. S. Kirk, J. E. Craven and M. Schofield (Cambridge: Cambridge University Press, 1957, rpt. 1983), p. 245.

[32] Heidegger, *Parmenides*, p. 5.

Beginning begins again. The sacred space of the grove and the gospel here overlap. 'Dionysus vs. the Crucified' yields to both Sophoclean tragedy *and* the Christian Passion, one embracing the other.

> In the beginning, there can only be dying, the abyss, the first laugh.
>
> In the beginning, there is an end. Don't be afraid: it's your death that is dying. Then: all the beginnings.[33]

And so, in the garden marked out for innocence or transgression, in the sacred grove of fury or protection, in the place of threshold between what we have been and what we will be, we find ourselves with a new way of speaking, a new mode of consciousness, as we enter and as we depart. Here the rhetoric of play gives us the limits of our speech, and within these limits we find a chasm we cannot traverse, but which calls us from within. 'We must move on, move on!' We move on in a certain knowledge that what we move from and what we move to is always determined by how we are moving. Even the inexorability of Oedipus' fate gives way in the final hour to a certain determination and discovery that, despite the enfeebling of harsh years, is self-directed:

> Follow me, O my children,
> come this way. I stand revealed at last, look,
> a strange new role for me – I am your guide
> as you were once your father's. On, onward!
> No don't touch me, let me find that sacred grave myself
> Where the Fates will bury Oedipus in his land.[34]

And even if, for Oedipus, his outcome is still controlled by the gods, and the location of his grave predetermined, these moments are, for us, unknown sites, and we move onward in the seriousness of our play that promises re-creation at the very place of unknown. This journey is the text that is our life, recognized in our artifice, our rhetoric, our masks. We might wonder how the ancient mask of Oedipus would have been drawn and shaped for his final moment on the stage, as he bids his children to follow and casts his blessing on Theseus. But that bidding and that blessing is upon us too, and we shape that mask ourselves according to how we accept that blessing, how we keep the revealed place hidden, or keep the hidden placed revealed – how we play out the future.

The unknown of this future is a call to imagination. Not to shrink back but to move forward, into the darkness and the chaos, and to forge anew. It requires the strength of creative minds, but not the abandonment of discipline. It requires the joy of experiment, but not the loss of critical assessment. It requires the breaking of boundaries, but not the forsaking of limits. We must make new answers, but not desert the old questions. We must give up our selves, but not deny our capacity for self-innovation. We must not be afraid to rewrite ourselves.

---

[33] Cixous, *Coming to Writing*, p. 41.

[34] Sophocles, 'Oedipus at Colonus', lns. 1749–1754 (p. 376).

When you have come to your end, only then can Beginning come to you.[35]

Let me end where I began.[36]

The beginning of Sophocles' life becomes the end of Sophocles' work, which becomes a new beginning.

The beginning of the Word becomes the end of the Word, which becomes a new beginning for all words.

We rise on these words, we rise as we craft them, shape them, rhyme them, judge them, one against the other. We rise as we site them, sound them, sing them, soaring higher and higher, rhapsodically, until, at some unseen height, which is also a soundless depth, the words themselves give way, and there is nothing. A resounding nothing. A crucial nothing. Between question and answer, between Omega and Alpha, a pregnant nothing. A vital nothing. An immortal nothing. A rapture. A rapture of unspeakable beauty ...

---

[35] Cixous, *Coming to Writing*, p. 41 (repeating T.S. Eliot in 'East Coker' of the *Four Quartets*).

[36] Sophocles, 'Oedipus at Colonus', ln. 709 (p. 322).

In the beginning there is coming to truth, through the word, as yet unspoken.

Index of Names